£4

THE GREAT WESTERN RAILWAY

A New History

Frontispiece A scene that could only have been on Brunel's Great Western Railway. A 2–4–0 locomotive, No 14, is bound from Bristol to Paddington at Bathampton, giving its passengers a spacious and smooth journey by the standards of the time, the late 1880s. But the writing is already on the wall. The locomotive is in fact a convertible and will spend most of its years running on the narrow gauge after the broad's abolition in 1892. The substantial difference between the two guages (7ft 0¼in and 4ft 8½in) is clearly shown in this action shot. We are fortunate that the broad gauge created so much interest among early photographers; on the title page opposite 4–2–2 *Lord of the Isles* is dressed for a ceremonial occasion on 24 June 1873. (*Both Locomotive & General Railway Photographs*)

THE GREAT WESTERN RAILWAY

A NEW HISTORY

with 8 colour plates 38 black-and-white plates
and 13 figures including maps

Frank Booker

DAVID St JOHN THOMAS
DAVID & CHARLES
Newton Abbot · London · North Pomfret (Vt)

British Library Cataloguing in Publication Data

Brooker, Frank
The Great Western Railway: a new history.—
2nd ed.
1. Great Western Railway—History
I. Title
385′.0942   HE3020.G8

ISBN 0–946537–16–X hardback
      0–946537–21–6 paperback

First published 1977
Second impression 1980
Third impression 1981
Second edition with extra illustrations 1985

Printed in Great Britain
by Redwood Burn Ltd, Trowbridge
for David St John Thomas and
distributed by David & Charles (Holdings) Ltd
Brunel House   Newton Abbot   Devon
Distributed in the United States of America
by David & Charles Inc
North Pomfret, Vermont 05053, USA

Preface and Acknowledgements

The Great Western Railway has intrigued and fascinated me ever since I came to know and travel on it in the early 1930s. When I set out to write this book I early became aware that the chief problem was not going to be a lack of published sources but, for many aspects, an overwhelming abundance of them. I do not profess to have read or seen all of them (although I hope I have been aware of the most useful) nor do I think anyone could in all honesty make such a claim. But I have taken ideas and information not only from many books and publications but also from many people in attempting to distil a straight-forward narrative of the railway's history from the time of its birth until that sad day on 1 January 1948 when its proprietors had to hand it over to the State. The Great Western was not the oldest railway, but it was among the first of the country's great trunk lines, and it is the only major railway system in the country that is still familiarly known by its original engineer's name. Its history is also probably richer in incident and achievement than any other, or at least it seems so to me. If reading this book prompts others to turn to and explore that history further, that in itself would be the richest reward for writing it.

I have to acknowledge a deep debt to the help and kindness of many people. Among those I should particularly like to thank are the Archivist and staff of the British Transport Commission Historical Records Office, London (these records have now been transferred to the Public Record Office); the Western Region Public Relations Officer and staff at Paddington; the Swindon Local History Library; Mr W. Best Harris, formerly Librarian of the Plymouth Public Library, and through him the staff of the

7

Local History Section of that library for generous help with many books. I also acknowledge with special gratitude the kindly help and advice of Mr Kenneth Leech of Chippenham, Mr Bernard Yandell of Plymouth, Mr Richard Angove of Penzance, and Mr W. R. E. Jones, former Western Region Public Relations Officer at Plymouth, who afforded me many facilities and helpful introductions.

Additionally I owe a significant debt to Mr C. R. Clinker for his valuable criticism of the manuscript and his invariably kindly advice. He has saved me from numerous mistakes, tempered some of my opinions and enabled me to reinforce the narrative at many points.

Finally it is doubtful if this book would ever have been written but for the encouragement and patience of Mr David St John Thomas.

Publisher's Note

That this book should have gone through three substantial printings in its first few years speaks for itself. It was, and remains, the only well-balanced single-volume history of the Great Western, covering social as well as strictly railway matters. The author, my first boss, has alas died, but his work lives on. For this new edition I have added several more black-and-white illustrations and introduced a touch of colour. Though a few matters mentioned in Chapter 7 have moved on, it does not seem necessary to amend the text in any way. This new printing comes out as we prepare to celebrate the GWR's 150th birthday, and for readers interested in persuing the subject in greater depth, I have edited jointly with Patrick Whitehouse a substantial commemorative volume with an introduction by the Western Region's general manager and contributions by many well-known authors. It is called *The Great Western Railway: 150 Glorious Years*. Frank Booker would have loved the occasion.

David St John Thomas

CHAPTER 1

The Anatomy of Greatness

More books have been written about the Great Western than about any other railway. This one most certainly will not be the last, for, as the age of steam recedes, the thicket of railway history tends to get even denser. More facts become available, more people write books about railways and, as perspectives lengthen, new shades and nuances come into play to provide more and more variations on the railway theme. This is particularly so with Great Western history. Brunel has been dead for more than 100 years, but few of the great Victorian engineers live more vividly in the present through their work, or through speculation over their influence. Among more or less contemporary figures, Churchward in Great Western circles has been almost canonized. An aura of god-like omniscience has enveloped this great locomotive engineer, and the specialized field of the engine and locomotive practice of the country's most independently minded system has attracted an awe-inspiring and still growing shelf of studies all to itself. As well, picture books, pamphlets, brochures, folders, guides, reminiscences and even poems have all contributed (and still do) to the ground theme of 'God's Wonderful Railway', a presumptive title which in itself makes such publications compulsory reading for the addict.

Amid all this the Great Western was also an enthusiastic admirer of itself. For of all railways it was the most determinedly professional and successful in self-advertisement, whether on posters or hoardings, or in persuasively projecting its image through a house magazine which, in appearance, content and circulation was often copied and envied but never surpassed. Where the books and pamphlets left off, the screen took over, holding audiences captive in dimly lit halls. Nor did it end there. For 'boys of all ages' winter evenings and long journeys could be whiled away assembling Great Western locomotives out of hundreds of jig-saw pieces. The slogan 'Go Great Western' and the name plate 'made in Swindon' had the force of a commandment and the guarantee of a jealously prized trade mark.

For a railway, then, about which so much has been written, what more remains to be said? One answer is that a remarkable story is always worth retelling. There was so much more to the GWR than the Cornish Riviera Limited or even Churchward's engines. Throughout its history achievement was uncannily balanced by failure, ill-luck or misjudgement. Pick up at random almost any book (MacDermot's apart) and somewhere or another will appear the phrase either stated or implied 'the railway that is truly great'. But where did this greatness lie? Behind that question lies a riddle to which there have been many guesses. Some might find the answer in the railway itself, or in Churchward's locomotive achievement. Some would see it in the still discernible image of its original builder, or in the way the continuous main line, which still binds the far west to the capital, was built up. Others again take the title for granted. The one point of unanimity would be an unquestioning acceptance that somehow or another it deserved the title.

It was most certainly a remarkable railway, but a true portrait must also show warts and blemishes. It was a railway which indeed spanned much of the western half of the country like a giant, but a giant flawed and limping at critical periods of its life from wounds self-inflicted, the pursuit of prestige beyond its means, or the pouring out of money into a declining coalfield when the world was turning to oil.

No other railway preserved for so long the splendid image of its designer yet suffered so grievously because of him. The broad gauge may have contributed to giving the world its first express trains, but its adoption proved a Himalayan blunder which exhausted the company's original capital and frustrated its dream of linking hands with the New World, while the search for easy gradients to accommodate it hung round its neck like an albatross for fifty years the taunt of 'The Great Way Round'.

But if Brunel's mistakes arose from engineering conviction and experiment, his successors' errors and rigid attitudes more often sprang from deliberate policy which constantly provoked challenges to its regional domination. The London and South Western Railway might never have been welcomed into Plymouth had it not been for sheer frustration at the poorness of broad-gauge facilities. Threats to the GWR's separate existence as a railway continued until the end of the last century and even into this. In 1895 there were still interests in South Wales strong and active enough to threaten the promotion of a new South Wales Railway from Cardiff to London—a threat sufficient to urge the Great Western into accelerating the building of its Wootton Bassett–Patchway line to relieve congestion at Bristol and to reduce fares and coal rates to and from South Wales. More disturbing was the near-revolt, in 1902, in its very heartland. Plans then for an independent line from Avonmouth and Bristol to London attracted a capital of £6 million and the enthusiastic support of Bristol interests in by far the most ambitious challenge the western city had ever offered to the existence of the railway it had helped to form. It was not the opposition of Paddington which killed the scheme but Parliament's doubts about the capital being forthcoming.

Until the end of its days an ingrained trunk-line mentality meant that the best of its main-line services were superb but its cross-country services from the West of England to the North via the Severn Tunnel and Shrewsbury were generally wretched. Conservatism and rigid class-consciousness kept third-class passengers from its trains for too long. It was not altogether alone in this, but even in the palmy days of Collett's 'Kings', 'the zenith of passenger train service', to use Mr O. S. Nock's term, the Great Western condemned its third-class fares on its longest non-stop train to travel jammed together and sitting bolt upright, their luggage overflowing into the corridor.

Ridding itself of Brunel's broad gauge occupied the company for nearly thirty years until 1892. After this and until 1914 it achieved a revolution in management and a lead in locomotive design unmatched on any other system. From World War I it emerged, if grey and careworn, yet in better fettle and better placed to grasp the opportunities of peace than any of its competitors. Even fate seemed to be on its side, for the bogy of nationalization which appeared in the early 1920s vanished before a gift which Fortune appeared to offer to the company while wearing her fairest smile. When other companies were losing their identities in amalgamation with uncomfortable bedfellows the Great Western alone was kept intact. But thereafter Fortune's smile became twisted. The South Wales coal railways and docks, handed to the Great Western under the 1921 Railways Act, were to prove not so much a bargain package as a poisoned chalice from which the company drank deeply with traumatic effect. Wales and its coal became not a treasure-house of expected profits but a grinding liability through falling markets and economic depression. Money lavished on docks to deal with exports that never approached their pre-war volume earned no return. By the early 1930s a company which less than ten years before had delighted its shareholders with a near-record dividend of 8 per cent was earning insufficient to pay 3 per cent and had itself become the greatest single user of the coal it planned to carry and export at a profit to others. It was still staggering from the economic aftermath of World War I when it lurched into World War II. By the time that had ended the brave dreams of a great revival were already beginning to dissolve before the approaching anonymity of Western Region which 1948 ushered in.

But a railway's story is not wholly contained in the way in which it moved traffic from one point to another. Railways, like rivers, knit up and assume the characteristics of the countryside they pass through. To peer only at the factual framework of the GWR's history and ignore its regional background is to see it in only one dimension and to overlook a factor which contributed as powerfully as any other to the legend and title of its greatness. Apart from the thin finger it poked into an alien North Country, no other railway was more of a piece with the territory it served. It shared its conservatism, its idiosyncrasies and aloofness, all of them characteristics rooted in a region which historically and in outlook differed much from the rest of the mainland.

It was no accident that in designing Temple Meads station Brunel made it less of a terminus than the headquarters and departure point of a railway serving a community that regarded London as a distant trading outpost. Convenience later dictated that Paddington should become the administrative centre, but the heart and soul of the railway remained in the West and in that West Country city which contributed three-fifths of the capital which brought it into being.

This was apparent immediately one entered a Great Western train. Not only in operation and appearance but even in smell it was markedly unlike any other. The retention of the sonorously antique title of Superintendent of the Line, the differences in signalling arrangements, the characteristic engine whistle, even the heavy gold braid which made its inspectors appear like functionaries of an imperial court, seemed to emphasize in an outward and visible manner a region where the attitude to life of its inhabitants was moulded and shaped by older allegiances and even by language into passionate and deep-seated loyalties which were muted or forgotten on the mainland. This was true not only of Wales but of Cornwall. When Brunel brought the broad gauge into Cornwall there were still people living whose grandparents could recall the Cornish language being spoken, a tongue rooted in a Celtic past which is increasingly pervading the present.

This sense of working in, and serving, a region suffused by the legends and often guided by the loyalties of older traditions, was sharpened by differences of geography, geology and even of climate. A passenger leaving Euston, King's Cross or St Pancras was whirled through a countryside where the South merged imperceptibly into the Midlands and the North without any striking change in the prevailing green, brown and grey of the landscape. But in travelling to the West the very colour of the soil changed from brown to red. As the climate became softer and moister, stations and sea fronts were fringed with palms. The scents and scenes were of the south with the sea on hot, still days, as blue as the Mediterranean between the Greek islands. To reach into Cornwall, surely the nearest experience in England to entering a foreign land, Brunel rose to the full height of his powers in spanning one of the strongest river boundaries south of the Tweed and across which the Briton still eyes the Englishman with suspicion. In serving and penetrating these remoter areas, jealous of their older traditions, the railway identified itself with them, and in turn captured something of their voice, spirit and character. Despite its bustling, metropolitan airs, a 'westerne wynde' was always sighing through the vast roof-span of Brunel's Paddington and the surge and thunder of the toiling Atlantic seemed never far away.

Even in South Wales where, more than anywhere else in its territory, the Great Western stared into the smoke-blackened face of industry, the picture remained in essentials the same. If it took much away it gave back to South Wales a great deal in return. The mineral wealth of the Rhondda attracted many outside adventurers, among them an old enemy, the LNWR, which in tapping the heads of the valleys as it reached towards Pontypool and Newport, did so only to sip at the lucrative coal traffic. But the GWR gave South Wales a through coal route to the capital and the English south-coast ports at a time when steam was displacing sail. Only in the north by the banks of the Mersey (like the Southern in Devon and Cornwall) did the GWR remain an outsider, establishing a presence but exerting little influence.

Yet even its regional domination and flavour do not provide a complete answer to the riddle of what made the Great Western great. Greatness is often a blend of fact and illusion, and if its source cannot precisely be indicated it is nevertheless wrong to imply that it did not exist. The continuation after nationalization of a Great Western tradition in steam until its final extinction by oil in the 1960s has no place in this record. In any case it could only echo or complement something which the railway had built up, sometimes brilliantly, sometimes painfully, in over 100 years of existence as a public company serving its customers and paying its shareholders dividends. And it is perhaps this overall story of its life which provides the firmest clue to its title, to its aura of unimpeachable integrity, its sheer difference from other railways. It is a story that is remarkable, dramatic, but also often strangely moving, and all those factors are components of greatness. The broad v. narrow controversy had the force of a political issue dividing the country. Out of the ignominy, disaster and failure of the early GWR services between Paddington and Maidenhead sprang the world's first express trains. The GWR opened up the holiday lands of the West Country, defying the Channel storms to lay and maintain a railway along the South Devon coast which still affords one of the most breath-taking seascapes in Europe. Further inland the tidal Severn was wrestled with and tunnelled under to bring out the riches of the Rhondda, while over its tracks, where Devon merges into Somerset, mail from the New World to the Old was speeded to its destination for the first time at more than 100 miles an hour. Nearer our own times the cancer of industrial decline which gnawed its vitals in South Wales was bravely masked by the glamour of the 'Cheltenham Flyer'.

Striding in and out of this story, like figures on an ever-changing stage, are a succession of personalities who reveal that remarkable men as well as machines went into the making of the Great Western Railway. Great and famous though he was, there is a pathos in the triumph and failure of the broad gauge that still poignantly clings to the memory of 'bold Brunel'. It hovers, too, over the shade of Daniel Gooch, who, after proving with his own engines the superiority for comfort and speed of the 7ft track, had to bow to its final and inevitable extinction before the encroaching narrow gauge. The first decades of the century saw Churchward and Collett make the name of Swindon a talisman in the world of locomotive design and performance. Along with them, and still haunting the corridors of Paddington, is another figure who as much as anyone else sums up an era of Great Western Railway history. It is the ghost of the quicksilver Felix Pole, whose mild gaze from behind his thick pebble lenses belied his record as one of the great managers of the GWR.

The 'Castles' and the 'Kings' have gone. The chocolate and cream livery on the main line is now only a memory. Church-ward's 'Stars' and Gooch's great eight-footers have their place in locomotive history, and the great brass domes of Dean's stately singles now only hint at their polished splendour in pictures. Today one can travel faster, more cleanly and in immeasurably greater comfort over former Great Western trunk routes than was ever possible in the days of steam. But never again will one travel with the same sense of fulfilment and excitement as when Paddington ordered the coming and going of its servants and the Swindon-designed engine had Welsh coal in its grate and bore on its tender the letters GWR.

CHAPTER 2

London to Bristol

THE LIVERPOOL EXAMPLE

In the autumn of 1832 four businessmen gathered in an office where Temple Meads goods depot now stands to discuss the bringing of a railway to Bristol. The idea was not new. Since 1824 there had been at least six separate proposals, some ludicrous when not impracticable, to bring that 'grand improvement, the locomotive steam engine' to what was still spoken of as the second town in the kingdom. Each had withered and died through lack of money and continuing interest.

This time, however, there was the exciting example of the Liverpool and Manchester Railway. Then nearly two years old, its success 'had come upon the scientific world like a miracle'. While Bristol still depended upon poor roads and tenuous canal links over which goods took weeks and sometimes months to travel to and from her docks, at Liverpool bales of cotton which had taken longer to get to Manchester 30 miles away than to come 3,000 miles from New York could now be delivered from the Mersey docks in under a day. So marked were the railway's advantages that surveys had been undertaken to link Manchester with Birmingham and Birmingham with London, thus providing a trunk rail route from the Mersey to the capital.

The Liverpool undertaking had ushered in the railway age. At Bristol, where the docks were deteriorating and trade was being lost to the Mersey, it rekindled an old desire. Merchants and public men saw in the new application of steam power a way of arresting Bristol's decline and strengthening her hand against the Merseyside port which was her greatest rival. By the end of the year a committee had been formed to consider the possibility of a railway to London. Its members represented Bristol's chief corporate and commercial interests as well as the Bristol and Gloucestershire Railway, a grandiose title disguising a small horse tramway connecting the city with a colliery on its outskirts. On 21 January 1833 the committee had its first public meeting. Funds were voted for a preliminary survey and estimate to build a railway from Bristol to London, and four members of the committee were appointed to select an engineer. It was the threshold of one of the most remarkable chapters in British transport history.

ISAMBARD KINGDOM BRUNEL

The young man whom the small sub-committee appointed on 7 March 1833 was Isambard Kingdom Brunel. Almost immediately his name came to dominate an undertaking with which it has remained linked ever since. There were to be other appointments, among them Charles Alexander Saunders, who as the railway's first secretary and in effect general manager was destined in E. T. MacDermot's words 'to do more for the Great Western Railway than any other individual, Brunel himself not excepted'. But for everyone today who can instantly recall Saunders there are a hundred to whom the Great Western Railway means Brunel.

He was twenty-seven when appointed and not entirely a stranger to Bristol. His plans for a suspension bridge across the city's Clifton Gorge had been preferred to those of Thomas Telford, then the foremost bridge builder of the time. He was also the engineer for the proposed improvements to Bristol's floating harbour where shoals were causing merchant ships to run aground. If lack of money had prevented work on both, their acceptance had established a local reputation for him. But few would then have prophesied his wider fame as an engineer. When later it had been established people were to describe him variously as bold, eccentric, talented, visionary, and, depending on whether or not they were admirers of the broad gauge, a crank or a genius.

This conflict of impact illustrates a man almost too many-sided to be comfortably confined within the term 'engineer'. He brought to his work the extra dimension of an artist's eye and also sometimes an artist's flamboyance. Those who disliked him often wrote him off as an exhibitionist. The difficulty of placing Brunel is not helped by his unusual background. Half French, half English (the 'Kingdom' came from his English mother's maiden name), his father, Sir Marc Brunel, was a Norman who fled the Terror in France to become a notable engineer in England and the first man to tunnel under the Thames. Through his father and his further education at a Lycée, French influences remained with the younger Brunel, subtly colouring his thought and influencing his ideas. The counterpart of the famous flat arches of Maidenhead bridge can be seen over the Seine. There is a grace and suppleness about many of his fixed land structures contrasting markedly with the massive, formal northern heaviness of Robert Stephenson, his great rival. In the grandiose largeness of his ideas he resembles another Frenchman, Ferdinand de Lesseps, who wanted to build the Trans-Siberian Railway but instead dug the Suez Canal.

Not only his social background but his appearance set Brunel apart from his contemporaries. In England the bluff, workaday George Stephenson, father of Robert, rumbling in a thick Northumbrian accent, was to many the archetype of the early Victorian railway engineer. Bristol, however, saw not a rugged northerner, but a nimble, highly articulate young man, olive-skinned, barely 5ft tall, with fastidious hands and widely spaced eyes under a firm, arched brow. Overwork, frustration and worry were later to change him until contemporaries saw a 'faintly ridiculous sturdy little man with a big bullet head on which he wore top hats enormous both in size and diameter along with shabby clothes'. The shabby clothes (often smothered in cigar ash) caricatured a man who strode over the whole field of civil engineering and would have been puzzled by twentieth-century specialization. Thus he ranged far beyond railways to pioneer ocean steam travel, replacing wooden ships with iron and sails by the screw propellor.

Brunel was one of the greatest of nineteenth-century bridge builders, but he also left his impress on harbour works at Sunderland, Bristol and Plymouth. Once launched on a scheme he was as careless of shareholders' money as he was of his own.

He thought more quickly and saw farther than most people. When something was wanted in a hurry Brunel could come up with a plan, whether for a portable hospital for the army in the Crimean War or for a new design of gun turret. Like all strongly original men, he fancied, in Gooch's words, that he could always do things better himself. He seldom delegated, and when he did, often had to achieve his aims through imperfect instruments. Himself larger than life, his favourite expression was 'grand', and sometimes sheer size seems to have fascinated him for its own sake. The ill-fated *Great Eastern* steamship which finally killed him with its problems was the largest of its kind for fifty years and sprang from a mind that was always challenging and frequently outranging the technical resources of his time. He was the last of the great Victorian engineers who approached and solved their problems with a sense of total technical, administrative and economic commitment. More complex and interesting as a man than George or Robert Stephenson, richer in personality than most of his other contemporaries, no other nineteenth-century figure made a more permanent, many-sided or significant contribution to the Victorian industrial achievement. When death cut him down he was still only fifty-three.

In the spring of 1833, however, Brunel was in no mood to foresee his end. The new railway was to be his greatest single-handed contribution to Victoria's England and the outline survey for it his first and most pressing task as its engineer. It was needed within two months. Helping him was W. H. Townsend, the surveyor and engineer for the Bristol and Gloucestershire Railway, and one of three other unsuccessful candidates before the sub-committee.

Their instructions were to survey a route which, in linking Bristol with London, would also provide good access to South Wales and the west of England. In the north the Stockton and Darlington and Liverpool and Manchester Railways chugged their way through a hinterland growing ever more smoky and crowded with mills and factories. In the west Brunel was to run his line through a countryside still bathed in the pastoral afterglow of Georgian England. The woollen industry, largely powered by water, had not polluted it. Bath with its curving terraces had not yet been industrialized. Coaches rattled over a Great

West Road which in places had been improved to a surface 'as smooth as a die with no stone larger than a marble'. Over it the night mail could reach Bath from London in ten hours.

A trunk railway route, however, had to pay much more attention to gradients. Brunel's first problem was whether to go south or north of the Marlborough Downs, which separated the Avon and Thames valleys. The builders of the 86-mile Kennet and Avon canal, opened in 1810, had chosen the southern route, enabling them to serve Devizes, Hungerford, Newbury and the woollen town of Bradford-on-Avon. But its summit was 200ft higher than the north and this had meant installing seventy locks to haul 60 ton barges up and over the Downs.

Such a summit discouraged Brunel, who turned instead to the north with its easier gradients and better access to South Wales. The reward was to be an almost level main line for more than seventy miles, with the minimum of curvature. The disadvantage was the absence of any large centre of trade between Reading and Bath. When challenged about this, Brunel is said to have retorted that the Great Western 'was a gentleman's railway'. Such sayings are the very stuff of tradition and legend for if he ever made the remark it was with his tongue in his cheek, the railway from the beginning being conceived as a fast trade artery over the shortest distance between Bristol and London. Moreover the northern route would make it easier to reach into the Midlands and beyond through Gloucester which was to be served by another railway shortly to be built to join the Great Western at Swindon. The fact that events at Gloucester were to block dramatically the first broad-gauge approach to the West Midlands was something still hidden in the future. In the meantime access by the main line to London was left to await the final choice of a metropolitan terminus site.

THE PARLIAMENTARY STRUGGLE

Brunel's preliminary survey was completed within a month. It fixed a route which now had to be filled out in a more detailed survey for a parliamentary Bill. As this went ahead the promotion of the new railway, hitherto very much a Bristol committee affair, was widened in scope and influence by the formation of a complementary London committee. The two met jointly for the first time on 22 August 1833 in the London office of George Gibbs, an influential Bristol Merchant Venturer. His cousin George Henry Gibbs was later to keep an invaluable diary of the railway's first months. At this meeting the title of Great Western Railway seems to have been adopted and here, too, Brunel was first introduced to Charles Saunders of the London committee and took an instant liking to him.

By now the cost of joining Bristol to London by a railway had been estimated at £2,805,330. The figure was announced in a buoyant prospectus issued in September which showed the railway as expecting an annual revenue of £747,752 from goods, cattle and passengers (in that order), a 'total arrived at not on a mere calculation founded on probabilities but deduced from careful inquiry into the facts'. The capital was to be £3 million in £100 shares of which Parliament required half to be subscribed before a Bill for the railway could be presented that year.

Already it was well into autumn. Saunders, mainly responsible for raising the capital, found an apathetic and distrustful public. Despite his efforts, only a quarter of the £3 million needed had been promised by the latest date for delivering the Bill. The directors, in a hurry, went ahead, applying for powers to build a line from Bristol to Bath and between Reading and London 'as a means of facilitating the ultimate establishment of a railway between London and Bristol'.

This meant leaving a vague gap in the middle—a heaven-sent gift to the opposition when the Bill came before Parliament. Their counsel condemned it as neither 'great' nor 'Western' but 'a head and tail of a concern seventy-two miles apart which could never be joined by a body'. Landowners, farmers, canal and coaching interests united in objections which seem ludicrous today but were real at the time. For eleven days Brunel, as the railway's chief technical witness, answered questions and rebutted fallacies with a readiness and skill which profoundly impressed his hearers and not least George Stephenson. The latter's tribute that he could imagine a better line but did not know of one has echoed down the years. The elder Stephenson was not always to be so accommodating. The father figure of Britain's railways could be touchy about rivals, and Brunel, although still not widely known, appeared a force to be reckoned with in the up-and-coming railway world. Stephenson was later to lump the broad gauge with the atmospheric railway experiment as 'the greatest humbug in the world' and to describe Brunel as 'the best fellow in the world to tell a lie and stick to it'. But at this vital time he lent Brunel invaluable support. After fifty-seven days of continuous debate the Commons approved the Bill. Not so the Lords, who threw it out, arguing that there was no financial security for it.

This was more a setback than a disaster. Despite the form in which it had been presented, the need for the railway had been proved. A new prospectus widened the issue of shares and Saunders went back to his 'sad and harassing work' of attracting money, a task in which the directors and even Brunel lent a hand. By the end of February 1835 sufficient had been promised to enable parliamentary consent to be sought for a complete line of railway between Bristol and London, where it was proposed to use the London and Birmingham Railway's Euston Square terminus as a joint station. The vagueness of the whereabouts of the railway's eventual home in London is a curious feature of these early Great Western Bills.

The second parliamentary fight still encountered stiff opposition. The Eton schoolmasters who saw the railway as contaminating the morals of their young men demanded a wall 10ft high for nearly four miles to shield them from it. They forced a clause (skilfully eluded by the company) forbidding the opening of a station at Slough. Another troublemaker was the proposed Basing and Bath Railway. Its promoters planned a line from Basingstoke to Bath passing south of the Marlborough Downs— the route Brunel had rejected. The admittedly greater gradients would be so balanced, they claimed, as to cancel each other out, an assumption the Parliamentary Committee chairman disposed of by remarking that this would make the Highlands of Scotland ideal for railway building. The Basing and Bath Railway soon disappeared from history but its parent, the London and Southampton, the second trunk line to be built out of London, was destined to reappear in the guise of the London and South Western Railway and to harass with more success the Great Western's southern flank.

More serious and potentially damaging was the continuing opposition to the long tunnel Brunel planned under Box Hill between Bath and Swindon. This was to run for nearly two miles on a 1-in-100 incline with a curve a quarter of a mile from the bottom. The genuine and widespread alarm it excited was not entirely misplaced, as an incident shortly after its opening proved. The opposition defeated themselves, however, with Dr Dionysius Lardner's fantastic forecast of passengers crashing to their deaths in trains roaring at uncontrollable speeds of 120mph in the tunnel. This, Brunel pointed out, was impossible. Friction would reduce the speed to little more than 50mph, while the steepness of the incline, he explained, was less than half that of the Burlington Arcade in London about which no one had ever complained. Although the dangers of Box tunnel deserved a more credible advocate than Dr Lardner, the furore over them was largely shadow boxing. The need for the railway had been established; the question was the best route. Parliament came down on Brunel's side. On 31 August 1835 the Bill for 'the line laid down by Mr Brunel' from Bristol to London via Bath, Chippenham, Swindon, Maidenhead and Reading with branches to Trowbridge and Bradford-on-Avon received the Royal Assent.

BRUNEL'S BROAD GAUGE

It had been an expensive birth costing nearly £89,000 in legal and other fees. Scarcely had the promoters finished congratulating themselves than they were called upon to consider a proposal about which history still argues. This was their engineer's suggestion of a width of 7ft between the rails instead of the 4ft 8½in adopted by Stephenson and most others. In laying out his exceptionally straight and level road Brunel had been impressed by its great potentialities for speed. A wider gauge than usual would be a means towards attaining this.

The adoption initially of the 7ft or broad gauge and all that sprang from it will always set the Great Western apart from other railways. There are still diehards who believe that the company's worst mistake was to abandon it. Today any discussion of it is bedevilled by hindsight and knowledge unavailable to

Brunel. Yet the idea even then of a wider gauge was not peculiar to him or as revolutionary as is sometimes made out. In the 1830s there were a number of engineers who were dissatisfied with George Stephenson's arbitrary adoption of the 'coal waggon gauge'. They thought, too, that a wider one would be safer and would permit more powerful engines. Brunel's distinction lies in being the first to adopt it on a trunk railway and to prove his case. In essence, he claimed that it made for greater speed, safety and smoother travel. 'The public will always prefer the conveyance', he wrote, 'which is most perfect and speed within reasonable limits is a material ingredient in perfect travel.'

Almost all that Brunel claimed for his 7ft gauge was achieved. Whenever it was allowed to show its paces, travel on it was almost always faster, certainly more comfortable and generally safer. Its first-class carriages were eagerly sought after for their roominess, and in collisions broad-gauge engines tended to remain on the track. Brunel's great blunder lay elsewhere. It was in his decision to adopt 7ft in isolation. He had come on the railway scene five years too late. With the Stockton and Darlington and Liverpool and Manchester Railways Stephenson had done more than demonstrate the advantage of steam traction; their 4ft 8½in 'narrow' gauge had consolidated a pattern destined to prevail over most of Europe. Brunel, in fact, gave away his own case in admitting that 7ft was not suitable for all railways, especially where there were curves. By adopting it he cut off the Great Western at a stroke from the fertilizing benefits of easily interchangeable stock. At a time when other trunk lines were being planned or nearing completion on a uniform gauge he was still thinking in terms of separate systems serving only their own territories.

Yet the problem created by a different gauge had been glimpsed before even a mile of his new railway had ever been laid. It was soon apparent that the decision to adopt it would depend in the first place on whether the London and Birmingham Railway then nearing completion would allow its Euston terminus ('Square' had by now been dropped) to be shared with the Great Western. This would mean Great Western traffic running for a short distance over a third rail on the London and Birmingham's narrow-gauge track. 'If they object', Brunel in effect told his directors, 'we must abandon our gauge.' The problem was solved by the London and Birmingham directors refusing to entertain a joint terminus. The Great Western board were thus forced to seek one of their own at Paddington. This was a turning-point for Brunel. There was no need to bother about others. Problems of interchange were banished from his mind by an overwhelming vision of broad-gauge trains running in and out of their own London terminus and making others conform by sheer superiority. At least this seems the most probable explanation. No one knows for certain.

Thus the broad gauge made its bow to history through the refusal of a rival railway to have anything to do with it. On 29 October 1835 the Great Western directors adopted their engineer's proposal. At the time it seemed not only to make sense but to be a signal to others tempted to challenge the Stephenson practice. On the other side of London the directors of the Eastern Counties Railway sanctioned a 5ft gauge (although they were soon to abandon it) for their line eastwards from London, while the Board of Trade considered recommending one of 6ft 2in for railways in Ireland.

LONDON TO MAIDENHEAD

The acceptance of his gauge was a major triumph for Brunel. Building the railway to accommodate it was now to occupy him for the next six years. He had already decided that it was to be the best rather than the cheapest—'the finest work in England', as he was to write in his diary. But he had to start almost from scratch. The comparable parallel today is building a motorway, but, unlike motorway engineers, Brunel had no large body of precedent to work upon. George Stephenson had blazed a trail, but his 'style' on the Liverpool and Manchester Railway, according to Sekon, was 'already universally acknowledged by all competent judges to be of a very contracted and niggardly description'. We know now that Stephenson had strict instructions to keep within his estimate, a consideration Brunel seldom worried about. Brunel, too, was working to much more ambitious dimensions which forced him to make rules and experiment as he went along. The result was to prove the most sustained and formidable challenge ever offered in this country to the Stephenson tradition.

Within weeks of the passing of the Great Western Bill work started at both the London and Bristol ends, although London was to see the first trains. From Paddington the line was taken through Acton and carried 70ft above the Brent Valley on a viaduct built of London stockbrick. The bridges in their architectural contrast early set the style of the new railway. The eight elliptical arches of the Brent or Wharncliffe viaduct spring from stone-capped piers tapered to give an Egyptian effect, 'the first of several examples where Brunel was to call on the past to add architectural dignity to the new steam age'. Some sixteen miles further on, Maidenhead bridge, crossing the Thames on two of the flattest and largest arches ever to be built in brick in Britain, was in startling contrast and a splendid example of its builder's sensitive eye for proportion. Yet such arches, it was confidently predicted, would collapse under their own weight. One newspaper even sent a special correspondent to see it happen. But Brunel's calculations were exact. A slight flattening of the eastern spans, an effect preserved fifty years later in widening the bridge to take quadruple tracks, was not its engineer's fault but that of the contractors for removing the centerings too early.

By the end of 1837 work was sufficiently forward to raise hopes of an early opening of the $22\frac{1}{2}$ mile section between Paddington and Maidenhead, or more strictly Taplow, for Maidenhead's main-line station was not opened until 1 November 1871. Brunel had already circulated to the makers some ideas and suggestions for locomotives, and the first weird fruits, the engines *Vulcan* and *Premier*, had been delivered from the manufacturers in November 1837. More important for the railway's future, he had found in Daniel Gooch a locomotive superintendent to look after them. Gooch, not then twenty-one, had grown up among engines and the men making them. George Stephenson, as a family friend, had even dandled him on his knees. Gooch was enthusiastic about the broad gauge, particularly the advantage of 'having so much room to arrange the engine'. But on taking up his appointment he saw something which filled him with misgiving. Eight of the engines ordered by Brunel had now been delivered. With the exception of *North*

Star, a Robert Stephenson engine on which Gooch himself had worked, he eyed them with alarm. All had very small cylinders and boilers but very large wheels. He doubted whether they had enough power to pull themselves along, let alone a train. These fears were soon to be realized.

By June 1838 the London and Maidenhead section was ready for opening. The public had been prepared for it by a well-contrived publicity campaign. There had been whispers of speeds of 100mph by locomotives drawing carriages rivalling stagecoaches in size, but far more comfortable.

'Among all the great lines of this country, not even excepting our good and great railway Adam the Liverpool and Manchester,' wrote Herepath's *Railway Magazine,* 'no one has ever more intensely concentrated public opinion on it than the Great Western. Nor is this confined to England. . . . A short time now will decide whether Mr Brunel's plans are worthy to be followed or not.' *The Times* had already made up its mind. The new railway was 'a stupendous undertaking [throwing] completely in the shade all those lines already open to the public whether regard is had to the magnitude of the scale on which the arrangements have been made, the power and speed of the engines, or the extent of the contemplated traffic'. After an 'experimental trip' the paper's special correspondent came away awed by the splendour and size of first-class carriages furnished 'in a scale of comfort which it will puzzle the next generation to surpass.' If this flair for advance publicity was not unique to the new company (it was in fact common to all the major early railways), its effect was as subtly brainwashing as today's more sophisticated advertising methods. Surely, but firmly, the public at large had been conditioned into expecting something not only spectacular but unexampled and epoch-making in the realms of everyday travel.

THE CRISIS OF CONFIDENCE

These anticipations were rudely jolted. The opening of the railway on 4 June and in the weeks immediately following was certainly spectacular but in a way which made a mockery of many hopes and promises. There was trouble from the start with Brunel's elaborate and unorthodox permanent way. Stephenson had laid his rails on stone blocks. Brunel, seeking a more rigid road, had laid light 43lb bridge-type rails on continuous timber baulks secured to transoms at 15ft intervals to keep the gauge. This made a timber framework which was 'stitched' or pegged down to wooden piles driven between the transoms on each side of the rails. The piles had remained firm, but insufficiently tight ballasting and settlement had caused the rails to sag between the piles, and passengers had a switchback ride which, allied with a side motion, threatened to shake them and the coaches to pieces. The engines, too, fulfilled Gooch's gloomiest fears. They were under-powered, broke down or left the track, throwing the timetable into such confusion that the public were informed when a train was due but not when it would arrive. George Henry Gibbs, arriving at Paddington on 7 July, found the engine *Vulcan* off the rails and sunk to the axle.

> This led to an accumulation of trains and people and in an attempt to correct the evil another engine got off the line and sank in the same way. The consequence was that many hundreds of people were disappointed and the four o'clock train did not reach Maidenhead till past 10. I was so sick of the sight I made off.

Few railway openings anticipated with such high hopes had been more inauspicious. It seemed that the very virtues for which the broad gauge had been extolled were those in which it was most deficient. But apart from the piling which was early seen as a failure, some of the other faults were teething troubles. Thus the carriages, built by workmen more familiar with horse coaches, had been fitted with springless iron, while a 'dreadful thumping' from their wheels arose from uneven iron tyres. The trouble with the locomotives, however, went deeper. With one exception (Robert Stephenson's *North Star*), they reflected Brunel's theories about reducing friction and providing low centres of gravity and also his instructions to their makers about weight and piston speeds. They proved totally unsuited to their purpose. Gooch, now newly wedded, found himself leaving his wife to spend most of his days and nights 'rebuilding in some measure half of the machines I was expected to work with'. But for his single-minded devotion at this stage, the new railway might well have collapsed in ignominy before its train service had even been established.

Suddenly, while Gooch toiled at his engines, a great storm blew up, threatening not only the railway's but Brunel's future. It had been rumbling in the background like summer thunder; the fiasco of the opening saw it burst.

The loudest noises came from the so-called 'Liverpool party' of investors, who, following the success of the Liverpool and Manchester Railway, were putting into steam traction money which had earlier gone into canals. Their aid to the Great Western at its birth should not be dismissed lightly. Without them it would have been hard put to it to find some of its initial capital. Some of this northern money was substantial enough to justify its owners' representation on the board. They were astutely kept off it by the suspicion that once on it Liverpool interests would dominate Bristol's. But an even stronger source of discontent was the northern party's dislike of Brunel. In their eyes George Stephenson was the only man to be trusted to build railways. Brunel was an unknown outsider, a crank whose unorthodox methods had failed. Wild and exaggerated rumours began to fly. They depressed the company's shares. Annoyed and alarmed, George Henry Gibbs prompted the directors to issue a 'tranquillizing report'. This, while admitting an 'uneasy movement of the carriages due to faulty ballasting and springing', hotly denied that the 'plan had failed and that the rails must be altered'. Unimpressed, the critics demanded a place on the board and called for the appointment of a second engineer. Brunel made it clear that he would resign rather than work with a second man.

As the crisis ebbed to and fro throughout July, George Unwin Sims, the Great Western chairman, stepped in. Brushing aside the Liverpool demand for a second engineer, he took up instead an earlier suggestion of Brunel's to call in independent engineers to report on and survey the line. But it proved difficult to find anybody. Robert Stephenson adroitly declined and so did James Walker, President of the Institute of Civil Engineers. Eventually two agreed. They were Nicholas Wood of the Stockton and Darlington Railway, who was probably at that time the country's leading practical authority on permanent way construction, and John Hawkshaw, the twenty-seven-year-old engineer of the Liverpool and Manchester Railway, whose appointment, it was hoped, would placate the Liverpool critics. Their instructions were wide. They were to report not only on the railway, its gauge and track, but on the efficiency and construction of the engines. Thus even before it was completed the broad gauge was forced to justify its right to exist.

Hawkshaw in October set the general tone of the two reports although in more emphatic terms. He condemned the gauge as calculated to leave the railway in isolation (a prophetic remark) and thought the engines too heavy, although the latter was hardly Gooch's opinion. On the permanent way, about which the directors particularly wanted advice, he was tersely enigmatic. 'The mode adopted in laying the rails,' he wrote, 'is, I think, attempting to do that in a difficult and expensive manner, which may be done at least as well in a simple and more economical manner.' Gibbs was incensed, condemning the whole report as 'ill-natured . . . the greater part of which might have been written without going near the line'.

Wood took much longer to produce on 12 December eighty-two closely written pages in which he appeared willing to wound but afraid to strike. His one positive and unqualified criticism condemned the piles holding down the track. Gibbs pithily summed up Wood 'as not absolutely opposing our gauge but tending to show we should do better without it'. The directors decided to put both reports before a meeting early in January to decide once and for all the railway's future.

Meanwhile, the fate of the 'stupendous undertaking', still not yet half completed, hung uneasily in the balance. Although improvements had been made to the carriage springing and track (which was now far superior to the hard-riding London and Birmingham system laid on stone blocks), hostility to Brunel still smouldered. The locomotives, too, remained unreliable, a fault they shared, incidentally, with the under-powered Bury locomotives of the London and Birmingham Railway. But Brunel's engines appear to have become so bad in December that Gibbs twice exploded into intemperate attacks on Gooch, questioning his 'competence for the supervision of that department'. This stirred the board into action. Going over Brunel's head they demanded a report on the engines from Gooch, presenting him with the dilemma of telling the truth and yet remaining loyal to Brunel. For his pains Gooch got a stinging rebuke from the latter but also a demand from the directors to prepare plans for new engines. Within two years these new engines were to transform the locomotive fortunes of the new railway. Meanwhile, Brunel, waiting through the dark months of November and December 1838, was brought to the depths of wretchedness. Like all mercurial temperaments, he was easily plunged into depression. Harassed, overworked, he also felt isolated. He still believed in himself, but only one man on the board, Charles Russell, seemed firmly behind him. Even Gibbs, earlier a staunch champion, began to wonder if, after all, the solution was not a second engineer. Brunel remained firmly against this. As the dark December days limped slowly to their end he made it plain once again that rather than share his office he would resign.

Suddenly light shone out of darkness. One of the more puzzling aspects of Nicholas Wood's woolly and vaguely depressing report had been the poor showing in trials of *North Star*, the company's only reliable engine. According to experiments conducted by the ubiquitous Dr Lardner, *North Star*, while capable of hauling 82 tons at 33mph, had to have her load reduced to a mere 16 tons for a maximum of only 41mph in which her coke consumption rose from 1·25lb to 2·76lb per ton mile. Such figures appeared to 'refute all the boasted advantages of the broad gauge'. Lardner maintained and Wood agreed that this falling off in performance was due to wind resistance caused by the greater frontage of the broad-gauge engines.

Neither Gooch nor Brunel, who regarded Lardner as a fool, could bring himself to believe this. An inspection of *North Star* soon revealed the trouble. It was not wind resistance, but a badly positioned blast pipe with too small a nozzle to urge the fire. Throughout most of Christmas Day 1838 Brunel and Gooch worked side by side in the coppersmith's shop at the railway's West Drayton sheds. They fashioned a new nozzle, or as Gooch described it 'a small round orifice', and then repositioned the blast pipe. The effect was spectacular. On trials *North Star* now took 40 tons at 40mph and burnt less than a third of the quantity of coke. Gibbs was heartened and impressed. The wavering directors, among them many Bristol ones thoroughly frightened at Brunel's resignation threat, regained their nerve. On 29 December *North Star* took them from Paddington to Maidenhead in a train weighing 43 tons. At an average speed of 38mph start to stop, it consumed only 0·95lb of coke per ton mile.

The journey saved the broad gauge and Brunel. The storm which had threatened the existence of both finally blew away at the shareholders' meeting on 9 January 1839. After Hawkshaw's and Wood's reports had been presented the directors solidly voted to keep the 7ft gauge 'as conducive to the general interest of the company'. The improved performance of *North Star* was then produced as a trump card, previous knowledge of it having been withheld, says Gooch, 'to spring it as a mine against our opponents'. Only on the question of the piling did the directors accept criticism, agreeing with Brunel that it should go and that a heavier rail should be substituted. The opposition rallied half-heartedly with an amendment that 'Hawkshaw's and Wood's evidence proved that Brunel's plans were injudicious and expensive and therefore ought not to be proceeded in'. In a poll they were decisively beaten by a 1,647 majority.

Thus the broad gauge emerged to resume its way through the West of England without further checks. Yet had the critics played their cards more astutely they might well have stopped it in its tracks. Hawkshaw had been explicit. He had prophetically warned that 'if railways were just commencing in this country an addition of a few inches, five or six at most, might be made; but the advantage to be gained by making it will in no manner compensate the evil that will arise from a variety of gauges in this country'. Had this been intelligently taken up, the critics' case would have been unanswerable. Brunel in his written reply to Hawkshaw's report never returned a convincing answer. There was not one to make. The broad gauge had survived not because Brunel was proved right but because Hawkshaw's prophecy was shrugged off. Within five years it was to be fulfilled.

BOX TUNNEL—THE FINAL LINK

Meanwhile, far from the squabbling shareholders in London, work on the railway had been forging steadily ahead. The temporary station at Taplow remained the terminus until July 1839.

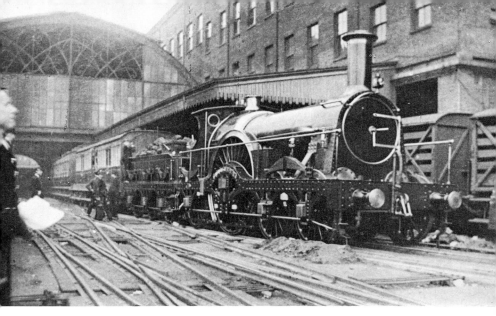

With little doubt the part of Great Western history overshadowing all else was the far-sighted vision by Brunel of a broad-gauge railway network. By 1866 the 7ft gauge extended throughout the 326 miles between Paddington and Penzance and also into South Wales and towards the West Midlands; yet already, by then, it was in decline. *Plate 1 (above)* The last broad-gauge train headed by 4-2-2 *Bulkeley* stands waiting to leave Paddington on 20 May 1892. *Plate 2 (below)* The western extremity of the ultimate Great Western system, Penzance: a former Bristol & Exeter 4-4-0ST, one of a class of twenty-six locomotives, some of which finished their lives in Cornwall before the final conversion of the broad gauge, waits to leave with a train for Paddington. (*Locomotive & General Railway Photographs; Collection of Richard Angove*)

The men who built and ran the Great Western Railway. *Plate 3 (top left)* Daniel Gooch, Locomotive Superintendent and later Chairman of the Great Western Railway, seen here in a painting by Sir Francis Grant completed in 1872 and recently acquired by the National Portrait Gallery in London. *Plate 4 (top right)* A photograph of Isambard Kingdom Brunel, Engineer of the GWR until his death in 1859. *Plate 5 (bottom left)* Sir Felix Pole, General Manager of the GWR in the daunting twenties from 1921–9. *Plate 6 (bottom right)* G J Churchward, Locomotive Carriage & Wagon Superintendent 1902–16, and Chief Mechanical Engineer 1916–21. *(National Portrait Gallery; Radio Times Hulton Picture Library; British Railways)*

In reaching it, apart from the crossing of the Brent valley and the Thames, only the occasional embankment had been needed to maintain the grade.

Thereafter, the scale of the landworks sharply increased. Between Maidenhead and Reading loomed Sonning Hill through which Brunel, discarding a tunnel, drove an open cutting two miles long and 60ft at its maximum depth. The work was carried on through a winter of storm and gale which turned the Thames valley into a great lake. Mud blocked the culverts and forced horses and men to a standstill. 'Hurry, hurry, hurry', pleaded Brunel, but the mud remained master for days on end. Human tragedy was added to frustration when George Unwin Sims, the chairman, committed suicide, worried, it was said at the inquest, by the insanity of his sister and perhaps by the fact that 'he had overdone it what with the Bristol and Exeter and other companies'. Sims had been a weak chairman; his death opened the way for a far stronger man in Charles Russell, who had upheld Brunel in his hour of trial. A striking figure as a man and a moral force as a personality, Russell was now to emerge as one of the greatest of early Victorian railway chairmen.

Completion of Sonning cutting cleared the way to Reading, opened for traffic on 30 March 1840. From Reading the railway swerved from the Kennet and the southern flank of the Marlborough Downs to go north-west through the Goring gap between the Berkshire Downs and the Chilterns to Didcot. From there its westward course was resumed through the Vale of White Horse to Swindon. By July nearly forty-one miles had been laid in eighteen months.

Further west the Bristol section was edging east to meet it. Jealous of their importance, the Bristol board, scorning expense, were determined to give their section its own special stamp of grandeur. With Brunel's enthusiastic co-operation, the dramatic limestone terrain through which it passed was matched with tunnels, bridges and viaducts which added a dimension of their own to the landscape. By 31 August 1840 Bath had been reached from Bristol. In December, the London section had reached Hay Lane near the old market town of Wootton Bassett. By the close of the year only twenty-four miles out of the total of 118¾ remained to be finished.

Wootton Bassett was five miles west of Swindon, where the railway's arrival had been celebrated by the brothers James and Thomas Edwards with an exhibition of old English single-stick play. The sleepy, decaying market town of Swindon, where less than 2,000 people lived, lay clustered at the top of a hill. Below the town was a large area of flat ground. Here the promoters of a railway from Cheltenham planned to join their line with the Great Western, a decision which helped prompt Gooch and Brunel in October 1840 to choose the fields between the railway and the town to site the Great Western's principal repair and locomotive shops.

By this time Gooch's powerful six-wheel 'Fire Fly' class engines, which had sprung from the designs he had been ordered to prepare in 1838, were coming into service. As they did so the train service gradually improved. With their 7ft driving wheels the 'Fire Flies' could gallop at 60mph between London and Swindon over a track that for seventy-seven miles never exceeded a gradient of 8ft per mile. But westwards, over the forty-odd miles between Swindon and Bristol, steeper contours demanded two inclines of 1-in-100. These Gooch planned to work by engines with smaller driving wheels. Swindon was thus ideally suited for engine changing and maintenance. From now on a new Swindon began to grow at the foot of the old, to achieve renown as a locomotive centre and infamy for the rest of the century as a compulsory refreshment stop.

Slowly the eastern and western sections of the railway drew together until ninety-nine miles out of London there remained only one link to be joined. This was the great tunnel under Box Hill, between Chippenham and Bath, where a south-western spur of the Cotswolds reaches out 400ft above the level of the railway. Underneath it, for two miles, Brunel bored the 'monstrous, extraordinary, most dangerous and impracticable tunnel at Box'.

Five years in the making—nearly a year longer than planned —and costing £100 a yard, Box tunnel was an archetype of the heroic pick-and-shovel labour of the early Victorian railway age. Guided only by the light of guttering candles, human muscle, helped by horses and one ton of gunpowder a week, tore from the bowels of the hill 247,000 cubic yards of Bath stone and fuller's earth. Wages were between 14s and 20s a week. For this pay more than 100 labourers lost their lives while others poured in a steady stream into the Bath United Hospital dazed with concussion, delirious from alcohol or helpless from fractured ribs and thighs, broken backs, and severed legs and feet. Drowning was another hazard. Twice water nearly overwhelmed the workings, one inrush in November 1837 overpowering the pumps to rise 56ft in one of the shafts. In the last six months nearly 4,000 men and 300 horses were thrown in on day and night shifts. When finally in March 1841 both ends of the tunnel were joined, the two roofs, despite the gradient, were found to form an unvarying line, while the side walls were within an inch and a quarter of each other.

It was the longest tunnel in the country when completed. Brunel crowned the western end with a magnificent masonry portico, the extra width of the broad gauge emphasizing its dimensions. But neither architectural adornment nor engineering achievement could dispel the aura of fear which hovered for months over the great black hole in Box Hill. Nervous passengers preferred to go over it by coach rather than through it by train. Nor did its immediate working do much to allay their fears. The Board of Trade even thought it ought to be lit, a suggestion Brunel managed to dodge. The night after its opening Gooch himself was nearly killed in it, having to reverse an engine he was piloting to race backwards to safety before another one coming down on the same single line, the only one then open. 'Had not the tunnel been pretty clear of smoke we must have met and crashed in mid-career and the crash would have been frightful cutting short my career also', he recalled later with some feeling.

Nevertheless, the completion of Box tunnel with or without its imaginary dangers had made a continuous line of railway between London and Bristol. On 30 June 1841 the directors in a beflagged train left Paddington to reach Bristol in four hours, and Bridgwater over the first section of the broad-gauge Bristol and Exeter Railway five and a half hours later. As they journeyed they must have felt like strangers entering the vast portals of a strange new world. Between Paddington and Bristol the countryside through six counties had been cut, bridged, embanked and tunnelled on a scale scarcely hitherto approached in the land.

Along the way porticoes, stations, bridges and viaducts reflected the architectural styles of the centuries to proclaim a line designed to exploit to the utmost the power of steam. In doing so they exhibited the grip of an engineering giant. The line marched into Bath from Bristol over a viaduct of seventy-three arches and in Bath itself the station, bridges and carefully curved retaining walls were being finished in Bath stone to harmonize with the spa's Regency terraces. At Temple Meads station, where the last rail into the Bristol terminus, it was said, was laid scarcely an hour before the first train steamed in, passengers looked up to behold a massive roof of 72ft span—wider than that of Westminster Hall—covering completely five lines of railway. Outside, the style of a great main-line terminus was being carried on in the Perpendicular Gothic of the approach buildings, housing among other offices the board room where the shareholders' half-yearly meetings were to be held regularly until 1858. But at Paddington there was still a makeshift air. Here, on land which the Bishop of London had been persuaded to part with for an 'enormous price', Brunel, pressed for time, had put up a temporary station on a site earmarked for the goods and engine sheds. The archways of Bishop's Road bridge were to serve as a London gateway of the railway for thirteen years before Paddington was completed.

Thus was built, between 1835 and 1841, to dimensions unapproached before or since on any other British railway, the Great Way West. Its engineer, almost unknown seven years earlier, was now mentioned in the same breath as George and Robert Stephenson. People gazed on his finished handiwork with awe. It was, they said, 'a most prodigious work'. Prodigious too, for those days, had been the cost, nearly £6,500,000 or £57,000 a mile. Yet although the total was three times the original estimate, it was still less than one third of the £20 million absorbed in canal investments between 1793 and 1815 at a time when the country had spent £1,000 million in defeating the French. Moreover, the railway was already beginning to expand. Even before trains had run over its entire length, broadgauge rails were reaching from it towards Devon and Cornwall and a way was being prepared to the Midlands and South Wales.

CHAPTER 3

Expansion and Colonization

ON TO EXETER

Within two decades of the first train steaming into Bristol from London, Brunel's railway, with trifling exceptions, had expanded to the geographical limits it was to work in for the next 100 years of its independent life. It had made its mark in the north, reached Weymouth in the south and gathered South Wales, much of Devon and most of Cornwall into the broad-gauge fold. In scale, variety and interest it was an achievement which affords few parallels in British railway history, and it can be compared with a military campaign in which territory was fought for, conquered and colonized, but also lost and abandoned. Moreover, from 1846, the colonization was carried out when, as a broad-gauge system, the railway was virtually under sentence of death.

Appropriately, Bristol, which had seen the railway's beginnings, also saw the first bud branch from its trunk when in 1836 the Bristol and Exeter Railway was incorporated. Like its greater neighbour, this was essentially a 'Bristol company' with many shareholders (and at one time two directors) in common with the GWR. The latter also leased and ran it to save the owners from financing purchase of their own rolling stock, although staff and everything else was provided by the B&E company. Built to the broad gauge, it struck out across the flat lands bordering the river Parrett to reach Bridgwater by 14 June 1841 (sixteen days before the Great Western main line of which it was an extension was fully completed) and Taunton on 1 July 1842. Brunel was its engineer, although his assistant William Gravatt did much of the work. By 1 May 1844 it had opened over the whole of its seventy-five miles to Exeter. On that day, for the first time in history, a traveller could eat a midday meal in Devon's county town and be dining again $5\frac{1}{2}$ hours later in London, 144 miles away.

EXPANSION TO THE NORTH

Expansion to Exeter had been trouble-free. The path of northward colonization proved harder. In the same year as the Bristol and Exeter, the Cheltenham and Great Western Union Railway had been promoted as an independent broad-gauge line to link Cheltenham (via Gloucester) with the Great Western at Swindon. By themselves its promoters never achieved this. Short of money, held to ransom by landowners, the dispirited shareholders sold off their line, still unfinished, in July 1843, to the Great Western, the latter completing it to Gloucester in 1845. In the previous year the broad-gauge Bristol and Gloucester Railway had also reached Gloucester, already the terminus of a narrow-gauge railway from Birmingham. Then for the first time broad and narrow gauge glared at each other across the platforms of the same station. Soon the name of Gloucester was tolling like a knell in broad-gauge ears.

This was due to Gloucester's strategic position as a centre for all Midland traffic to and from Birmingham and Bristol. As early as 1840, Gloucester had been joined to Birmingham by the narrow-gauge Birmingham and Gloucester Railway. An extension from Bristol to Gloucester to make a continuous narrow-gauge line to Birmingham was a logical development, and this was begun in 1841 by the Bristol and Gloucester Railway Company. Almost immediately complications arose. For the Bristol and Gloucester Railway was in essence the little Bristol to Coalpit Heath colliery tramway whose owners had assisted at the Great Western's birth in Bristol. Now it was building a narrow-gauge railway in the heart of broad-gauge territory. The situation became intolerable when, with the Bristol–Gloucester line still uncompleted, it became known that the Great Western was to absorb the Cheltenham Railway over which the one-time tramway company (whose colliery line had been Bristol's first railway) hoped to enter Gloucester by laying narrow-gauge rails thereon. The Bristol and Gloucester company saw their line hemmed in at both ends by a giant neighbour and themselves probably next on the menu to be swallowed. Anticipating by three weeks the Cheltenham Railway takeover, the Bristol and Gloucester capitulated (13 April 1843), making their railway a broad-gauge satellite. When in September 1844 broad-gauge traffic began to flow over their line Gloucester became the first town in the kingdom to experience the new phenomenon of the 'evil of the break of gauge'. The spectre foreseen by Hawkshaw had appeared; it was full of menace for the future.

From now on, with its traffic chaos artfully aggravated by the Birmingham and Gloucester's traffic manager, Gloucester became a bogy station, an object lesson of the evils of differing gauges. A powerful anti-broad-gauge lobby grew up. Among its sympathizers were some of the directors of the Bristol and Gloucester company. Despite their entry into the broad-gauge fold, the hearts and interests of many of them remained with the narrow gauge over which most of their traffic originated. Trade prospects began to prove stronger than sentiment for the broad gauge. This became clear in January 1845 when the two companies formed an unofficial directors' committee to manage the two railways as one through route. Although not an amalgamation, each company retaining its independence, it was next door to it.

It was also a move full of warnings which at Paddington went largely unheeded. Remote from the delay and disorder at Gloucester, it appeared to the Great Western board that a formal takeover approach to the two companies would bring the broad gauge into Birmingham itself. But by now a large number of Bristol and Gloucester shares had changed hands, leaving the GWR no longer the dominant voice. This became apparent when Paddington finally made its offer to buy both lines. The boards of the two companies said neither Yes nor No, but demanded £5 per share more than Paddington offered.

Events now moved quickly. Saunders temporized, promising an answer within three days. The delay let in a smarter operator. John Ellis, the Quaker deputy chairman of George Hudson's newly formed Midland Railway, was a man whose large woollen interests had suffered from Gloucester's delays. Reacting with alarm to tidings he heard on a train journey of negotiations to 'admit the plague of the broad gauge to Birmingham', he lost no time. When Saunders refused to improve his offer Ellis stepped in with a better one of his own. Matching Midland stock against Great Western cash, along with guarantees on outstanding Bristol and Birmingham liabilities, he snatched the two lines from under Saunders's nose. On 3 August 1846 the two lines were separately absorbed by the Midland Company. At one stroke the Midland gained a trunk line from Birmingham to Bristol. In its first full encounter with the narrow gauge the broad gauge had not only been out-manoeuvred but publicly humiliated.

The capture by the Midland of a through route from Birmingham into the heart of Bristol ranks as one of the most brilliant coups in railway diplomacy. It was also one of the most lasting, for the route remained a Midland line into the heart of the Great Western empire even after the 1921 Railways Act. But its consequences in the 1840s were to be even more startling. In forcing the Great Western to approach Birmingham and Wolverhampton via Oxford it precipitated the decisive trial of the gauges and brought Paddington to the banks of the Mersey.

Oxford had been reached from Didcot by the broad gauge in 1844; many Great Western shareholders thought it should be the Company's 'farthest north'. But these were wildly speculative times with the second 'railway mania' only two years in the future. In this heady climate the north-west Midlands and particularly the busy triangle bounded by Birmingham, Wolverhampton and Stourbridge beckoned as an enticing area of trade still to be exploited by railways. It was here that the north touched hands with the south through older transport links joining the Bristol Channel with the Humber, the Mersey and the Thames. Between this growing industrial area and London the sole rail approach to the capital was Robert Stephenson's fiercely monopolistic London and Birmingham Railway. The Great Western found itself under increasing pressure from manufacturers and industrialists to provide a competing line. If they did not do so it was clear that some other company would.

In the race to fill the gap the bitter memory of the Midland's coup at Gloucester faded as the Great Western sought to carve a new broad-gauge route from Oxford to the heart of the West Midlands. The first steps were the promotion (1844) of the broad-gauge Oxford and Rugby and the Oxford, Worcester and Wolverhampton Railways. Rugby was then the foremost railway centre in the Midlands, a funnel through which the London and Birmingham, with the Midland Railway from Derby, poured all their traffic from Birmingham, Derbyshire, Yorkshire and places beyond, to London and the south. The threat of a broad-gauge line reaching out to it touched sensitive narrow-gauge nerves. The London and Birmingham in alliance with the Midland rushed plans before Parliament for a railway which would not only compete with the proposed broad-gauge lines but threatened an extension from Oxford to Didcot to join the LSWR's Basingstoke and Didcot Junction Railway. It was the first of many threats to cut the Great Western system in two.

The midland counties, which an earlier canal age had laced with waterways, now faced the prospect of being tunnelled and embanked for rival railway gauges. As the two sides took up positions Parliament turned over the contending Bills to a special Board of Trade committee of five—the 'Five Kings' of railway history. They wasted no time. By January 1845 the Five Kings had made up their minds in favour of the London and Birmingham's proposed London, Worcester and South Staffordshire Railway. This meant giving the whole of the district north of Oxford to the narrow gauge. In weighing up the merits of the broad and narrow gauge systems the Five Kings not only remembered the confusion at Gloucester but pointedly noted that the narrow gauge was running faster trains.

This stirred Paddington into action. In the following March the Great Western's show-piece, the Paddington–Exeter express, was accelerated to cover the 194 miles in 5 hours dead, a time reduced two months later to $4\frac{1}{2}$ hours. Armed with this proof of broad-gauge powers, Saunders and his board resubmitted their slighted Rugby and Wolverhampton Bills. The same committee of five now threw out the London and Birmingham proposals in favour of the broad-gauge schemes north of Oxford, temporizing their approval with a proviso for a third inside rail for narrow-gauge use over the Oxford and Rugby line, a third rail for the Oxford, Worcester and Wolverhampton Railway being provided for in its original Bill.

This was a startling reversal of roles. The London and Birmingham with its Midland accomplice now found itself in the position of the Great Western at Gloucester. A prize within reach had been snatched away. They advanced in wrath and with noisy cries to stir up renewed opposition before Parliament adopted the committee's report. Almost at once they were stopped dead in their tracks by a sally from an unexpected quarter.

THE WAR OF THE GAUGES

No one had watched more closely the parliamentary battle over the Oxford and Wolverhampton lines than Captain Mark Huish. From his office in Liverpool he administered as secretary and general manager the strategically situated Grand Junction Railway, completed in 1838 to link the Liverpool and Manchester Railway with Birmingham. Huish was one of nature's buccaneers. Aggressive, bullying, calculating, his portrait also shows the sharp features of a persecutor. Before coming to railways he had served with the East India Company in Bengal, a province noted for its tigers. The captain's fierce intimidating snarls, his swift predatory pounces were in the coming months to bear an uncanny resemblance to that animal.

Huish had no particular affection for the broad gauge; he had even less for the monopolistic tactics of the London and Birmingham. He saw the latter trying to dominate not only the area it served but looking for a way to Wolverhampton and the Mersey with the help of small provincial lines north of Shrewsbury. Huish set out to frighten the L&B by offering the Great Western a shared competing line from Lancashire to London. To achieve this the Grand Junction was promoting a Birmingham and Oxford Railway to join the Great Western's Oxford and Rugby line at Fenny Compton, fifteen miles short of Rugby. This would give the Grand Junction independent access to London over Great Western metals. In return Paddington was offered a path through Birmingham and Shrewsbury to Liverpool and Manchester with the assistance of the Grand Junction, which offered to lay broad-gauge rails on its system.

Huish's startling offer broke upon the railway world in a famous circular to Grand Junction shareholders issued on 11 June 1845. If it surprised them, it fell on the London and Birmingham like a thunderclap. They read, trembled and collapsed. Within a year the L&B had been frightened out of existence as an independent company, to reappear with the Grand Junction and other lines as the London and North Western Railway. Huish's broad-gauge bluff had gained him a railway empire of 587 miles of railways and canals. It was his most spectacular coup. Ensconced in 1847 at Euston as the LNWR manager, he was to rule from there with almost despotic power, spending the rest of his railway life fighting the broad-gauge rival he had enticed into his territory.

The broad gauge, meanwhile, prepared to advance into the heart of the industrial Midlands. Huish's offer, after some hesitation, had been taken up; the fact that he now disowned it served only to increase Paddington's determination. Stirringly worded petitions began to circulate: '50 miles an hour versus 25. Coaches before waggons. The Blessings of the Broad Gauge for the Northern Districts. Safety and Speed before cramp and delay. Brunel for ever! Hurrah!'

If this was heady music for broad-gauge supporters, there were others who looked upon an extension of its 'blessings' as an impending disaster. Although the Bills for the Oxford and Rugby and the Oxford, Worcester and Wolverhampton Railways were to receive the Royal Assent on 4 August 1845, their passage through Parliament had been strongly opposed. The clash of the gauges at Gloucester had made a profound impression on many people. At the one point in the country so far where the broad and narrow gauges had met head-on it seemed that 'the West of England was as completely isolated as if a river too wide to be bridged lay between it and the rest of the kingdom'. Handling goods between broad and narrow gauge trains was estimated to cost the equivalent of another twenty miles of carriage.

It was this that worried Richard Cobden, the arch apostle of free and unrestricted trade. Cobden was all for the spread of railways, but insisted that they should be of uniform gauge. For this reason he had opposed, although without complete success, both the Great Western's Oxford and Wolverhampton Bills. On 25 July 1845 he raised the gauge issue again. This time Parliament listened to him. A royal commission would examine the whole question of the rival gauges 'and whether or not it would be expedient and practicable to take measures to bring Railways already constructed or in process of construction in Great Britain into uniformity of gauge'. Thus for the second time the flaw Brunel had built into his railway at birth was threatening its existence.

Parliament matched Cobden's mood of urgency. Within little more than a fortnight (12 July 1845) the Gauge Commission had been appointed. Its members appeared an oddly assorted trio. They were 'our trusty and well beloved' Sir Frederic Smith, formerly Inspector General of Railways; Peter Barlow, the mathematics professor at Woolwich Academy whom Gooch, in his memoirs, says he heard described as a 'fat old buffer'; and George Biddell Airy, the Astronomer Royal. Airy's appointment also caused some mirth. 'The only paper of a practical nature we have seen from the pen of the Astronomer Royal', according to a commentator quoted by Sekon, 'went to prove that in practice a short connecting rod gave out as much power as a long one, and we fear that such an investigation is not likely to impart much confidence in the practical wisdom of his calculations.'

This sarcasm was misplaced. The Commissioners were far from being fools, although they worked in a climate full of distraction. Cobden had made the gauge issue a public question at a time when railways were entering into the nation's way of life. People talked of 'railway time', of 'getting up steam', and reckoned distances in the hours and minutes of railway timetables. The second 'railway mania' bringing, within two years of the first, 168 Acts authorizing nearly £60 million in capital for new lines, was at its height, spilling over into speeches, pamphlets, books and tracts. Stirred on by Huish, the LNWR, jealous of the reputation for fast and comfortable trains that the broad gauge was building up in the West, was to appoint an official solely to create a public opinion in favour of the narrow gauge.

Steering a middle course, the Commissioners examined forty-eight witnesses. Of these thirty-five were narrow-gauge partisans;

of the remainder only four, Saunders, Brunel, Gooch and Seymour Clarke (the Great Western traffic manager), supported the extreme width of 7ft. It was Brunel who gave the inquiry a practical push. He suggested tests between broad- and narrow-gauge engines of equal weight. The narrow-gauge faction, less enthusiastic, countered by demanding that the broad-gauge trials should be held first. Brunel, confident in Gooch's engines, also wanted an extended test for broad-gauge speed and endurance over the whole 194 miles between Paddington and Exeter. This also brought objections. In the end the trial routes finally selected were London and Didcot (53 miles broad gauge) and York and Darlington (45 miles narrow gauge), the latter being a particularly straight and level road.

Thus at nearly opposite ends of the then British railway system broad and narrow engines were put through their competitive paces. In speed and performance the broad gauge proved markedly superior. Gooch's 7ft single *Ixion* of his 'Fire Fly' class, a design then at least five years old, was taken from daily service to achieve 60mph drawing an 80 ton train. The brand-new narrow-gauge 4–2–0 engine with 6ft 6in driving wheels and a long boiler was nearly seven miles an hour slower, while a second narrow-gauge trial engine, a 2–2–2 and equally new, left the road after only twenty-two miles and turned over.

On most counts it appeared a convincing broad-gauge victory. But the commissioners' overriding concern was not with speeds. It was about the 'very serious evil of the break of gauge' which no solution proposed to them 'was calculated to remedy in any important degree'. Among other things this meant that, apart from the expedient of mixing the gauges (which the Commissioners disliked), they saw no evidence of any method other than hand porterage to transfer goods between them. This is difficult to understand but appears to have been so, and the absence of such aids remains one of the baffling mysteries of the broad gauge. Brunel himself had at times suggested transferable containers and had even sketched plans for a simple hydraulic hoist for lifting them. When the Bristol and Gloucester went over to the 'broad' its directors had been promised 'a very simple arrangement for the transfer of whole loads of goods from the waggons of one company to another'. Gooch tells us that a machine was constructed at Paddington which could lift narrow-gauge wagons complete upon broad-gauge platforms. No such device ever appears to have been used. In the upshot the commissioners' report was generally against Brunel's system. They acknowledged its speed and generally easier motion at 'high velocities', but with more than 1,900 miles of narrow gauge they recommended the latter as more convenient and better suited 'to the general traffic of the country'.

For the broad-gauge camp this was a profound shock. Saunders, with the help of Brunel and Gooch, immediately rushed in with a 'very carefully prepared answer'. In restating what, in essentials, was the official case for the broad gauge, Saunders saw the whole controversy as a cloak for a narrow-gauge monopoly and insisted that goods could be mechanically unloaded from one gauge to another with perfect safety and facility. But, as Gooch himself admitted in his memoirs, this, as far as the gauge itself was concerned, was bolstering up a weak case. 'I never had any faith in any of these plans as workable in practice', he was to write later.

Nevertheless, Saunders' persistence led to a certain amount of rethinking. Swayed perhaps by his overall eloquence, and the fact that it was unrealistic to expect the Great Western to abandon the whole of its broad-gauge track, Parliament and the Board of Trade did some tinkering with the commissioners' report. The result was the Gauge Act of 1846 which said No in one breath to the broad gauge but gave a qualified Yes in another. For while it upheld the commissioners' recommendation of a ruling gauge for the country of 4ft 8½in, the broad gauge was allowed to stay where it had been sanctioned on present and future lines. It still lay in the power of a committee on any Bill to authorize the broad gauge if it thought fit.

But in reality Cobden had gained his point. Whichever way it was looked at, the practical effect of the Gauge Act was to sentence Brunel's system to death. Although it was to be another fifty years before the physical evidence of his great experiment finally vanished, no significant extensions to it were passed by Parliament after 1846. Its 'blessings' remained largely unfulfilled, not least through the inaction of its owners. Left to itself, it was now to wither and die.

The Great Western Railway many of us remember. A pre-nationalisation shot of 'Castle' No 5007 *Rougemont Castle* nearing Reading on an up Swansea express. *(Colour-Rail, J. M. Jarvis)*

Another genuine Great Western photograph. 'King' No 6018 *King Henry VI* at Exeter St David's on the down *Torbay Express*. Note the spotless rake of roof boarded coaches, though many Great Western expresses in the immediate post-war era continued to be of very mixed stock. Also note the red headlamps.
(Colour-Rail)

But long before this process set in, the clash of battle between the gauges was to continue ringing round the kingdom. Huish in the north and the London and South Western Railway in the south were to carry on the war for almost ten more years. In the West Midlands it helped keep the Great Western out of Birmingham until 1852.

Once at Euston, Huish had run up his true colours. He promptly disclaimed all responsibility for the Birmingham and Oxford Junction Railway over which he had earlier offered to lay broad-gauge rails. This left the Birmingham railway shareholders stranded and looking for sympathy from the Great Western. Huish's response was to launch an all-out competitive war to prevent Paddington taking them over. The Birmingham and Oxford Company's seal was forged, its shares parcelled out among Euston clerks and porters who with other hangers-on packed its meetings to force the company to lease itself to the LNWR. The Birmingham and Oxford board became divided and brought to a state of civil war. It was a rehearsal of tactics which Huish was to perfect later on over the approaches to the Mersey. For nearly three years a spate of Acts, Petitions and Injunctions occupied the Lords, Parliament and Chancery as Huish and the North Western board dodged and feinted to keep the Great Western out of their territory. The struggle ended when the Great Western (1848) bought both the Birmingham and Oxford and its short continuation line, the Birmingham, Dudley and Wolverhampton Railway. The latter, despite its title, ended not at Wolverhampton but 1½ miles away at Priestfield Junction, where it was joined by the narrow-gauge Oxford, Worcester and Wolverhampton Railway, that other broad-gauge promotion which had in the meantime gone wrong. The acquisition of the Birmingham railways, on which mixed gauge was laid, cost the Great Western £30 5s for each £20 share of the combined capital of £1,700,000. If it was a bargain for the shareholders it was also an important extension of the broad gauge. From Oxford through Banbury to Fenny Compton (over the Oxford and Rugby line) and from there through to Birmingham and Wolverhampton, the broad gauge had gained access to the heart of the West Midlands, toppling the LNWR monopoly of the London and Birmingham traffic. A substantial

reminder of this old, forgotten, far-off railway battle can be
seen still. It is the embankment from two miles north of Fenny
Compton to Rugby on which work was abandoned but which is
clearly visible from the main line today.

These abortive works were a small price to pay, however, for
the victory that had been gained. From 1 October 1852 Birmingham could now be reached from Paddington in 2¾ hours
over a distance of 129 miles. But this was not all. In opening the
door into Birmingham the Great Western saw on the horizon a
glittering prize that seemed to be beckoning to them from less
than 100 miles away. This was the wide estuary of the Mersey
where Birkenhead looked across to Liverpool and its lucrative
ferry traffic.

BROAD GAUGE TO THE MERSEY?

The Mersey's lure had by now become irresistible. At Leaming-
ton's Royal Hotel on that October day when the Great Western
had first run into Birmingham, the 180 directors and guests
gathered to celebrate the occasion made the dining room ring
with a resounding toast. It was 'The broad gauge to the Mersey'.
The time was now indeed approaching for Paddington to reach
out to the great river on which Liverpool's shipping was
crowded, but it was to be over narrow- and not broad-gauge
rails. And it was to be led into the promised land by its bitterest
enemy, Captain Huish, who ruined himself in doing so.

The setting was self-contained for the coming drama. Apart
from the North Western's line through Crewe to Chester, the
approach to the Mersey lay over three small narrow-gauge independent lines—the Birmingham and Shrewsbury, the Shrewsbury and Chester, and the Chester and Birkenhead Railways.
Over their total of eighty miles they offered a ready-made route
from Birmingham through Wolverhampton, Shrewsbury and
Chester.

But it was a route through an area which in railway politics
was highly sensitive. Huish, now head of the largest railway con-
federacy in the kingdom, looked upon it as North Western
territory which he had taken careful steps to guard. Through
loans, leases, price arrangements and running agreements with
the adjoining Stour Valley and Shropshire Union Railways he

Edwardian elegance: *Plate 7 (above)* Two of William Dean's stately 4-2-2s, Nos 3076 *Princess Beatrice* and 3002 *Atlanta*, head a down express through the fields of Acton in the early years of the present century near the point where today's Old Oak Common high-speed train maintenance depot stands. *Plate 8 (below)* Dean Badminton class 4-4-0 No 3297 *Earl Cawdor* heads a Paddington–South Wales express at Goring troughs in 1898. The coaches are some of the first standard GWR clerestory roofed vehicles with through gangways to allow inter-coach access. *(Locomotive & General Railway Photographs)*

Locomotive experiments: *Plate 9 (above)* French compound Atlantic No 103 *President*, one of three de Glehn compound locomotives which Church-ward brought over for trials on the GWR to compare with his own designs. Many features, although not compounding, were later embodied in Great Western locomotives and some, such as bogie design, found their way on to locomotives of other British companies. *Plate 10 (below)* The first British Pacific, GWR No 111 *The Great Bear*, was completed by Churchward in February 1908. Apart from its prestige value it was clearly built as an exercise to see whether an engine of this size could perform any better than the four-cylinder 4-6-0s of the same period. Its route availability was very restricted and in 1924 it was rebuilt into a Castle class 4-6-0. *(Locomotive & General Railway Photographs)*

had almost completely surrounded the Shrewsbury lines and had given them little opportunity for independent working, especially against the LNWR. But the Shrewsbury shareholders were heirs of a warlike past. Their handsome main station nestled at the foot of a Norman castle, a reminder of battles against marauders of earlier years. In October 1849 they cocked a snook at Huish by announcing and confirming their intention of cutting rates for passenger and freight traffic over their own railways. Although within their rights, it was a provocative gauntlet to throw to one of the most formidable railway managers in the kingdom. The war the Shrewsbury companies courted soon came. Within weeks the Chester station, which they partly owned, was attacked and the Shrewsbury and Birmingham railway clerk was man-handled from his office. His tickets followed after him. The Shrewsbury company's timetables were torn down and chains and posts obstructed the station approaches.

Elsewhere the construction of the Stour Valley line, of which the Shrewsbury and Birmingham Railway was part owner, was deliberately delayed. Traffic on canals, which were important feeders to the railways, was obstructed, and fares were slashed to a point where ten miles could be travelled for the price of a penny ticket. Only the Birkenhead Railway, declining to compete against the LNWR, escaped Huish's wrath. Instead, it aided him by refusing to take through third-class bookings from the Shrewsbury lines. Two years of warfare with Huish brought the Shrewsbury companies to the brink of ruin. In 1851, exhausted, overwhelmed and bankrupt, they appealed to Paddington for help.

Pre-occupied with its own effort to reach Birmingham, the Great Western had hitherto been on the sidelines of the Shrewsbury war. It was now drawn into it. Saunders answered the hard-pressed companies' appeal with an agreement, supervised by a joint management committee, for a mutual interchange of all traffic between them and the Great Western. If this was little more than a moral prop, it was sufficient to goad Huish to fresh fury, but this time aimed indirectly at his great rival. All the tactics rehearsed to keep the broad gauge out of Birmingham were now paraded to drive a wedge between the Shrewsbury companies and Paddington. Their shares were bought up, their meetings packed and the forged seal (this time the Birmingham and Shrewsbury's) brought out again. For three years Huish raged up and down the Mersey approaches biting, bullying and snarling until finally his tactics recoiled on him. The rigged polls, packed meetings and the forged seal had no legal validity. Nothing he did could shake off the Great Western's grip. At the same time the North Western was losing money. Dividends had remained halved since 1846. Keeping traffic off the partially completed Stour Valley line for nearly two years had alone cost them nearly £80,000 in revenue.

Peace came to the Mersey battlefields on 1 September 1854 when the 'fighting Shrewsburys' thrusting aside all efforts to work with the North Western, amalgamated with the Great Western. This brought Paddington at one bound to the city of Chester. But although an important territorial gain it was less than a full-scale broad-gauge triumph. Powers to lay the broad gauge over the Shrewsbury systems were refused. Instead, the Great Western had to enter Chester on narrow-gauge rails and in doing so took over and operated its first narrow-gauge engines and track. Moreover, Huish had bankrupted the Shrewsbury companies. The Great Western had to spend its own current revenue to pay a guaranteed 3½ per cent to the Shrewsbury shareholders.

With the Shrewsburys gathered into the Paddington fold there now remained only fifteen miles separating the Great Western from the prize it was pouring out so much treasure to reach. It was here that Huish had the last word. His 'terrorized ally' the Chester and Birkenhead Railway, which completed the link, slipped through the Great Western's grasp to remain vindictively sulking outside the amalgamation agreement until 1860. Then it came under the joint ownership of both the LNWR and the Great Western. Through this loophole the North Western and not the Great Western gained the lucrative Mersey ferry traffic. It was Huish's sole victory after nearly ten years of war over the Mersey approaches. It meant that Paddington finally limped to the Mersey at Birkenhead, with running powers into Manchester, hand-in-hand with its enemy.

So ended the dream of 'the broad gauge to the Mersey'. For

the Great Western it was partial victory achieved at the expense of an operating liability. To push on to Birmingham after the Grand Junction's defection made sense. But north of Wolverhampton ambition took over from common sense. There were many shareholders who questioned the logic of linking a railway built to serve Bristol with the environs of a port which was its greatest competitor. The lure of the Mersey cost the Great Western nearly £10 million in loans and other expenses to bolster up unprofitable undertakings. It brought its own shareholders' dividends tumbling. Nor was the public offered, north of Shrewsbury, any striking advantages over the service provided by the LNWR. A 'number of fast trains and a good many exceedingly slow trains' which Ahrons observed at the end of the nineteenth century remained the Great Western operating pattern until the end. The sloughing off of the so-called Northern Division was the least regretted loss when nationalization overtook the GWR in 1947.

But if the struggle impoverished Paddington, it destroyed Huish. Discredited and distrusted, he resigned from the LNWR in 1859 after twelve years as its general manager. Ten years of bitter warfare with the rival he had originally invited into his territory had left battered and dented the LNWR hegemony he had striven so single-mindedly to build up. Yet with all his faults, and they were many, under him it had also grown to greatness. By 1851, with a capital of almost £30 million, it was not only the richest and largest railway in the country, but the largest joint stock company in the world. In struggling to retain the Mersey approaches Huish had fought the right battle but in the wrong way. It called for the cunning of the fox rather than the spring of the tiger. A present-day railway historian (T. R. Gorvuish) has called Huish 'one of the most influential executive managers of the early Victorian age' and has described his achievement between 1846 and 1851 of drawing the Midland, Lancashire and Yorkshire, East Lancashire and Manchester, Sheffield and Lincolnshire Railways into alliance with him 'the most striking feat of railway diplomacy at the time'. In doing this he was one of the first to see the value of alliances with neighbouring lines. He pioneered the development of railway management and was in advance of his time in encouraging the uniform acceptance of through traffic. But mid-Victorian railway memories were short. When Huish died aged sixty-eight in 1867 the *Railway Times* dismissed him tersely in the words 'De mortuis nil nisi bonum'. It was left to his family to remember him more gratefully through a personal fortune of £50,000.

STORMING THE CITADEL

There remains to be told the ironic epilogue to the Great Western's northern conquests. It is woven into the story of the Oxford, Worcestershire and Wolverhampton Railway over whose authorization, along with the Oxford and Rugby Railway, the Great Western had gone to war in 1845 to defend its 7ft gauge. The OWW, 'Old Worse and Worse' as it came to be called, repaid its parent by stabbing it in the back. While Russell and Saunders were wrestling with Huish, it turned itself into a narrow-gauge railway.

The quarrel which led it to do so had its roots in two causes— the refusal of the Great Western, then itself hard pressed, to back with an unlimited guarantee the cost of building the Worcester railway, whose shareholders, in turn, saw in Paddington's adoption and purchase of the two Birmingham railways the potential reduction of their own to a secondary loop line. These grievances, manipulated by two unscrupulous and strong chairmen, were used as an excuse to delay by ten years, through a series of shifts and evasions, the completion of the OWW. Seven years after its authorization it still had only thirty-six miles of line open and no money left to buy locomotives or rolling stock. In defying Paddington, it not only threatened to gain independent access to London, but, in collusion with Huish, passed much of its Worcester–London traffic through to Euston. When in 1854 its main line was finally completed it had laid broad-gauge rails only in a few places on the down line: there was no intention of ever using them and no broad-gauge train, save an inspecting officer's special to Evesham, ever ran over that railway's entire length. Thus a line promoted to extend the broad gauge ended by adding to the facilities of the narrow.

The real significance of the OWW's rebellion became plain in the 1860s. In 1858 it had made its peace with the Great Western, which, sick and tired of a rebellious daughter, waived its own broad-gauge rights. Two years later, having made itself an independent company and torn up, or sold off, most of the broad-gauge rails it had laid, it changed its name to West Midland Railway. In doing so it absorbed two small narrow-gauge concerns—the Worcester and Hereford and the Newport, Abergavenny and Hereford Railways. The title of West Midland Railway was to prove short-lived but the manoeuvres which had brought it into being included an important proviso. This was a pledge that neither the West Midland nor the Great Western would back any competing line to London.

But the smell of intrigue and double dealing was never far away from the OWW despite its changed title. Barely two months after the West Midland Railway was born, a proposal for a competing London line was revived and a Bill for it brought into Parliament in 1861. Its solicitors were connected with John Parson, a one-time chairman of the OWW who had been notorious for evading the pledge to lay broad-gauge rails. The Great Western had little stomach for the threatened fight. Unable or unwilling to meet its foes, it suddenly announced that it was joining them. On 30 April 1861 an astonished railway world learned that the Great Western and the West Midland Railways were to amalgamate.

It was a decision that profoundly altered the Great Western system. From now on its narrow or standard gauge commitments became equal in importance if not in prestige (although, except from Swindon's ivory tower, this was now wearing thin) to the broad gauge. In a triangle of country with Shrewsbury as the apex and Pontypool and Oxford as the bases a further 280 miles of narrow-gauge territory had come under Paddington's control, expanding the railway from 647 miles (mostly broad) to 1,104 miles, of which 369 were narrow and 189 common to both. But it also emphasized the isolation of the 7ft gauge. For although the West Midland acquisition included a large tract of territory that might otherwise have fallen into North Western hands there were now breaks of gauge at more than twenty places. Honouring an earlier promise, and to help the interchange of traffic from the 190 miles of the West Midland system, a third rail was put in between Reading and Paddington. On 14

August 1861 a narrow-gauge train ran into Paddington and by 1 October a regular narrow-gauge service had been established. The big citadel had been stormed and had capitulated.

This was the ironic end of the great battles to bring the 'blessings' of the broad gauge to the north. They had ended by bringing the narrow gauge into Paddington itself, the very heart of the broad-gauge empire.

POWER FROM THE PRINCIPALITY

For all the effort and treasure poured out to reach the Mersey, the Great Western north of Shrewsbury established little more than a presence. In contrast the bringing of the broad gauge to South Wales was not only more peaceful but of profoundly greater industrial importance. Although the vast anthracite fields between Llanelly, Swansea and Neath were being exploited by 1836–7, the mineral wealth of the Rhondda further east lay comparatively unexplored until 1850. In bridging the Wye at Chepstow in 1852 to give South Wales a continuous rail route to London and the south coast, Brunel turned one of the keys unlocking the coal of the Rhondda. Before he did so the Upper Rhondda was a wild, untouched mountainous region 'where the lark sang and a Sabbath stillness reigned'. It was never to be the same again. As sail gave way to steam the furnaces of ships' boilers became increasingly hungry for the dry, fiery steam coal of South Wales. Over the South Wales Railway, first as a mere trickle, but later in an avalanche that compelled the building of the Severn tunnel, was to come much of the coal which fuelled the Navy and the world's merchant fleets.

Unlike the north beyond Birmingham and Wolverhampton, South Wales was legitimate Great Western territory and had been looked on as such since the railway was first incorporated. The problem was getting into it. Brunel wanted to branch off from the Swindon and Gloucester line at Stonehouse to cross the Severn between Fretherne and Awre, a route only ten miles longer than the future direct line through the Severn tunnel. Local opinion was hostile to this. Instead, when the South Wales Railway was expressly sanctioned as a broad-gauge line in 1845 the approach was fixed via Gloucester, although this added fifteen miles to the journey from London to South and West Wales.

The GWR provided a quarter of the railway's capital and leased it for working. By 1850 it was finished over the 75 miles from Swansea (itself reached by a branch) to Chepstow and a year later to Grange Court on the Severn's west bank and 7½ miles from Gloucester. From Grange Court the Great Western-sponsored Gloucester and Dean Forest Railway took it across the river to Gloucester. Only the Wye needed to be bridged to make a continuous rail link from Swansea to Paddington via Gloucester and Swindon.

It presented the most formidable water challenge Brunel as a railway engineer had up to then encountered, for the Wye matched its beauty with peculiar problems. It not only had the second highest tidal range in the world, over which Brunel had to provide a 50ft clear heading above high water, but difficult land approaches. At Chepstow the river's left bank was flanked by a 120ft limestone cliff while the opposite shore was a mudflat at low tide. Thus the river had to be approached at one end by using the cliff as an abutment and at the other by a massive embankment, leaving a total length of 600ft to be bridged, of which 300ft was the river gap. For an all-in cost of only £77,000 Brunel carried two lines of railway over the river on a modified suspension bridge, the chains hanging from the ends of a horizontal tube circular in section and 9ft in diameter. When completed it was his first large iron bridge, and his ugliest. Lessons learned in floating out the 138 ton tubes for positioning on the bridge piers came in useful seven years later when he was to bridge the Tamar with one of his most handsome structures.

With the bridge's completion for single track in 1852 (the second followed in April 1853) Swansea could be reached in seven hours from London. Also by the end of 1852 the line had been extended thirty miles over the neck of the Gower Peninsula in Carmarthenshire to Pembroke. The original plan to complete it to Fishguard was shelved in the aftermath of the Irish potato famine. Instead the line was terminated at New Milford (it became Neyland in 1906), opposite Pembroke Dock. The building here of a harbour for the Irish packet service was a striking example of a port brought into being by railway enterprise. Brunel found the area scarcely inhabited; he left it a settlement with a deep-water harbour capable of taking the largest vessels, although one which for years was never sure of its name. In Great Western timetables it was New Milford, but to the port's inhabitants Neyland. Forty years later, when Fishguard supplanted it, New Milford disappeared and Neyland resumed its rightful name, which the Post Office keeps today—although the inhabitants prefer New Milford.

In 1863 the South Wales Railway sold out to the Great Western. It was a move hastened by the latter's amalgamation with the West Midland system which offered an alternative and competitive route to South Wales. But its existence could not subtract from the pioneer achievement of Brunel's original line. Through him South Wales was no longer a remote part of the Principality, approached by stormy sea lanes and indifferent roads. Moreover, by its mere presence the South Wales Railway had accelerated the growth of the coal industry. In 1845 there had been only seven pits in the Aberdare Valley. Before the broad gauge had been completed to New Milford there were sixteen, and twelve more were being opened. In 1855 the first trainload of Rhondda coal was sent to Cardiff, a trickle before the avalanche. As the industry expanded, Brunel's broad-gauge line became criss-crossed by independently owned narrow-gauge lines built to give the mineral-rich valleys an outlet to the sea. Their building emphasized the handicap of the 7ft gauge which found itself more and more isolated as the coal trade grew. The earliest and richest of them, the Taff Vale between Cardiff and Merthyr Tydfil, had been engineered by Brunel himself in 1840, chiefly as an outlet for the Dowlais iron works, but even before it was opened in 1841 pit development prospects had compelled the addition of two branch lines. With the others in the fullness of time it was to become Great Western property. Meanwhile, because of this web of small coal lines, mineral traffic over the broad gauge remained minimal for many years, one coal train to London a day sufficing. But already Cardiff was showing signs of supplanting Newcastle as the nation's 'coal metropolis'. In the Rhondda itself twenty new pits were to open between 1865 and 1875, polluting its clear streams, overwhelming its green beauty and shattering its pastoral stillness for ever.

When the Bristol and Exeter Railway reached its Devon terminus in 1844 many people in that county saw their first train. The extension of the broad gauge into Devon and Cornwall in the years that followed came over the tracks of the South Devon and Cornwall Railways, both of which had Great Western representation on their boards. Between them they brought an extra dimension to the nation's life. Before the railway, Dartmoor, the north and south coasts of Devon, and above all the Cornish peninsula, were remote enough from the rest of the kingdom for a journey to them to resemble a pilgrimage. In bridging the Tamar at Saltash, Brunel did for the south-west what he had achieved for South Wales seven years earlier in bridging the Wye. Slowly at first but with ever gathering appeal the era of the western holiday lands dawned. Today more people in Britain have holidays in Devon and Cornwall (24 per cent of the population in 1976) than in any other part of the country. Most now come by road, but their parents and grandparents made the journey over the route pioneered by Brunel's railway. To them the Riviera was not a stretch of the Mediterranean coast but the name of the Great Western train which took them to the wide sands and rolling surf of Perranporth and Newquay and stopped at its 'farthest west' at Penzance, just short of the fabled land of Lyonesse.

The Great Western, through its associates, came to dominate South Devon and Cornwall, but south and east from Exeter it was a secondary railway. The enemy before which it retreated was an old antagonist, the London and Southampton Railway, which by 1839 had become the London and South Western. If less fiercely belligerent than the LNWR under Huish, the LSWR was more astutely directed. Its challenge long outlasted the gauge war and had still to be reckoned with in the early years of the twentieth century. The battle which it provoked in the south while Paddington was still at grips with Huish in the north sprang largely from the Great Western's proposal in 1845 to extend its Berks and Hants Railway (Reading, Basingstoke,

Newbury and Hungerford, the latter a temporary terminus) to join the Paddington-assisted Wiltshire, Somerset and Weymouth Railway at Westbury. Behind this was a plan to shorten the distance between Paddington and Exeter by cutting out Bristol through a new direct broad-gauge line from Yeovil via Crewkerne, Honiton and Ottery, called the Exeter Great Western Railway. Such a line would have greatly shortened the distance between Exeter and Paddington.

The scheme was frustrated by the LSWR which promoted a rival London line via Salisbury, Dorchester and Yeovil. For ten years, while this and other broad and narrow schemes in the south were fought for in and out of Parliament, the countryside between Exeter, Salisbury and Weymouth 'rang with the clamour of the gauges'. Bells were pealed and cannon fired to announce the victorious promotion of a line; a comma turned upside down or a letter misplaced was sufficient to condemn a whole scheme. At public meetings the English language was tortured and turned upside down to express the passionate feelings of the rivals. Thus a gentleman at Yeovil declared that 'he stood upon the broad gauge of truth and could not be opposed but on the narrow gauge of selfishness and interest'. By the time the war had ended, the LSWR, which had once undertaken not to go farther west than Salisbury and Dorchester, was in sight of Exeter (reached from Salisbury via Yeovil in 1860) and had leap-frogged into Cornwall to acquire illegally the little Bodmin and Wadebridge Railway. The Great Western, in turn, gained its Berks and Hants extension and pursued its own path to Weymouth, from Westbury through Frome and Yeovil on the Wiltshire, Somerset and Weymouth Railway. It was also given powers in 1848 to promote what is now the present direct route to Exeter via Westbury, Castle Cary and Taunton. The concession was a barren one. The costs of the struggle with Huish, together with the after effects of the 'railway mania', left it without funds to start the work, and the powers lapsed. Nearly sixty years were to go by before the scheme was taken up again.

From Warminster the Great Western reached out to Salisbury in 1856. When it finally steamed into Weymouth from Yeovil on 20 January 1857 (the LSWR did so from Dorchester the same day) it marked the farthest point of broad-gauge penetration in the south. The rest of the country between Exeter, Salisbury and Dorchester fell to the LSWR, almost solely because Parliament preferred, for defence reasons, a narrow-gauge line along the south coast. Thus Bridport and Lyme Regis, just over the border in Dorset, and Sidmouth and Exmouth in Devon, were all lost to the broad gauge and with them the chance of a common Great Western development of the whole of the Devon and Cornish resorts. Moreover, in reaching Exeter the LSWR gained a springboard for Mid-Devon and North Cornwall and in so doing was eventually to rub shoulders with the Great Western in Plymouth.

THE 'ATMOSPHERIC CAPER'

Nearly thirty years before this happened, however, the Great Western itself had reached Plymouth through the South Devon Railway, which in prolonging the broad gauge for another fifty-nine miles from Exeter was to trace a saga of experiment and failure which still puzzles and intrigues posterity.

The South Devon received the Royal Assent for its Bill on 4 July 1844. The GWR, the Bristol and Exeter and the Bristol and Gloucester Railways provided £400,000 of its authorized capital of £1,100,000 and eleven of its directors. Encouraged by Brunel, the new infant almost immediately showed itself to be highly unorthodox. Barely had it been born than there came hot-foot to its promoters the brothers Joseph and Jacob Samuda with a momentous proposal. They offered their patent of the atmospheric system of traction. This was then operating between Kingstown and Dalkey on the Dublin and Kingstown Railway in Ireland and was later to be adopted by William Cubitt for the London, Croydon and Epsom Railway.

In principle, the atmospheric idea, which had been around for thirty years, was beguilingly simple. Instead of being pulled by steam engines, carriages were to be propelled by compressed air pumped through a pipe between the rails. On top of the pipe was a continuous slot in which ran a piston attached by a hinged connecting rod to the leading coach. Pumping engines along the line created in the pipe a vacuum in front of the piston which was then pushed along by air pumped in behind. A hinged leather flap, a key feature of the Samuda patent, was to keep the pipe airtight. There was no noise, smoke or smell. It seemed to be the nearest thing on land to a bird's silent flight in the air. Experiments, it was claimed, showed that 70mph could be attained in conditions similar to those on the South Devon Railway. So confident were reports that when the system was adopted the South Devon shares shot up £5 in value.

The South Devon directors took their cue from Brunel, who warmly recommended the scheme. But George Stephenson dismissed it all as a 'great humbug'. His son Robert, and Joseph Locke, the engineer for the LSWR, were also decidedly against it. What would happen, Robert Stephenson asked, if a pumping engine broke down? Would not a whole section of the line be immobilized until the engine was repaired? The question was never answered, but if it ever arose in Brunel's mind it was overridden by one more pressing. A key feature attracting him to the atmospheric system was his worry whether steam traction could work the South Devon's curved and hilly route between Newton Abbot and Plymouth. To keep down costs it had been laid out with exceptionally steep inclines. Although by 1840 steam locomotives had been sufficiently improved to take gradients of 1-in-40 he doubted their ability to work the South Devon track to broad-gauge standards. The atmospheric system could take steep gradients. He had been impressed (as were Board of Trade inspectors) with the trials he had seen and with the performance of atmospheric trains on the Dublin and Kingstown Railway.

'As a mechanical contrivance,' Brunel reported to the South Devon board, 'the atmospheric system has succeeded perfectly as an effective means of working trains by stationary power whether on long or short lines at a higher velocity and with less chance of interruption than is now offered by locomotives.' The South Devon were induced to make further savings by building their line single instead of double to accommodate the Samuda system, which, in the enthusiasm of the moment, it was planned to extend into Cornwall.

But there were features about the South Devon likely to tax any form of traction, let alone one comparatively untried. Any railway between Exeter and Plymouth had to skirt the granite mass of Dartmoor. After a flat coastal run from Exeter to

In the early days of British Railways the true GWR lives on. 'Hall' class No 4949 *Packwood Hall* with its original chimney passes Starcross with a down Penzance train. *(Colour-Rail, P. W. Gray)*

Another 'Hall' beside salt water but in very different circumstances. No 4978 *Westwood Hall* leaves Kingswear with coal for Torquay gasworks. This was an important and regular traffic and like many persisting into BR days was of purely local significance, never even reaching the nearest main line junction. *(Colour-Rail P. W. Gray)*

Newton Abbot, Brunel ran his line along the southern foothills of the Moor to reach Plymouth through Totnes, 'with the design of accommodating the greatest area of population in the district to be traversed'. This meant that between Newton Abbot and Plymouth the line had to climb, dip and curve over a deeply folded countryside crossed by five rivers. The Dainton Banks, or inclines, between Newton Abbot and Totnes, with gradients of 1-in-57 and 1-in-36, along with severe curves, 'form one of the most trying pieces of railway in Great Britain'. At Wrangaton, seven miles from Plymouth, the summit of the line is 462ft above sea level. Eastward out of Plymouth Hemerdon Bank presents drivers with a 1-in-40 gradient for $2\frac{1}{2}$ miles.

It was over this route, condemned to be the bane of generations of engine drivers, that Brunel now prepared to propel trains by air. In Paddington Charles Russell, the Great Western chairman, mindful of the company's £150,000 stake in the South Devon, was decidedly lukewarm. 'The Great Western', he wrote on 14 December 1844, to Thomas Gill, the South Devon chairman, 'can by no means be considered favourable to the atmospheric principle with the present small amount of experience.'

This upset Mr Gill, but neither he nor Brunel were to be swayed from their purpose. The latter went ahead ordering 4,400 tons of piping, specifying 'good, solid metal run from the pig and not from the stack', and called for weekly deliveries of 220 tons at Bridgwater, Exmouth and Totnes. Gradients already made steep for the sake of economy were made even steeper for the new system. Thus instead of spreading the climbing evenly between Newton Abbot and Plymouth he grouped it into four steep planes, two facing each way, for which larger-diameter atmospheric pipes and bigger pumping engines were to be provided.

An atmospheric train service had been promised by July 1845 from Exeter to Teignmouth where the line skirted the sea barely 20ft from the high tide mark. It did not arrive until a year later (30 May 1846), and was worked by steam and not atmospheric traction. In spite of Brunel's decided opinion that the 'mere mechanical difficulties [of the atmospheric system] can be overcome', it was apparent that almost everything had to be experimented with afresh, while the installation proved far more costly and protracted than had been expected. Nor did other things go well. The tidal Exe at one point seemed an 'unfathomable swamp' yielding no bottom for a bridge, even 40ft down. A persistent easterly gale stopped all work on an important retaining wall for nearly four months.

There was a strike by the navvies. They wanted (and got) fortnightly instead of monthly pay. Drawn mainly from the southern counties and working for between 2s 6d and 4s 3d a day, they were a less masterful breed than their counterparts in the Midlands and North, but had much the same habits. 'When they were in liquor there was nothing you could do with them', the Rev J. R. Thompson, of Totnes, told the Commission on Railway Labourers. He also found them and their children living 'in a state of wildness which made it impossible for their parents to send them to school'.

The morals and living conditions of these navvies and their families were also causing much concern to the South Devon directors at this time. It was the Rev Mr Thompson, however, who saw at first hand the squalor in which they lived. He found barrack-like buildings where between 150 and 200 men, women and children 'lived and slept exposed to each other'. Close to Marley tunnel, near Totnes, built to keep the railway from spoiling Sir Walter Carew's view, he found others crowded into 12ft square turf and mud huts built against hedges and banks. 'I have never seen anything to be compared to them' he told the incredulous Parliamentary Commissioners, who thought the lodging 'of these industrial armies of the field like the lodging of her Majesty's forces should be the care of the state'. In towns like neighbouring Totnes the navvies were the prey of shopkeepers fleecing them 'for provisions not of the quality which they ought to be for the money paid' and which cost them 20 to 30 per cent more than other people. So lived and worked the men who built the South Devon Railway.

The 'atmospheric caper', as Devonians called it, was now being unfavourably noticed in the press, which fed on the criticism and scorn of a public who, when not complaining about the delay, doubted whether the railway would ever work when it was completed. By 30 December 1846 the railway had reached

Newton Abbot, but it was still not atmospheric. Difficulties with the pumping engines meant that locomotives had to be hired from the GWR to work the service.

Meanwhile Joseph Samuda had come to stay at Dawlish and Brunel himself was regularly in Totnes and Plymouth. Hard driven and increasingly irritable, he frequently lost his temper with critics and particularly with William Praed, who found his country seat at Teignmouth in full view of the vulgar new railway. Praed's persistent protests led Brunel to explode that he sounded 'like a kettle tied to a cur's tail'; local wits retorted that this might equally apply to the new railway and its builder. The Midland Railway, which had absorbed the Bristol and Gloucester, was also becoming restless. Remembering the £50,000 dowry which the latter, on becoming part of the broad gauge in 1843, had contributed towards the capital of the South Devon, they exacted a promise that the atmospheric working should not go beyond Totnes.

They need not have worried. Although the pipes had been laid to Totnes they were never used. When the railway to Totnes from Newton Abbot opened on 20 July 1847 it was worked by steam. Even this was a considerable relief to Brunel who wondered whether even steam traction would take the Dainton incline out of Newton Abbot. 'I never saw Mr Brunel so anxious,' wrote Gooch. 'Relying on the atmospheric transport he had made these steep inclines and he feared there might be difficulties in working them. These difficulties disappeared with the day of opening . . . it seemed a great relief to Mr Brunel to find it was so.'

Two years late and still experimental, a regular service of four atmospheric trains at last began to operate between Exeter and Teignmouth in September 1847 and to Newton Abbot in January 1848. Over a mainly level route the trains proved at least as fast as steam, the highest speeds being an average of 64mph (maximum 68) with a load of 28 tons, while 35mph was averaged on the same section with 100 tons. Even so Gooch's despised steam engines were always in readiness in case of breakdowns. Brunel became a little more cheerful. 'Notwithstanding numerous difficulties I think we are in a fair way of shortly overcoming the mechanical defects', he wrote to the South Devon board in 1848.

Thomas Gill, with a child-like faith in the whole experiment which never wavered, was announcing that it had proved so successful that locomotives had been entirely withdrawn between Newton and Exeter.

They were soon back. Despite Brunel's optimism in a report intended chiefly, perhaps, for boardroom eyes, the whole experiment was rapidly approaching collapse, dogged by problems 'for which only imperfect remedies could be found'. The most troublesome was the failure of the leather valve to seal the pipe after the passage of the connecting rod. 'Little holes would be left here and there and a very small aperture soon increased in the attempted exhaustion of the pipe by the stationary engine.' There were other troubles. Water from condensation collected in the pipe. The vacuum drew the natural oil out of the leather, making the valve pervious, while the compound used to seal it was often sucked into the pipe by the rush of oil. Pumping engines broke down. Their overstrained cranks also snapped off. Because of the difficulty of keeping the pipe airtight, the engines had to deliver three times more horsepower than estimated. The end came in June 1848 with the discovery that the leather along the whole length of the continuous valve, the most important part of the system, was disintegrating. The chemical action of iron oxide and tannin had turned it into a blackened, decomposed tissue causing whole sections to tear apart like paper. The only remedy was its complete renewal, estimated to cost £25,000.

Atmospheric working had by then cost nine times more than calculated and three times that of locomotive traction. Brunel, who had staked some of his own money, realistically recommended its abandonment. Only the chairman, Thomas Gill, wanted to continue. In an acrimonious boardroom tussle he was overruled and a capital loss of nearly £400,000 (probably £10 million in modern values) of which only £50,000 was regained was written off. Gill resigned and Brunel insisted on receiving only a minimal retaining fee until the South Devon was completed to Plymouth. On 9 September 1848, steam took over the working of all atmospheric trains. The Italianate pumping engine houses (there were eleven in all) between Exeter and Totnes became known as Brunel's follies.

High speed: during the 1930s the GWR entered the high speed stakes and even went as far as shrouding two locomotives, King class No 6014 *King Henry VII*, and Castle class No 5005 *Manorbier Castle*, with pseudo-streamlining around the cab and front end. *Plate 11 (above)* No 6014 is seen with the down Bristolian near Bathampton in March 1936. *Plate 12 (below)* No 5005 heads up between Cheltenham and Gloucester with the Cheltenham Spa Express, known by its nickname 'The Cheltenham Flyer'. For a time during the 1920s and early 1930s it was the fastest train in the world with a start to stop average speed between Swindon and Paddington of 71·4mph in 1932. This was soon overtaken as diesel traction in other parts of the world gradually took the lead in high speed running. *(Locomotive & General Railway Photographs)*

Right up to World War II the GWR was noted for its many branch and local services, although cuts during the 1950s and '60s eliminated most of them. *Plate 13 (above)* A main line stopping train between Swindon, Bath and Bristol seen near Bathampton soon after the turn of the century with a mixture of four- and eight-wheel coaches and headed by an 0-4-2 tank, one of a number of small classes employed on this sort of work. *Plate 14 (below)* Churchward 44XX 2-6-2T No 4410 seen in British Railways' days with the single-coach Princetown–Plymouth branch train which climbed up the remote and bleak fastnesses of Dartmoor. *(Locomotive & General Railway Photographs; Western Morning News)*

So ended the atmospheric experiment. It had been worked on a little over 20 of the railway's 59 miles, badly bruised Brunel's reputation and left for posterity some puzzles. Where was the provision for traffic growth? How could points and crossings have operated with the pipe in the middle of the track, for links with branch lines? Was the constant trouble with the pumping engines due to their makers having been influenced by Brunel's ideas? It had been a similar story with his railway locomotives. They too had proved inadequate for their tasks.

Atmospheric ventures elsewhere in the country (some eighty-two companies had been established for building them) were all eventually to be abandoned. Yet the South Devon experiment will always remain a tantalizing dream of what might have been —an eccentric foreshadowing of electric traction without the attendant horrors of electrocution. When it worked there was much in its favour. William Hunt, a prominent West Country journalist and a close observer of the then railway scene, sums it up best:

> I much regret its failure for it rendered railway travelling safe and pleasant. It made explosions and collisions impossible. There was no vibration, no noise of steam, no suffocating smoke or nauseating effluvia; but, alas, the travelling was uncertain.

Left with a permanent handicap of steep gradients and severe curves between Newton Abbot and Plymouth and forty miles of single track which it had later to double, the South Devon limped to its terminus at Millbay on 2 April 1849 to give Plymouth a service of six trains daily to and from Exeter. Because of the huge debt incurred on the atmospheric experiment, the South Devon had nothing left to spend (except for the immediate Plymouth area) for expansion. Most of the additions in other parts of its territory were made by local companies, with some assistance from the South Devon, which generally assumed responsibility for running them. In this way, by the time it was enfolded in the arms of the Great Western in 1876, the South Devon had extended through Torquay to Paignton, Brixham and Kingswear, to Moretonhampstead and Ashburton, and had crossed into Cornwall via Tavistock to Launceston, establishing in that ancient capital of the Duchy the only broad-gauge terminus in north Cornwall.

E

CORNWALL—BROAD AND NARROW GAUGE

Starting from the South Devon's inconveniently sited Millbay terminus (through trains had to reverse in and out of it), the Cornwall Railway, linking up with an older narrow-gauge company, was now to carry the broad gauge from Plymouth through the Cornish peninsula to Penzance, the most southwesterly town in the kingdom.

Among the shires and counties knit together by nineteenth-century British railway development, the Royal Duchy of Cornwall had characteristics which set it apart. Celtic, inward looking, isolated, its people looked to the mainland across a wide river which separated Cornwall from Devon and 'the Briton from the Englishman'. Behind this barrier they preserved the traditions of strange saints commemorated by churches standing among farms, fields and settlements with names prefixed by tre-, pol- and pen-, symbols of the old and then practically dead Cornish language. A quarter of the population burrowed underground for a living, emerging on Sundays to sing hearty revivalist hymns in Dissenting chapels and bethels. 'Fish, tin and copper', the age-old toast of Cornwall, reflected the sources of its wealth, to which the nineteenth century was to add china clay. Yet this isolated peninsula, its granite spine swept bare of trees by the fury of Atlantic gales, had developed through metal mining an engineering expertise only equalled in the early nineteenth century by the coal industry. Richard Trevithick, 'the Cornish giant', had taken out a patent for a railway locomotive long before Stephenson's *Rocket* appeared. A steam blast, an important feature of all subsequent steam locomotives, is thought to have been one of Trevithick's basic inventions. Cornwall's first railway, which joined a group of copper mines with the north-coast harbour of Portreath, was in everyday use by 1812, and in the 1820s and 30s the west of the county had an industrial railway system as advanced as anything in the north. The $9\frac{1}{2}$ mile narrow-gauge Hayle Railway (later developed to Penzance as the West Cornwall Railway and to become part of the Great Western main line) was authorized in the same year as the first Great Western Bill was thrown out of the Lords—a year that also saw the authorization of the Bodmin–Wadebridge Railway, the first in the kingdom to run an excursion train. Yet not until 1859 was a Cornishman able to travel the length of his county by a continuous line of railway.

For this, Cornwall's prickly individuality, political factions and lack of capital, particularly the latter, were mainly responsible. A direct line to London had been toyed with as early as 1835. Businessmen in Falmouth, looking in that year for a counterpart on land to the swift-sailing packets calling for orders at their port, thought they had found one in a project for a Cornwall Central Railway. This was a narrow-gauge promotion planned to pass through central Cornwall to Launceston, and thence to Okehampton, Exeter, Salisbury and London. Sanctioned by the Commons, it was thrown out by the Lords, only to be revived in 1845 stiffened with the backing of the LSWR. By this time the passing of the South Devon Bill had brought a promise of Great Western support for a broad-gauge railway from Plymouth to Falmouth running nearer the south coast than the Cornwall Central. Politics hovered over the rival schemes, Liberals supporting the central and Tories the coastal line. The Tories won, the central Bill being thrown out of Parliament on technical and commercial grounds. Thereafter it receded into the background to be a potential LSWR threat which was never to materialize. But had it done so it might well have been the better line, a faster and more direct route to London and the rest of the country. As it was, the clash in Parliament over the rival central and southern schemes was Cornwall's nearest glimpse of a gauge war.

The broad-gauge railway which emerged from this encounter had the backing not only of the Great Western but of the Bristol and Exeter and South Devon Railways. Brunel, whose reputation had weathered the atmospheric fiasco, surveyed and settled on a route which, although slightly modified in the early 1900s, was nearly as difficult to work as the South Devon's. Crossing the Tamar out of Plymouth it climbed to two crests of 435ft and 350ft between Liskeard and Truro, dropping in between to sea level and rising a further 420ft between Truro and Redruth before levelling out to Hayle and Penzance. Over the fifty-three miles between Plymouth and Truro there were thirty-

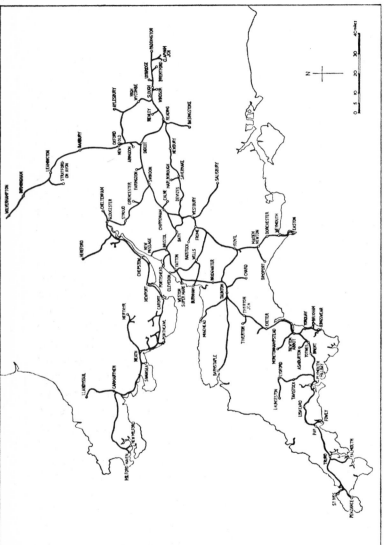

Fig 1 Map of Great Western and allied broad gauge lines including lines with mixed gauge, showing the maximum extent of Brunel's 7ft gauge. By the time the last broad-gauge branches to Ashburton and St Ives were built in the 1870s the broad gauge had already disappeared from much of South Wales and some other lines.

four of Brunel's famous timber viaducts, 'the like of which had never been seen before and will never be seen again'. Built up either on masonry or timber piers according to the type of country to be crossed, they creaked alarmingly as trains passed. In all they totalled over four miles in length, crossing valleys and tidal creeks at heights never attained again until modern skyscrapers. All were to be gradually replaced after the 1870s, most by masonry structures with clear spans higher than church towers.

Construction of the line was an affair of stops and starts, largely through money troubles. Scarcely had the first earthworks been started in 1847 than riots broke out, people claiming that the navvies would eat all the food—a not irrational fear in a county where the staple diet for many was potatoes, inferior bread and pilchards. The navvies were dismissed but then almost immediately the money ran out. All work came to a standstill until 1852 when the capital was reorganized and a decision made on Brunel's recommendation to build a single instead of a double track, although bridges and tunnels were made to double-line standards. Still money remained short. Nearly 36,000 shares were forfeited because the holders could not be made to pay their calls. In June 1855 the broad-gauge companies stepped in by agreeing to lease the railway from Plymouth to Truro and conditionally guaranteeing interest on shares. Before this the contractor for the Truro–Falmouth section had gone bankrupt and all work on that line was temporarily abandoned. Instead, the hard-up company concentrated on completing the line between Plymouth and Truro. Not until 4 May 1859, thirteen years after it was sanctioned, was this section officially open for traffic.

Two days earlier the Prince Consort had come down to name and open the bridge by which Brunel had carried the railway over the Tamar's 'silver stream'. What he saw was one of the finest monuments of Britain's railway age, its designer's masterpiece. To span the river at Saltash where it is 1,100ft wide and 70ft deep Brunel had thrown across two 450ft arched tubular spans joining in mid-river on four cast-iron columns secured to a central underwater pier. The spans were high enough to give the Navy's tall ships passing up and down a clear heading of at least 100ft above high water.

In building the bridge Brunel had profited from lessons learned in spanning the Wye at Chepstow. The central underwater pier anchored on hard rock 80ft below high-water level had been built up to river level by masons working in a pressurized diving bell—the first use of a compressed air caisson in civil engineering. The two 1,060 ton trusses or spans, each made up of an arch-shaped circular tube 16ft 9in wide and 12ft 3in high, were prefabricated on the Devon shore and floated on pontoons from which they were gradually jacked into position. Suspension chains of linked plates connected the tube ends, the chains' inward drag being balanced by the outward thrust of the tubes against the land abutments. This makes the whole structure a combination of arch and suspension bridge and as such it is the world's only chain-link suspension bridge that carries express trains.

Seven years in the building, and altered to take a single instead of double track, it cost £225,000. Even the hard-up Cornwall Railway acknowledged a bargain. 'Considering the extraordinary difficulties which were overcome and the magnitude of the operation, it is believed there is no engineering work in existence more economically completed', its directors noted in their succeeding half-yearly report. In gratitude they placed over the shore arches the inscription 'I. K. Brunel, engineer, 1859' in the large raised letters the traveller still sees today.

Although he had masterminded the floating of the first truss into position in September 1857, Brunel was not present when the Prince Consort opened the bridge. He was then ill from the disease which helped to kill him four months later and which has given rise to the deathless, but totally untrue, local legend, that he committed suicide by jumping into the river from the bridge.

Nine more years passed after bridging the Tamar before the Cornwall Railway was completed throughout. Falmouth, where prosperity had declined when the packet trade finally left in 1844, was linked to Truro on 24 August 1863. It was not, however, by the main line it had dreamed of thirty years earlier, but by a branch on which there were eleven more of Brunel's famous viaducts. Four years later (1 March 1867) the first broad-gauge passenger train steamed into Penzance from Truro. It did so over the older road of the narrow-gauge West Cornwall Railway realigned and altered to take mixed-gauge traffic under an agreement by·which the west Cornwall company, too poor to do the work itself, was absorbed in 1866 by the associated broad-gauge companies.

Thus, twenty years after parliamentary approval, the Cornwall Railway was finally completed over its seventy-eight miles from Plymouth to Penzance. In building it the broad gauge sang its swan-song and made its last great colonizing gesture before the tide of narrow-gauge conversion set in. With its completion, Penzance, which looked towards the western approaches to the kingdom, could clasp hands with the nation's capital in the east at Paddington.

The 300-odd miles of continuous railway which made this possible remain one of the most majestic and enduring monuments of broad-gauge enterprise.

CHAPTER 4

Near-Disaster—to the Golden Age

EARLY VICTORIAN GROWTH

By the middle 1860s the GWR was unlike any other railway in the country. Paddington administered an empire made up of two distinct and opposing halves. In one the broad gauge, based on Swindon, stretched from Paddington through Bristol to Penzance in the west, through Gloucester and Swansea to Neyland in South Wales and to Weymouth in the south. In the other, the narrow gauge with locomotives based on Wolverhampton was bounded by London, Oxford, Worcester, Newport, Shrewsbury and Birkenhead.

The broad gauge in mileage and territory had passed its zenith and was beginning to decline. Generally first-class passengers had travelled on it (and were to continue to do so for some time although in increasingly shabby coaches) in more comfort and often faster than on standard-gauge lines. By 1848 Gooch's great 8ft singles, unlike any other engines in the country in size and power, were doing the journey between London and Bristol in $2\frac{1}{2}$ hours. Between Paddington and Swindon the average speed was 59mph, nearly twice as fast as on any other railway. Although economies drastically slowed some of these times after 1852, the nearest man had hitherto come to such speeds had been on the racecourse, and to symbolize the power and triumph of steam the company had named its crack Paddington express the 'Flying Dutchman', after the Derby winner of 1849.

Earlier Queen Victoria had summed up the experience of broad-gauge train travel. After her railway journey in June 1842 from Slough to Paddington, making her the first reigning monarch to travel by train, she noted in her diary that it was free from dust, crowd and heat. The queen travelled with certain privileges. Because she was nervous, speeds were kept down to 35mph. She also had her own coach (at that time, the first eight-wheeled railway carriage in the country). Even so, less exalted travellers had a ride almost as comfortable in the first-class carriages. Most of the Great Western's broad gauge coaches had six wheels, which were safer than four. An exception were the early first-class posting or saloon carriages. These took eighteen people and 'were fitted up in a style of elegance not met with in any railway conveyances in the kingdom (save only the royal carriage)'. There were luxurious couches, cushions and sofas and 'even tables on which people may eat, read or play chess'.

Second-class travel was more spartan in carriages which, although roofed, were open at the sides to the wind and rain. At least one passenger was held by a coroner's jury to have died from cold and exposure 'while travelling in a second class carriage on the Great Western Railway'. Even they were better off than third-class travellers, 'persons in the lower stations of life', as Saunders called them in 1839. Looked on as little more than freight and less valuable than cattle, they sat in a 'variety of miseries' on benches in open trucks or uncovered wagons. Gladstone eased their plight a little by his Cheap Trains Act of 1844. This compelled the company to carry them at 1d a mile and give them some protection from the weather. To comply with this their open truck became for a time a wagon rather like a milk van 'with small Venetian ventilators at the top which admitted a moderate amount of air and served as windows'. A journey in such wagons from Bristol to London took 9½ hours.

Although carriage design slowly improved, along with the lot of second- and third-class passengers, the earlier horse age still dominated the design of the Great Western first-class carriages built between 1844 and 1853. Their style, appearance and proportions were those of the stage coach which the railway had effectually banished into the remembrance of things past. According to Dyos and Aldcroft in *British Transport*, there were 116 coaches licensed to travel as far as Taunton and Exeter in 1834 and they performed 807 journeys a week. By the end of

1843 all had disappeared. After 1863, with the 7ft gauge declining, no new broad-gauge carriages were built, and repairs to them were reduced to a minimum. By 1870 their classification told its own story. They were divided into best express, second best, ordinary and excursion, the last 'never to be used in regular trains except in case of absolute necessity'.

Although accidents on early Victorian railways were sufficiently frequent for *Punch* to remark that medical students would learn more on railway tracks than in hospitals, the broad gauge generally had a deserved reputation for safety. In twenty years of working there had been only two really serious accidents, killing fourteen people and injuring thirty. One reason for this was that, unlike their narrow-gauge counterparts, broad-gauge engines tended to stay on the line after collisions. Gooch had proved this at the opening of the Birmingham line when, misreading a signal near Aynho, he drove the *Lord of the Isles*, heading a directors' train, into the back of a mixed passenger and goods train. The latter's rear trucks were splintered but *Lord of the Isles* remained on the line.

The company had a rigid minimum time interval between passenger and goods trains and its general safety record was also helped by the care Brunel and Gooch took in choosing drivers. Brunel's active mind found train driving boring. Great Western drivers and firemen were denied any shelter on the engine in case they dozed off or missed signals. They were also chosen 'for their mechanical rather than literary abilities', on the assumption that illiterate minds were less likely to wander.

In 1855 a telegraph superintendent was appointed, the first on any railway, but train working had earlier been assisted by installing Wheatstone's electric magnetic telegraph, although the system was not originally used directly to assist in train signalling. With wires running by the side of the track in an iron pipe, this was an early form of dial telegraph and had been extended from Paddington to Slough by 1843. It achieved sensational publicity on New Year's Day 1845 by helping to capture a murderer in a manner uncannily foreshadowing the part played by wireless in 1912 in arresting Dr Crippen. Even the two crimes were similar; only the poisons administered differed. The doctor used hyoscine to dispose of an unwanted wife; the Slough murderer used cyanide to lace a glass of stout intended for a discarded mistress. It was her 'piercing shriek' after drinking the stout that led to a message being passed over the 'electric wires' to Paddington enabling the police to make an arrest after the murderer alighted from the London train. The use of the electric telegraph to form part of block signalling in place of time interval working was a later development.

Between 1840 and 1847 when it had grown to be the second largest railway in the kingdom, the company had 11·2 per cent of the total railway receipts, and although this figure had dropped to 6·3 per cent in 1850, by February 1851 passenger and mail traffic (the Post Office began carrying mails over the system in 1840) brought in nearly £300,000 in a year, a figure that rose to £848,800 in 1855. Goods traffic accounted for another £436,000. High freight rates, however, brought active opposition, particularly from Bristol traders. In 1855 a number of them boycotted the railway, chartering instead a steamer for trading between Bristol and London, a competitive venture which after ten years ceased suddenly when the steamer was wrecked off Land's End. Despite this discontent, by the end of the decade goods carriage over the railway had climbed to nearly £500,000, bringing the total receipts of the company to well over £1 million.

There was steady progress at Swindon, now growing into one of the country's great railway towns. By 1846, when the first passenger train engine came from its workshops, the influx of labour had become so great that the Swindon lock-up was too small to house the drunk and disorderly. One navvy was rescued from it by his mates tunnelling under the floor. By 1861 Swindon's population, which in 1801 had been little over 1,000, had expanded to 6,856, and it was to double that figure by 1870. A seventh of the people worked for the railway. Hours in the engine shops and sheds were from 6am to 6pm, half an hour longer than at Crewe. In 1856 they were shortened to 56½ hours a week. There was gross overcrowding in the new town and hardly any sanitation. Cesspools overflowed into the road. In the face of dire medical warnings, the company reacted by building over 300 model dwellings arranged along a grid-iron pattern of streets named after cities served by the railway. A school and a church were built, and until 1850, when it became a victim of an economy cut, the company paid the vicar's stipend of £150 a year. The directors' solicitude for their workers extended to the graveside (as well it might, for there was an average of one serious accident a week in the workshops), a horse and hearse being supplied free for an employee's funeral. For dependants, however, the hearse had to be paid for.

Swindon also had another claim to fame. This was to be found in its celebrated refreshment rooms, 'the most gorgeously decorated in provincial England'. The high walls 'ended in elaborately decorated cornices, while winged cherubs blew trumpets and waved flower garlands among flowers painted on the high ceilings'. Although this artistry was not matched by the food and drink served during the compulsory ten-minute stop, the refreshment rooms, under independent management, generally showed a profit whatever the financial state of the company. In 1846 the latter was sufficiently buoyant to encourage the directors to support Ascot races by a gift of 300 guineas to run the Great Western stakes. Frowned on by more Puritan-minded members of the board, the subscription was reduced to 100 guineas in 1852. Four years later an economy cut extinguished it altogether. Thus ended the only national railway stakes in British racing history.

At Plymouth the company had built its first docks, designed by Brunel who travelled down to supervise their building, 'writing his illegible fist all the time and smoking'. Their situation close to the South Devon's Millbay station led in 1851 to the inauguration of a monthly steamer service to India, Australia and China. Steamer links with the railway had also been developed elsewhere. From New Milford, in South Wales, there was a packet service to Waterford, in Ireland. In 1857 Weymouth also saw the beginning of steamer traffic, although the company's direct involvement in steamer services through boat ownership was still sixteen years away. Not least, in 1854 the hole-in-corner arrangement at Bishop's Road bridge which had served as a London terminus gave way to the splendour of Brunel's new Paddington station which was to suffice without extension for another fifty years.

GREAT WESTERN RAILWAY.

NOTICE.

The Great Western Company give Notice that the conveyance of

PASSENGER & GOODS TRAFFIC

BY THEIR RAILWAY

WILL BE SUSPENDED BETWEEN

ROSS AND HEREFORD

AND BETWEEN

ROSS & GRANGE COURT,

For about a fortnight, during the latter part of August, for the purpose of converting the Line from the Broad to the Narrow Gauge, so as to form a Through Route between Gloucester and the North.

WELL-APPOINTED COACHES

WILL RUN BETWEEN

Hereford & Ross, and Ross & Grange Court,

During the time of the Alteration in the Line.

Hand Bills will be issued giving particulars of the running of the Coaches in connection with the Trains.

J. GRIERSON, General Manager.

PADDINGTON, *July* 27, 1869.

McCorquodale & Co., Printers, "The Armoury," Southwark.

Fig 2 Temporarily back to the horse-drawn age to allow the broad-gauge network to shrink. Many of the details of this notice are in the GWR mould that lasted well into the twentieth century

GOOCH GETS A FREE HAND

Until the middle 1850s, four men—Russell, Saunders, Gooch and Brunel—had virtually controlled the railway. With the approach of the 1860s death and retirement brought changes. Charles Russell, the 'man of honour' who had upheld Brunel in his darkest hour, was the first to go, retiring at seventy in August 1855 after twenty years as chairman. Almost immediately tragedy struck him down. Within a year his mind gave way, leading him, like his predecessor Sims, to die by his own hand. Four years later Brunel was in his grave, killed by overwork, frustration and a kidney ailment. In 1864 Saunders died worn out in the company's service, his end probably hastened by the hostility of some Bristol shareholders towards granting him a pension. He was blamed as the originator of the company's northern extensions when, in general, he had been opposed to them. His death left Gooch as the last of the great quartet. Gooch's engines, more than anything else, had shown what the broad gauge could do; he now saw it being increasingly challenged by the advancing tide of the narrow gauge. As well, he was at odds with a board 'little guided by the usual principles that govern men of honour'. In the summer of 1864 Gooch resigned, intent on employing his considerable talents in laying the first Atlantic cable.

He left a railway which was now in deep trouble. The cost of nearly twenty years' expansion had cut remorselessly into dividends. The 7 per cent paid in the last half of 1847 represented a figure not seen again for three-quarters of a century. Nothing at all was paid in the first half of 1858. Only the protests of outraged shareholders secured $1\frac{1}{4}$ per cent for the second half of that year, the lowest dividend the company ever paid. Additionally, the board, which since the amalgamation now included members of the West Midland and South Wales Railways, was distracted by sectional interests. Since Russell's death there had been six chairmen in ten years. Always in the background, too, was the problem of the 7ft gauge. On the pretext of interchange difficulties its very existence provoked attack on its territory. A renewed outburst of railway speculation in 1863 threatened the system at a dozen or more points. In February 1865 the independently promoted broad-gauge Vale of Neath Railway (Neath to Merthyr Tydfil with a branch to Aberdare) had to be absorbed from fear that the LNWR and Midland would use it to reach Swansea and the Aberdare mining area.

With chairmen coming and going the company drifted without firm guidance. As no one appeared willing to hold office longer than two years, the directors turned to the servant who had so lately left them. Still only fifty-six, Gooch in his year's absence had failed to lay the Atlantic cable but had become MP for the borough of Cricklade, although he found canvassing small traders 'detestable'. He did not want the chairmanship. 'There were too many men on the board with whom I had no inclination to work', he noted. The offer, however, was renewed. As his price Gooch demanded 'a completely free hand'. With this understanding he became chairman in 1865 of the railway he had earlier resigned from as locomotive superintendent. He took some months off to complete laying his Atlantic cable, a feat which earned him a knighthood. It was in September 1866 that he finally sat down to his railway duties.

The new chairman brought to his task a shrewd financial mind, but little imagination. With no magic panacea for a railway staring at bankruptcy, his was a policy of retrenchment. On taking over he found a state of affairs which 'horrified' him. 'Half a million of rolling stock had just been ordered, large new stations at Reading and Slough had been put in hand without any clear estimate of their cost or provision to meet them.' At Oxford there was a proposal to spend between £60,000 and £70,000 building new carriage works on a site which the winter rains flooded. This scheme was being strongly pressed, against the opposition of the university authorities, by the chairman, William Potter, whom Gooch thought was a 'vain, soft-headed fool blown about by any wind'.

Not only its own policies but outside events conspired against the company. The 'Black Friday' collapse in May 1866 of the bankers Overend and Gurney, along with other firms who had been over speculating, hit it hard. The collapse came when nearly £14 million of renewable debentures was in circulation and more than £1 million outstanding in temporary loans. Current revenue was raided to meet the crisis. Appeals to the Bank of England for a loan fell on deaf ears. The company was told to rescue itself. Shares began to tumble with rumours that it was unable to meet its debts. James Grierson, in the new post of general manager, expected to see the Receiver called in at any moment. Insolvency was only narrowly averted by the continued use of revenue and by offering shareholders additional preference shares instead of dividends.

From now on a policy of rigid economy stamped Gooch's conservative image on the company for nearly twenty years. Trains were cut, mileage reduced, repairs to broad-gauge stock kept to a minimum and stations left unpainted. The 'Flying Dutchman', the company's prestige speed symbol, disappeared from the timetables. The Oxford carriage works were quietly abandoned, to be built later at Swindon for £20,000 less. Only the fares and goods charges remained high, a potent source of complaint among passengers and traders. Brunel's railway, ended the sixties and entered the seventies lapped in deep lethargy—too poor to be enterprising, too mean to be smart. Even in the 1880s Foxwell was still noting that its porters handled passengers' luggage with heartfelt inertia.

But Gooch's drastic medicine worked. Other railways had been badly hit in the 1866 banking collapse; few weathered the storm so well as the Great Western. Dividends were being paid again by 1868. With their reappearance a decision had to be taken about that other pressing problem, the future of the broad gauge. This had now become not only a physical, but a psychological handicap, inducing a complacency in its superiority increasingly less justified compared with rapidly improving narrow-gauge standards. In 1867 there were roughly 1,500 miles of broad-gauge track with 700 engines. When in 1859 a shareholder had boldly proposed that it should be torn up for the narrow gauge he was shouted down. Now ten years later the dilemma was not whether, but when, it should disappear. In South Wales traders were solid for its removal. There were now breaks of gauge at more than thirty points cutting off the company from the fertilizing benefits of interchange traffic with other railways. Gooch, the last and perhaps the greatest broad-champion, had now with a heavy heart to prepare for its execution.

The Great Western Railway was one of the early pioneers in self-contained rail motor units in an attempt to cut operating costs on lightly-used services. The first appeared between Stonehouse and Chalford in 1903 and were gradually extended to many parts of the system. *Plate 15 (above)* This steam railcar is seen working up the main line near Acton. They had their limitations and were eventually replaced by the familiar push-pull trains with separate locomotive. *Plate 16 (below)* In the 1930s the GWR again tried railcars, this time with diesel propulsion, which successfully took over the working of many branches and main line stopping services. When British Railways was evolving its diesel multiple-unit programme in the 1950s it looked closely at the experience of the GWR with diesel railcars. *(Locomotive & General Railway Photographs)*

The Great Western had an enviable safety record, particularly during the present century with a remarkably low number of collisions. *Plate 17 (above)* In October 1890 an up broad-gauge express hauled by 4-4-0 saddle tank No 2051, with a lightweight express, collided head-on at Norton Fitzwarren with a goods train which had been shunted on to the up line for a down train to pass. The signalman cleared his signals for the express by mistake, having forgotten the standing goods train. From this accident lever collars were evolved to place over levers as a reminder to the signalman. *Plate 18 (below)* In 1906 the Great Western Railway conducted the first experiments with its mechanical-contact automatic warning system which was applied at distant signals and gave audible indications on the locomotive footplate. This helped to prevent drivers missing the signals or mis-reading them. The plunger under the motive power unit which engaged the track ramp, is seen here as fitted to a British Railways diesel unit. *(Locomotive & General Railway Photographs; British Railways)*

The first conversions began in a small way in 1866. By 1869 broad-gauge trains had ceased running north of Oxford, although this had been accelerated by the Oxford, Worcester and Wolverhampton Railway's abandonment ten years earlier of the broad gauge. Wales saw its last broad-gauge train in 1872. By 1873 some 200 miles of branches south of the main line in Berkshire, Wiltshire, Hampshire and Somerset had also been converted. Two years later mixed gauge was complete between London and Bristol.

LAST STRONGHOLD OF THE BROAD GAUGE

The last stronghold of the broad gauge was in the West Country over the Bristol and Exeter, the South Devon and Cornwall Railways. Here sentiment and affection wedded it to the area. Once past Newton Abbot, the traveller heading west came into another world. Timekeeping, as if reflecting the slower pulse of life, seemed scarcely to matter. The ugly, squat tank engines of the South Devon Railway toiled over a hilly and twisting line to Plymouth at 25mph. That company, still hard up after the atmospheric fiasco, gave its drivers liberal premiums for saving coal. Sekon, seeing a train ascending a bank at 6mph and rolling down the other side with steam off, remarked that it was certainly a vivid example of economy. On passenger trains journeys were a little faster, but could have unexpected distractions. Waves often came over the sea wall between Dawlish and Teignmouth, flooding the carriages. Passengers climbed on to the seats to keep dry 'or were amused by the screams from an adjoining compartment from some frightened females'.

The fastest train of the day, if on time, took 7 hours 5 minutes to do the 240-odd miles from Paddington to Plymouth. In December 1869 it was remarked by the Plymouth *Western Morning News*, almost as a matter of congratulation, that 'the 9.15am express from Paddington was less than an hour late reaching Plymouth and the mail only two hours late. These were the two worst instances and both of them showed a great improvement on last year.'

Poverty and a refusal to hurry also distinguished the Cornwall Railway. Without engines of its own, it relied on the South

LINE.　　　　　　　　　　　Week Days.

STATIONS.	N.G. 46 Bristol and Taunton Ordinary Goods.		N.G. 47 Empty Train.		B.G. 48 Paddington and Penzance Passenger.		N.G. 49 Portishead Goods.		B.G. 50 Creech and Taunton Goods.		N.G. 51 Taunton and Barnstaple Passenger.		52	
	arr.	dep.	arr.	dep.	arr.	dep.	arr.	dep.	arr.	dep.	arr.	dep.		
	A.M.	A.M.	A.M.	A.M.	A.M.	A.M.	A.M.	A.M.	A.M.	A.M.	A.M.	A.M.		
Paddington	....	....	....	....	....	5 30	....	....	....	....	....	....	....	....
Swindon	..	....	..	....	7 39	7 49	..	..	..	..	..	..	..	..
Nth. Somrst Jc	....	....	....	....			**R.R.**		....	....	....	....		
Bristol ..	..	..	..	9 0	9 0	9 15	..	..	..	..	..	..	..	..
Pylle Hill	....	8 30	—	—	—	—	....	9 20	....	....	....	....	....	....
Bedminster ..	—	—	—	—	—	—	—	—	....	....	....	..	..	....
Malago Sid. ..	**CR**		—	—	—	—	—	—	....	....	....	....	....	....
Portishead Jc.	—	—	—	—	—	—	9 13		..	..	..	..	..	..
S. Liberty S...	—	—	—	—	—	—	....	....	..	..	..	..	..	..
Bourton	—	—	—	—	—	—	..	..	..	..	..	..	..	..
Nailsea	—	—	—	—	—	—	..	....	..	..	..	..	..	..
Yatton	**CR**		9 20	....	9 35	9 38	..	..	..	..	..	..	..	..
Puxton	—	—	—	—	—	—	..	....	..	..	..	..	..	..
Worle Junc...	9 14		..	..	—	—	..	..	..	..	..	..	..	..
Worle	....	....	....	....	—	—	....	....	..	..	....	....	..	..
Wst-s-M	9 20	9 55	....	....	—	—	....	....	..	..	....	....	..	..
Uphill Junct.	10 0	10 18	..	..	9 51		....	..	..	..	..	..	..	..
Bldn. & Uphill	—	—	....	....	—	—	....	..	..	..	..	..	..	..
Brent Knoll ..	—	—	....	....	—	—	....	..	..	..	..	..	..	..
Highbridge ..	10 38	10 50	....	....	10 2	10 5	....	..	..	..	..	..	..	..
Pottery Sidg.	—	—	....	....	—	—	....	..	..	..	..	..	..	..
Dunball	11 0	11 10	....	....	—	—	....	..	..	..	..	..	..	..
Bridgwater	11 20	11 40	..	..	10 17	10 20	..	..	..	..	..	..	..	..
Durston	11 55	12 5	..	..	10 32	10 36	..	..	..	..	..	..	..	..
Chard Junction			..	..	—	—	..	..	..	10 55	..	..	..	..
Taunton	12 20	....	....	....	10 48	10 53	....	....	11 0	....	....	11 20	....	....
Notn. Ftzwarn	..	..	..	..	—	—	....	..	..	..	11 25	11 26	..	..
Victory Siding	....	....	....	....	—	—	....	..	..	..	....	....	..	..
Poole Siding..	....	....	....	....	—	—	....	..	..	..	....	....	..	..
Wellington ..	....	....	....	....	11 6	11 8	....	..	..	..	....	....	..	..
Whiteball Sid.	..	..	..	..	—	—	....	..	..	..	..	..	..	..
Burlescombe..	....	....	..	..	—	—	....	..	..	..	..	..	..	..
Sampford Sid.	..	..	..	..	—	—	....	..	..	..	..	..	..	..
Tiverton Junc.	....	....	..	..	11 26	11 30	....	..	..	..	..	..	..	..
Cullompton ..	....	....	....	....	—	—	..	..	..	..	..	..	..	..
Kensham Sid.	....	....	....	....	—	—	..	..	..	..	..	..	..	..
Hele & Bdnch.	..	..	..	..	—	—	..	..	..	..	..	..	..	..
Silverton	..	..	..	..	—	—	....	..	..	..	..	..	..	..
Stoke Canon ..	....	..	..	..	—	—	....	..	..	..	..	..	..	..
Stoke Canon J.	....	....	..	..	—	—	....	..	..	..	..	..	..	..
Cowley Bdg' J.	....	....	..	..	—	—	....	....	..	..	..	..	..	..
Extr.Tkt.Pltm	....	....	....	....	—	—	....	....	..	..	..	..	..	..
Exeter	..	..	..	..	11 50	11 58	..	..	..	..	..	..	..	..
St. Thomas ..	....	....	..	..	12 1	12 4	....	....	....	....	....	....	....	....
Newton Abbot	..	..	..	..	12 48	12 54	..	..	..	..	..	..	..	..
Plymouth	....	....	....	....	2 20	2 35	..	..	..	..	..	..	..	..
Penzance ..	..	..	..	..	6 25	..	..	..	..	..	..	..	..	..

Fig 3　A section of the Great Western service timetable for the use of staff, covering the former Bristol & Exeter line in 1886. In particular it shows the 5.30am from Paddington.

Week Days.

STATIONS.	K Mine-head Frght. SX	A Passenger. SX		∧ Passenger. SO 11th July to 22nd August, inclusive.		9.20 a.m. Torrington to Waterloo Passenger. SO		A 8.10 a.m. Newport Passenger. SO 4th July to 29th August, inclusive.		F 3.35 a.m. Acton Freight. MSX		B Passenger. SX	
	dep.	arr.	dep.	arr.	dep.	arr.	dep.	arr.	dep.	arr.	dep.	arr.	dep.
	a.m.	a.m.	a.m.	a.m.	a.m.	a.m.	a.m.	a.m.	a.m.	a.m.	a.m.	a.m.	a.m.
Paddington	....	—	5 30	—	7 40	..	..	..	..	...	...	....	....
Bristol	..	8 34	8 50	—	..	..	..	8 59	9 15	...	...	..	..
Highbridge (¶¶)◄━	....	9 18		...	....	....	....	9 18		....	...	....	....
Pottery Siding ...	...	—	—	...	....	....	....	3 minutes		....	...	....	....
Dunball	...	—	—	...	....	...	...	recovery		...	...	....	....
BRIDGWATER	..	9 30	9 33	...	....	...	....	Highbridge to Taunton		...	...	....	....
Westbury	....	....	..	....	9 44	..	....	..	....	7 39C	T7 44	....	..
Castle Cary ....◄━	...	....	..	...		...	....	..	....	8 59		....	..
Alford Halt	...	..	..	...	—	...	....	..	....	—	—	....	..
Kelnton Mandeville	...	..	..	...	—	...	....	..	....	—	—	....	..
Charlton Mackrell..	...	..	..	...	—	...	....	..	....	—	—	....	..
Somerton (Som.)....	...	..	..	...	—	...	..	..	....	—	—	....	..
Long Sutton & P'ney	...	..	..	...	—	...	..	..	....	—	—	....	..
Langport East	...	..	..	...	—	...	..	..	....	—	—	....	..
Curry Rivel Jct. ..	...	..	..	...	—	...	..	..	....	—	—	....	..
Athelney	...	..	..	...	—	...	..	..	....	—	—	....	..
Lyng Halt	....	..	..	....	....	....	..	..	..	....	....	....	..
Durston	..	9 41	9 43	...	....	....	..	..	....	..	..	..	..
Cogload	....	R L		M L		....	....	M L		M L		....	....
Creech St. M. Halt	....	R 9 48L		M 10 7½L		....	....	M 10 11 L		M 9 50 L		....	....
Creech Junction	....	R L		M L		....	....	M L		G L		....	....
Taunton East Jct...	....	R L		M L		....	....	M L		9 56E	T10 20	....	....
TAUNTON	10 0	9 53	10 1	10 10		....	....	10 10	10 16	—	—	....	....
Taunton West Stn..	....	M L		M L		....	....	M L		—	—	....	....
Fairwater Sidings ..	....	—	—	—	—	....	....	—	—	—	—	....	....
Silkmill	—	—	—	—	—	....	....	—	—	—	—	....	....
Norton Fitzwarren	10 7	—	—	—	—	....	....	—	—	—	—	....	....
Victory Siding	....	—	—	—	—	....	....	—	—	10 28	10 48	....	....
Poole Siding	....	—	—	—	—	....	....	—	—	—	—	....	....
Wellington (Som.)..	..	10 12	10 14	—	—	....	....	—	—	11 0B	E11 2	....	....
Whiteball Tunnel..	..	—	—	10 16		....	....	10 31		11 18		....	....
Burlescombe	....	—	—	—	—	....	....	—	—	—	—	....	....
Sampford Peverell..	....	—	—	—	—	....	....	—	—	—	—	....	....
Tiverton Junction..	....	N	—	1 mi	nute	....	....	2 min	utes	—	—	....	..
Cullompton	....			reco	very	....	....	reco	very	—	—	....	..
Hele and Bradninch	....	4 minutes		—	—	....	....	—	—	—	—	....	..
Silverton	....	recovery.		—	—	....	....	—	—	—	—	....	..
Stoke Canon	....	TX		—	—	....	....	—	—	—	—	....	..
Cowley Bridge Jct.	...	10 44		10 43		10 48		10 50		—	—	....	..
Exeter (Riverside) .	...	—	—	—	—			—	—	12 19	12 40	....	..
EXETER (St. David's)	....	10 47	10 58	10 45		10 51	10 55	10 53	10 58	—	—	.:	..
St. Thomas	....	—	—	—	—	....	....	—	—	—	—	....	..
City Basin Jct....	....	—	—	—	—	....	....	—	—	12 54	1 40	....	..
Exminster	....	—	—	—	—	....	....	—	—	—	—	....	..
Starcross	....	—	—	—	—	....	....	—	—	—	—	....	..
Dawlish Warren ...	....	—	—	—	—	....	....	—	—	—	Z	....	..
Dawlish	....	11 14	1115½	5 min	utes	....	....	—	—	—	—	....	..
Teignmouth	....	11 21	11 23	reco	very	....	....	—	—	—	—	....	..
Old Quay	....	—	—	—	—	....	....	—	—	—	—	....	..
Hackney	....	—	—	—	—	....	....	—	—	2 12	—	....	..
NEWTON ABBOT ...	....	11 31	11 39	11 15C	11 20	....	....	11 24	11 29	..	—	—	11 40
Aller Junction	....	11 42		11 43		....	....	11 32		..		11 43	
Kingskerwell	....	....	....	2 min	utes	....	....	2 min	utes	....	....	—	11 46
Stop Board	....	....	....	reco	very	....	....	reco	very	....	....	....	....
Torre	....	....	....	—	—	....	....	—	—	....	....	11 52	11 56
Stop Board	....	....	....	—	—	....	....	—	—	....	....	....	....
TORQUAY	....	....	....	11 34	11 39	....	....	11 43	11 48	....	....	11 58	12 0
Gas House Siding ..	..	....	....	—	—	....	....	—	—	....	....	—	—
Paignton	..	....	....	11 44		....	....	11 53		....	....	12 5	12 7
Goodrington Yard	....	....	....	—	—	....	....	—	—	....	....	—	—
Goodrington S.H.	....	....	....	..	..	..	..	..	..	....	....	12 9	12 11
Churston..........	....	..	..	..	..	..	..	..	..	....	....	12 16	X12 22
Stop Board	....	..	..	..	..	..	..	..	..	....	....	—	—
Kingswear C'sing ..	....	..	..	..	..	..	..	..	..	....	....	—	—
KINGSWEAR	....	..	..	..	..	..	..	..	..	....	....	12 35	—
Stoneycombe Siding	..	..	..	..	..	..	..	..	..	....	....	..	..
Dainton Siding....	..	11 47		..	..	..	..	..	..	....	....	..	...
Totnes ....◄━	..	11 55	11 58	..	..	..	..	..	..	....	....	..	..
Plymouth	..	12 43	1 0	..	..	..	..	..	..	....	....	..	..
Penzance...........	..	4 25	—	..	..	..	..	..	..	....	....	..	..

N—On Tuesdays, calls at Tiverton Junction 10.28 a.m. to 10.29 a.m.

Z—To be kept clear of 10.35 a.m. (SX RR) Paddington to Penzance, when that train runs.

¶¶—Highbridge and Burnham-on-Sea.

Fig 4   The same section of line is covered in this 1953 extract from the Western Region service timetable, also including the 5.30am from Paddington.

Devon for motive power. But its coaching stock was its own, particularly some first-class coaches built as an experiment in a 'thin but enduring wood'. The wood certainly endured, for one coach lasted until 1957, serving out its last years as the ground floor of a cottage. Trains which a local newspaper described as 'much given to dawdling' stopped at all stations, taking $2\frac{1}{2}$ hours to do the fifty-nine miles from Truro to Plymouth. To get from Paddington to Penzance a traveller often started in daylight and arrived in darkness. Still, this was much faster than the stage coach, even for third-class passengers, whose slow trains took 13–14 hours. And in any case speed was relative. Francis Kilvert, the diarist, returning from Cornwall in 1870, could speak of trains which 'flew through all the length of the western shires'.

Nevertheless, despite its imperfections, the broad gauge in Devon and Cornwall proved the most potent instrument of social change since the Norman Conquest. Some of these changes had been hard to accept. Away from the railway, inland market towns in Devon with age-old agricultural traditions began to decay; Exeter's canal lost its importance; the trade and ship-building industries of the small south-coast harbours withered and died. But for others there was an enrichment of life. Plymouth became the business metropolis of Cornwall when the railway reduced to minor importance overnight the age-old road link (today's A30) between Cornwall and Devon through Launceston. In South Devon, it determined the pattern of holiday development and settlement. Previously select watering places like Teignmouth, where Keats had once stayed, burgeoned. Torquay, which in 1801 had little over 1,000 people, could figure in an 1861 railway guide as a resort of 11,000, 'swelling to sometimes twice as much in the summer'. Where there was no railway, however, there was no resort. Thus Dartmouth saw Kingswear (reached by rail in 1864) blossomed at its expense while Salcombe with its cosy yacht harbour was to see the railway come only as far as Kingsbridge. Not until the coach and car supplanted the steam train in the late 1950s did the pendulum begin to swing back for some of these forgotten towns.

The pattern differed slightly in Cornwall. Already its richest mines were in decay, and in any case their mineral ores were shipped to South Wales for smelting. The holiday industry symbolized by the rise of Newquay (reached by passenger trains in 1876) was to blossom later in the century. But the railway boosted fishing and agriculture. It tempted fishermen out on Sundays. For the first time ever a day's catch off the Cornish coast could be sold in Billingsgate twenty-four hours later. Soon 1,000 tons a year were being sent to London. Newlyn grew to become the major fishing port of the county, a place it still holds. Regular train services meant also that meat could be despatched in quantity to London. So many oxen were slaughtered for the lucrative metropolitan market that they temporarily disappeared from Cornish fields. From the Isles of Scilly potatoes (flowers followed later in the century) were increasingly exported, the change from narrow to mixed gauge between Penzance and Truro in November 1866 saving as much as a day in handling goods. A more mixed benefit was railway time which the town clocks indicated by a third red hand. As this was twenty minutes later in Cornwall than in London it provided endless controversy in prosecutions over the licensing laws.

Until 1870 this broad-gauge world in the far south-west had been cosy and enclosed. Keeping mainly to the south coast (although through the Bristol and Exeter Railway it was to push out from Taunton to Barnstaple in 1873 and to Minehead from Watchet a year later), the broad gauge had taken in its stride the appearance of the LSWR at Exeter in July 1860, despite the latter's better-situated station there and its threat of competitive timing to London. But by 1871 the LSWR had crept to Okehampton and three years later to Lydford. From there it glared at Plymouth and menaced the broad-gauge hegemony in Cornwall. To this the broad gauge reacted by allowing third-class passengers on its secondary expresses (the LSWR admitted them to all its West Country expresses) and accelerated the 'Flying Dutchman' (restarted in 1869) to reach Plymouth in $6\frac{1}{4}$ hours, a timing which remained for the next twenty years. But the South Western's grip grew ever tighter. In 1874 under the very nose of the Great Western and its Bristol and Exeter counterpart it gobbled up with the aid of the Midland, the Somerset and Dorset Railway (Bath to Bournemouth), thereby robbing the Great Western of much through traffic from the Midlands to the south. Two years later it was in Plymouth itself running from Lydford over 'mixed' South Devon Railway track. It was not a very good arrangement but it heralded the coming of an active and competitive LSWR route from Plymouth to London.

In fighting off this stealthy, competitive challenge in its last stronghold the broad gauge was at a curious disadvantage. The LSWR masterminded its entire policy single-handed from Waterloo. The long Great Western main line from Paddington to Penzance, in contrast, was a combination of associated companies made of itself, the B&E, the South Devon and Cornwall Railways. They were administered by a joint committee which, although separate from that running the leased Cornwall Railway, handled through rates, fares and matters of day-to-day concern. It was an arrangement unique in the kingdom, but although it worked well it emphasized the isolation of the broad gauge in the West.

The increasing LSWR threat, made more sinister by the latter's plotting with the Midland (revealed in the Somerset and Dorset Railway coup), compelled a change. It came in 1876 when the three Devon and Cornwall companies amalgamated with the Great Western, giving the latter, for all practical purposes, direct responsibility for the whole broad-gauge route from Bristol to Penzance. The Great Western now not only had a better claim to its title but became the longest railway in the country. More important were three other immediate advantages: Paddington gained the unitary control it needed; Great Western third-class passengers soon benefited from the South Western's policy (1877) of abolishing express fares, thus compelling the Great Western to follow suit, although only to stations it ran to in competition with the LSWR; and lastly it brought back into Paddington's fold the Bristol and Exeter Railway.

END OF THE B&E

The Bristol and Exeter Railway had been frightened into amalgamation by fear of a Midland Railway takeover. It had parted from the Great Western in 1849 when its lease with the latter terminated and at a time when the Great Western sought to promote a more direct (ie not via Bristol) line from Exeter to London.

Declining Paddington's compensation terms but remaining a broad-gauge railway, it went on to pursue its own way for twenty-seven years.

The Bristol and Exeter had given Devon its first passenger railway, and when assuming its independence had nearly 100 miles of track ending at Bristol in a terminus once described as 'the most disgraceful, dangerous, difficult and unpracticable in Europe'. This was because of its arrangement at right angles with Temple Meads station, a curve being built to allow B&E trains to manoeuvre into the Great Western station. In 1854 it moved into handsome offices put up in the Jacobean style, the chief ornament today of its independent existence. By spur lines, absorption and leases the company gradually extended its mileage until by 1876 it had expanded its system to over 213 miles of which 138 were its own property. It took in places as far apart as Clevedon and Yeovil, Wells and Chard, Tiverton and Minehead. It helped Weston-super-Mare to grow from a place-name to a prosperous dormitory of Bristol, enabled Bridgwater (including Dunball Wharf, Burnham and Highbridge) to become the fifth coal importing port in Britain, and saw Taunton grow in population from 10,000 to 50,000. Over its main Bristol–Exeter line, on which by 1876 mixed gauge had been laid, poppies grew in such profusion that they appeared to wave to passing trains. Despite this floral gaiety it shared with its greater neighbour the distinction of running what were then the fastest trains in the world over a permanent way that was dubbed the Bristol and Exeter racecourse.

As well as the largest, it was also the most consistently prosperous, of the broad-gauge Associated Companies, its dividends never falling below 4 per cent. Claiming never to have lost a life by accident, it was nevertheless reviled by its users for the 'extreme illiberality of its system of management', another way of saying that its fares and rates were too high. These, for first and second class, were the highest in the country, while its third-class accommodation was among the worst, even by the standards of those days. Bristol traders found it cheaper to ship goods to Plymouth and Torquay and have them taken to Exeter by the South Devon Railway—a combined sea and rail journey three times as long but twice as cheap. When finally it

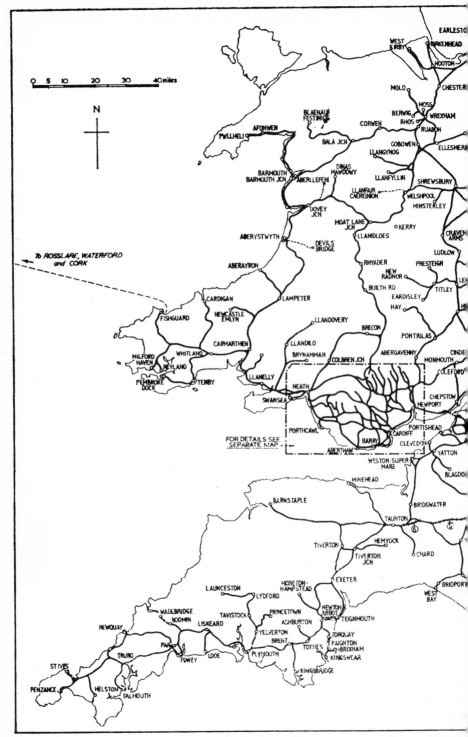

Fig 5 General map of the Great Western system at its maximum e

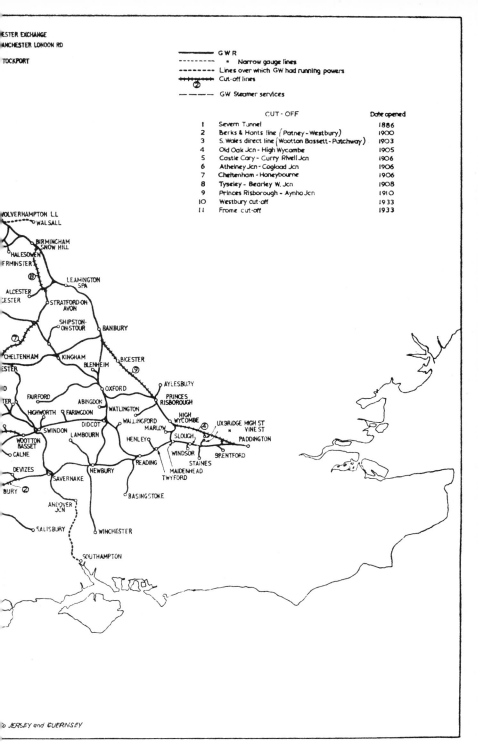

———————— G W R
---------- ▪ Narrow gauge lines
-------- Lines over which GW had running powers
+++++++++ Cut-off lines ②
— — — GW Steamer services

	CUT-OFF	Date opened
1	Severn Tunnel	1886
2	Berks & Hants line (Patney - Westbury)	1900
3	S. Wales direct line (Wootton Bassett - Patchway)	1903
4	Old Oak Jcn - High Wycombe	1905
5	Castle Cary - Curry Rivell Jcn	1906
6	Athelney Jcn - Cogload Jcn	1906
7	Cheltenham - Honeybourne	1906
8	Tyseley - Bearley W. Jcn	1908
9	Princes Risborough - Aynho Jcn	1910
10	Westbury cut-off	1933
11	Frome cut-off	1933

showing the cut off lines built at various stages in the company's history gave up its independence its faults were commemorated for posterity by an anonymous rhymester:

> Here lies from malediction free,
> The niggardly, grasping B&E:
> High fares and bad accommodation
> Made it renowned throughout the nation;
> In life its customers it bled
> And o'er the grave no tears are shed
> Save such as kind folk will be venting
> When their foes die without repenting.

THE SEVERN'S CHALLENGE

Ten years after Paddington had consolidated its West of England route (although its train services still brought more complaint than praise) the directors recorded the end of the most spectacular engineering task the company had undertaken since Brunel had built his original main line. This was the boring of the Severn tunnel to shorten the route to South Wales—the one great imaginative stroke of Gooch's chairmanship.

The Great Western had entered the 1870s still tightly held in his conservative grip but again earning a steady dividend. A dividend in March 1869 of $3\frac{3}{4}$ per cent, the highest for eighteen years, had climbed by 1873 to $6\frac{1}{4}$ per cent, the best for twenty-five years. It had been achieved, however, at the price of almost complete stagnation. Gooch too, was now almost a spent force and the railway he ruled highly unpopular. There had been a fitful glimpse of wider horizons when in 1872 a shipping department was inaugurated. Six years later there was a link with the French railways through the inauguration of a Weymouth–Cherbourg packet service. In 1889 the Great Western took over the Weymouth and Channel Islands steamer service.

Sixteen years before this, however, work had started on the Severn tunnel. The compulsion behind it was a strictly economic one springing from a phenomenon then scarcely without equal in industrial Britain. This was the growth of coal production in South Wales, which was now becoming the world's largest exporter of coal. From Cardiff northwards to the Rhondda and Aberdare valleys the countryside in little more than twenty years had developed into one vast coalfield. In the Rhondda alone twenty new collieries opened in the ten years from 1865 and production grew from a half million to 2 million tons a year. By the 1880s the total production in South Wales had reached 21·2 million tons a year; the influx of miners was pushing up Glamorgan's population faster than that of any other part of the United Kingdom. Cardiff had overtaken Newcastle as the nation's 'coal metropolis' and had expanded its dock accommodation five times since the railway opened. By now, too, railway control had been extended to the city's docks along with those of Barry and Newport.

Much of this coal, as shown earlier, was siphoned off for export over independently owned lines like the Taff Vale and Rhymney Railways running between the pits and the ports. But the Great Western, now standard-gauge and with a trunk line traversing the southern half of the Principality between the mountains and the sea, was the main outlet for its transport inland, particularly to London and the south-coast ports. Between the coalfields and southern England, however, the river Severn interposed a barrier almost as absolute as the ocean, with violent tidal rises of as much as 50ft and a bore, or tidal wave, which goes up the river 'at the speed of a galloping horse'. It forced the company's coal trains, both leaving and approaching South Wales, to make the circuitous and time-consuming detour via Gloucester. The single-line Bristol and South Wales Union Railway opened in 1863, despite being built to improve access between Bristol, Newport and Cardiff, afforded no real alternative. It shortened the route for passengers by a steam ferry from New Passage on the river's east bank to Portskewett on the South Wales Railway, but provided no freight facilities.

The need for a shorter freight route to and from South Wales was thus urgent. The dilemma was whether to go over or under the Severn. A bridge was at first considered when in 1865 the board gave support for a scheme by Sir John Fowler for a new trans-Severn railway which included a 2¾ mile viaduct across the river 100ft above high-water level. This would have been cheaper to build and easier to maintain and widen. But Gooch and his board gradually began to listen more and more to an engineer who advocated a tunnel. He was Charles Richardson who, while engaged on the South Wales Union Railway, had surveyed the Severn's bed and calculated its tides and distances. A tunnel under the river, he argued, could bring South Wales an hour nearer London, cut the running distance between Cardiff and Southampton by 61½ miles and knock away a substantial prop from the nagging taunt of 'The Great Way Round'.

Richardson, skilfully and persistently advocating his tunnel, won the day; Fowler's £1 million bridge scheme was dropped. An Act for the tunnel was passed in 1872, the first move in a battle with the Severn which the river nearly won.

On paper Richardson's plan was straightforward. It was for an eight-mile-long railway from Pilning (on the line from Bristol to New Passage) where it would pass in a tunnel under the Severn to Rogiet, in Monmouthshire, joining there with the South Wales Railway. Richardson's survey of the river bed had revealed a 400ft wide and 80ft deep fissure called 'the Shoots'. He proposed to bore 50ft under it, which meant lengthy approach tunnels inclined on gradients of 1-in-100 from both shores. This was sound enough as far as it went; unfortunately his survey paid too little attention to the Monmouthshire side of the river bank. This neglect was to lead to not one but several disasters.

Work started in 1873. At times half stifled, at others groping in darkness and drenched with water, the tunnel's builders battled for nearly fourteen years against unsuspected freshwater springs and the Severn's tidal surges—the most violent in Europe. Four times the workings were nearly drowned out; brickwork in the tunnel headings was torn apart like paper under the force of the invading water. The chief villain was the unsuspected 'Great Spring'. Tapped when a heading was driven into a fissure, it twice gushed into the tunnel, on one occasion drying up wells and five miles of the river Nedern on that Monmouthshire shore which Richardson had too lightly regarded. Twice diver Lambert, 'an heroic man of few words', using a hitherto unproved self-contained breathing apparatus, succeeded in closing the watertight doors which had been installed 340yd down the tunnel. Once eighty-three men trapped in a flooded shaft were only rescued in the nick of time by a boat. Flooding out at 27,000 gallons a minute, the Great Spring was finally mastered by being diverted into a shaft over which a permanent pumping installation still pours out 20 million gallons a day. By the time the tunnel was finished, Richardson had stepped down as engineer to be replaced by Sir John Hawkshaw who deepened the tunnel under the Shoots by another 15ft. It was the same Hawkshaw who forty years earlier had prophetically condemned the broad gauge.

On 9 January 1886 the first train, appropriately filled with coal, ran through the $4\frac{1}{2}$ mile tunnel; almost a year later (December), passenger traffic began. It had cost nearly £2 million, 'the price to be paid for bringing Cardiff one hour nearer London and Bristol'. The reward came the following year when 7,776 trains ran through it drawing nearly 242,000 wagons. The longest tunnel on Britain's railways, it might never have been completed but for Gooch's dogged tenacity and unflagging encouragement. It was his last gesture to the company he had served so well. Within three years of its opening he was dead.

INTO THE TWENTIETH CENTURY

The Severn tunnel had joined England to Wales under water; it also marked a watershed in Great Western history. During its building the railway had begun to stir from the long sleep Gooch had imposed on it. By the time it was completed it was marching with ever lengthening strides towards the twentieth century.

Gooch died in October 1889, to be buried in the quiet shadow of Clewer church near Windsor. An old (he was eighty-three), tired man, he had for some time displayed a 'quiet and somewhat phlegmatic style of getting through the heavy business devolving on him'. Although it had fallen to him to begin tearing it up, he cherished to the last the 7ft gauge his engines had done so much to justify. His daily business journeys from Windsor to London were made in a broad-gauge train specially kept for him. It was usually drawn by the *Iron Duke*, one of his 8ft singles, and kept for him polished to burnished splendour.

With Gooch's death a blast of fresh air blew into the boardroom. For the first time for over thirty years there was a chairman (1890) who was not a director. This was Lord Cawdor (later Viscount Emlyn), a Welsh peer of great business drive. He was to find an ideal partner in Joseph Wilkinson (later knighted), who, on becoming chief goods manager in 1896 after serving on the Buenos Aires and Pacific Railway, reinvigorated the goods department. In 1903 Wilkinson died to be succeeded by James (later Sir James) Inglis whom Felix Pole, himself no mean candidate, thought 'the finest general manager the company ever had'. Two years before Lord Cawdor's appointment the traffic department had been stirred up by N. J. Burlinson, who succeeded G. N. Tyrrell as Superintendent of the Line in 1888. Tyrrell, like Gooch, who was his staunch friend, had typified the broad gauge in repose. Cautious, anxious, scared of speeds over 40mph, he had dictated the timing of Great Western trains for twenty-four years 'until the company was running the slowest trains of any railway north of the Thames'. Foxwell in his *Express Trains English and Foreign* remarked that at this time 'the Great Western persists in treasuring a stock of trains running at little over 30mph, trains such as are dear to the French and German mind, but not to be thought of for an instant by any decent British company'. Burlinson banished this image. Each summer of his comparatively short reign saw new expresses put on, mileage increased and old trains accelerated, although with Dean's under-powered engines he could not do much about maximum speeds, which remained at little over 55mph until 1902.

There were changes in other directions. The stiff class attitude which frowned on third-class passengers slowly thawed. From 1872 the egalitarian Midland had been admitting them to all trains. After wriggling for years to avoid doing so, the GWR followed suit in 1882 when third-class passengers were admitted to all trains except the 'Flying Dutchman' and the so-called 'Zulu'. The latter, when it was put on between Paddington and Plymouth in 1879, the year of the Zulu War, was the company's first new express for seventeen years. In 1890 there first appeared the 'Cornishman', on what was then a fast schedule between Paddington and Penzance, which outpaced the 'Dutchman' and 'Zulu'. Two years later (March 1892) between Paddington and Birkenhead appeared the first corridor train heated by steam and affording lavatory access to all three classes—the only one at that time in the country. In addition passengers could summon the guard by an electric bell—a facility which appears to have been used only once and then by a small boy who rang it to find out what would happen.

From 1894, when Burlinson retired, the improvements in the train service were carried on by T. I. Allen, who in 1896 brought in restaurant cars between London and Bristol and Cardiff. In the same year Oxford was passed for the first time by a North Wales express which dropped there a slip coach instead. A more significant achievement was the inauguration in that year of the then longest non-stop run in the world when the first part of the down 'Cornishman' ran direct to Exeter (194 miles) in 3 hours 43 minutes. This was over Brunel's old route via Swindon which had been slightly improved in 1892 by the opening of the Bristol relief line to avoid Temple Meads station. By 1901 the 'Cornishman' had been speeded up to reach Exeter in 3 hours 38 minutes, Plymouth in 5 hours and Penzance in 7 hours 52 minutes. A year later came the first non-stop run between London and Plymouth—a special which carried King Edward VII and Queen Alexandra to the Royal Naval College, Dartmouth. Between 1889 and 1901 the growth of fast through expresses out of Paddington had increased more than two-fold while services on the northern line (Birmingham, North Wales and Birkenhead) had been transformed, in the words of the Rev W. J. Scott, 'by the most brilliant group of high speed expresses on the whole system—one of the finest in Great Britain in fact'. By then the number of runs at 50mph had been increased to 54 and the mileage to 4,349 compared with 9 and 310 in 1888.

During a single week-end in May 1892, four years after Gooch's death, the remaining 177 miles of broad-gauge track, all of it west of Exeter, became standard gauge. In all the history of the broad gauge few things were so well planned as its extinction in the area where it had lingered longest. At Paddington the general manager issued a fifty-page manual of instructions followed a week later by another thirty pages for the superintendents of the Bristol and Exeter divisions. Preparation on the track was equally thorough. Ballast was cleared, facing points made up in advance, nuts and tie bolts oiled, rails measured and cut and standard-gauge locomotives brought to the scene on broad-gauge trucks—for the latter a last indignity.

For the final task 4,200 platelayers and gangers were assembled from all parts of the system. Some of them gazed on the sea for the first time, convinced, according to Sekon, that even the tides were controlled by the company. They were billeted in goods sheds, waiting rooms and lineside tents and given straw and blankets for bedding. With them came their cooking pots for preparing gruel made from oatmeal provided so liberally by the company that the *Daily News* of the time thought it would 'probably give the Scottish compound a lift in public favour'. With a nice sense of direction, W. H. Wills, the tobacco magnate and a GWR director, gave each of them a packet of his Westward Ho! smoking mixture. Aided by these slender creature comforts they assembled at dawn on 21 May to banish the memory of Brunel from his last stronghold. As the gangers and platelayers worked west from Exeter, long lines of broad-gauge coaches and wagons were shunted east to Swindon where, in acres of dreary sidings, most of them awaited the breaker's hammer. By the evening of 22 May it was all over. Standard-gauge engines were now running over the company's entire system.

Thus in a space of thirty hours the public career of the broad gauge was terminated. It had cost nearly a million pounds to do so. Devon and Cornwall, which had loved it most and where it had lingered longest, let it go reluctantly. There were speeches (which made some trains late), mock funerals and the singing of 'Auld Lang Syne'. Coins placed on the line for the last broad-gauge train to run over were long treasured as family heirlooms. The Portreeve of Ashburton, who fourteen years earlier had welcomed with banners the first broad-gauge train to the little Dartmoor market town, decorated with black crêpe the last one to leave it. In London *Punch* looked on with moist eyes and broke into a doggerel parody of 'The Death of Sir John Moore':

> Not a whistle was heard, not a brass bell tolled
> as the corse o'er the sleepers was borne.
> Not a fog signal wailed from a halting throat
> O'er the grave where the broad gauge is buried.

For one man, however, a bell did toll. Overwhelmed with the responsibility of converting his 70yd length, a ganger at Torquay

The GWR was noted for some very fine bridges on its system. *Plate 19 (above)* The Royal-Albert Bridge is seen here under construction in 1858. It provided the physical link between Cornwall and the rest of England. The easternmost span is seen being jacked into position. *Plate 20 (below)* Brunel employed timber construction for many viaducts, particularly in the West Country. This is one at Collegewood on the Falmouth branch was the last to survive in Cornwall and was replaced in 1934 by a new concrete structure. *(Collection of Richard Angove; Dr Ian C Allen)*

Many railway buildings from Victorian times have been replaced by modern structures or have been drastically altered. *Plate 21 (above)* The terminal part of Bristol Temple Meads is seen here in the early years of the present century before rebuilding. *Plate 22 (below)* One of the surviving relics of the atmospheric traction trials between Exeter and Newton Abbot soon after the opening of the railway in 1847 is this pumping house at Starcross, part of which is still in existence today. *(Locomotive & General Railway Photographs)*

walked into the sea to his death. If this symbolized, in its most tragic form, the emotion felt by many at the final disappearance of Brunel's great experiment, the company itself was glad to see it go. Out of deference to Gooch while he was still living they had three times put off the date of its extinction, otherwise an unprogressive management had shamefully neglected a system which its rivals had generally treated with marked respect. If the Gauge Act was the first tragedy to befall the broad gauge, the second, and almost as great, was the refusal of the management to allow a public with a tremendous, if sentimental, regard for it to see what it could have done in regular service in its final years. No broad-gauge restaurant or corridor cars were ever built, and after 1860 new engines produced for it were virtually rebuilds. As late as 1889 *The Great Western Magazine* was complacently remarking that 'engines that work the broad gauge today are practically unaltered from those of as long ago as 1846'. Nor of all the great cavalcade of broad-gauge construction that crowded into Swindon on that May weekend was as much as a single coach spared for posterity. Had any been, the twentieth century could have better compared the legacy George Stephenson bequeathed them with the alternative Brunel offered.

The final extinction of the broad gauge enormously simplified administration, not least at Swindon. There still remained at Swindon, however, one vivid link with the past and the habits of other years. It was to be found in the notorious refreshment rooms. As a cheap way of getting them built the company in 1846 had given the contractors a 99-year lease on them at a rental of 1d a year. For fifty years lessees, with few exceptions, had reaped immense profits by enforcing under contract a ten-minute stop for all passenger trains. This was to allow travellers to consume 'Banbury cakes and pork pies (obviously stale)', bad coffee, which Brunel thought was roasted corn, tepid beer, and soup 'tasting like liquid fire'. The captive travellers also bought, among other things, 100,000 bottles of stout a year and tea which at today's prices cost them 15p a cup. It was the traffic delay rather than the price and quality of the food which finally stirred the company into action. In 1895 they bought out the lease, which still had forty-five years to run. The cost of £100,000 was made an annual charge on revenue and was not finally liquidated until 1920. The abolition of this compulsory stop cut journey times to the west by twenty minutes.

Timing was improved still further over the whole region by the new links (or 'cut-offs') and spurs planned in the 1890s and carried out in the early 1900s. Between them they made the most revolutionary contribution to quicker travel over the system since the railway's construction, ending for good the sneer at 'The Great Way Round'. Such a taunt had not been an exaggeration. Before the 'cut-offs' a holiday family setting out from Paddington for Devon found themselves after Reading heading first north-west to Didcot, then west to Bristol and then turning south to Taunton before resuming their westward course. To reach Birmingham by way of Oxford, Great Western trains had to travel 129 miles while LNWR passengers were whirled to the Midland centre over a route 16 miles shorter. Weymouth, to which the LSWR went direct from Waterloo, was only reached from Paddington by a meandering journey via Swindon, while the Severn tunnel, although it cut out Gloucester, had increased to well-nigh intolerable limits the congestion at Bristol.

In 1900 Weymouth was brought nearer by building a fourteen-mile stretch of new line from Patney and Chirton to Westbury. In 1906 a mixture of new track and the reconstruction of old single lines between Castle Cary and Cogload, near Taunton, where the old main line via Bristol was joined, knocked twenty miles off the distance between London and the West Country, thus completing a scheme Parliament had authorized in the 1840s. The Cornish Riviera Limited, which had begun life in 1904 by running non-stop to Plymouth, was transferred to the new route, reducing the time between Paddington and Plymouth of the world's then longest non-stop daily run from 4 hours 27 minutes to 4 hours 7 minutes—one minute being saved for each mile of shortening.

Congestion at Bristol was eased in July 1903 by the opening of the South Wales direct route, a new line cut from Wootton Bassett to Patchway a few miles east of the Severn tunnel. Although it meant boring a $2\frac{1}{2}$ mile tunnel under the Cotswolds, it cut the passenger train time between London and South Wales and prepared the way for the speeding up of communication with Ireland by the shorter cross-channel service soon to be inaugurated with the opening of Fishguard. In 1910 Paddington and Birmingham were brought within two hours of each other, partly over a Great Western–Great Central Railway joint line. Altogether, cut-offs and new links had meant building 139 miles of new line as well as 34 jointly with the Great Central. They extended the system's mileage to little short of 3,000 and gave it direct lines between all the chief towns in its territory.

LINERS AND MOTORS

This was still an age when steam power from coal ruled the passage of the oceans as well as transit over rails on land. Brunel's old dream of a continuous Great Western Railway all the way to Ireland and the United States saw its fulfilment in 1909 when the Cunard Line began routing to Fishguard the four-funnelled *Mauretania*, the largest liner afloat. New York was then brought forty miles nearer England, and transatlantic passengers, after landing, within five hours of London. Enticing liner traffic to Fishguard ('The Gateway to Europe', the GWR told its customers) by creating there a sheltered harbour connected to the main South Wales line had been an enterprise of faith largely completed by 1906. Behind its planning lay also the double aim of breaking the monopoly of the LNWR's Irish traffic via Holyhead and luring liners from the LSWR's Southampton docks. To achieve it, the shape of Fishguard's bay was altered by blasting away a huge slice of the 300ft high cliffs, the rubble helping to form a breakwater to impound more than a square mile of the Irish Sea. Safe, spacious, fog-free, the newly created port with its own hotel, power station and galleries for 1,000 head of Irish cattle typified the pre-1914 concept of inter-linked train and ship travel. Scarcely had it been completed than it proved to be a hostage rejected by fortune, for World War I abruptly cut off the North Atlantic liner traffic, and changed travelling habits led to Southampton being preferred when the war ended. Today the docks and station at Fishguard are underused and the landscaped walks for the hotel guests a memory. Planned to accommodate ocean giants, Fishguard derives its main income today from the Irish roll-off roll-on traffic. By contrast, Neyland (or New Milford), which it thrust back into obscurity, looks across to Milford Haven basking and expanding in the prosperity of oil.

Yet Fishguard, so arrogantly and confidently planned, typified the new and resurgent Great Western which had now firmly entered the twentieth century. The caution of Gooch and the timidity of Tyrrell had been left firmly behind on a system which, between 1888 and 1912, had accomplished a revolution in all its departments. It now competed on equal terms with the LNWR ('the oldest established firm in the railway passenger business', according to an Edwardian postcard) which between 1870 and 1900 had surpassed it in performance. The cut-offs via Westbury, Castle Cary and Langport, along with Churchward's powerful 'City' class 4-4-0s, had already decisively beaten off a LSWR challenge for the American liner traffic calling at Plymouth. The GWR's fastest trains between Plymouth and London were now forty minutes quicker than the LSWR's best. At Weymouth the company monopolized the Channel Islands steamer service. Further west, between Helston and the Lizard, deep in Cornwall, history of another sort had been made. On 17 August 1903 the company had sponsored the first ever railway-owned motor passenger service with a fleet of five second-hand Milnes-Daimler buses. Strange, primitive, hazardous vehicles they were. On hills the conductor walked beside the rear wheel with a wooden wedge in case the bus slipped back, while the driver had often to hand pump the fuel from the tank when the pressure valve failed. The water-bound roads of those days were so badly cut up by the solid tyres that the company had to lend the district council a traction engine to repair them. But for the Edwardians they were a new dimension in travel. Within two years nearly a million passengers had been carried on this and other omnibus services which followed in its wake. By August 1905 the company had fifty-eight passenger and eight goods motors in use and a headquarters office and repair shop had been established at Slough. Thus in the guise of a company-operated petrol bus feeder service came the forerunners of those road motor saloon coaches which, in other hands in the later 1920s, were to prove steam's deadliest rivals on land.

The pioneer Helston–Lizard motor omnibus services had been

ATTRACTIVE CIRCULAR RAIL AND COACH TRIPS

THROUGH THE

MENDIP HILLS

DAILY

(Sundays, Saturday, August 4th, and Monday, August 6th, excepted)

CIRCULAR DAY-TRIP TICKETS WILL BE ISSUED AS UNDER:—

No. 1 Tour.	No. 2 Tour.
To Winscombe by rail, thence by char-a-banc or brake† to Cheddar via Shipham, Charterhouse and Cheddar Gorge, returning by rail from Cheddar.	To Cheddar by rail, thence by char-a-banc or brake † to Winscombe via Axbridge, Compton Bishop and Webbington, returning by rail from Winscombe.

† Or other suitable vehicle.

FROM	TIMES OF STARTING.		
	For Tour No. 1.	For Tour No. 2.	
	A.M.	A.M.	P.M.
Clifton Down	10 35	10 35	12 27
Redland	10 37	10 37	12 29
Montpelier...	10 39	10 39	12 31
Ashley Hill	10 45	10 45	12 27
Stapleton Road	10 50	10 50	12 40
Lawrence Hill	10 53	10 53	12 37
Temple Meads...	11 15	11 15	1 33
Bedminster	10 40	10 40	1 38

No. 1 TOUR.—Passengers arrive at Winscombe by train at 12.6 p.m., and the chars-a-banc will leave Winscombe Station immediately after, arriving at Cheddar Station at about 2.15 p.m. RETURN TRAINS FROM CHEDDAR.—Trains leave Cheddar at 5a21 and 8b30 p.m.; also on Wednesdays and Saturdays only at 7.30 p.m.

No. 2 TOUR.—Passengers arrive at Cheddar by train at 12.22 p.m. or 2.42 p.m., and the chars-a-banc will leave Cheddar Station immediately after arrival of train due at 2.42 p.m., arriving at Winscombe in time for the train leaving Winscombe for Bristol at 5a28 p.m. Passengers may, if they so elect, remain at Winscombe and travel to Bristol by the 9.0 p.m. train, or the 7.42 p.m. train Wednesdays and Saturdays only.

a Passengers for Ashley Hill by this train wait at Temple Meads from 6.25 p.m. to 7.55 p.m., or they can return to Montpelier. Passengers by this train holding Bedminster tickets must return to Temple Meads. b Not to Ashley Hill by this train, but passengers holding Ashley Hill tickets can return to Montpelier.

Return Fares for the Circular Trips.

N.B.—Tickets are issued available for first, second, or third class by rail, according to fares shewn below, but there is no classification on Mr. Weeks' chars-a-banc or vehicles.

Tour No. 1.			Tour No. 2.		
1st Class.	2nd Class.	3rd Class.	1st Class.	2nd Class.	3rd Class.
5/-	4/-	3/6	4/3	3/3	2/9

The service between Winscombe and Cheddar will be performed by Mr. Alfred G. Weeks' well-horsed chars-a-banc (or other suitable vehicles).

Large parties should give notice not later than the day before to Mr. Weeks, Winscombe, to ensure ample accommodation being provided. Box seats (extra charge, one shilling) may be reserved by application to Mr. Weeks at least two days beforehand.

(Continued on page 22.)

For Special Notices relating to the issue of Excursion Tickets see page 2.

Fig 6　Road and rail excursions were popular even around the turn of the century with horse drawn vehicles as in this announcement taken from the Bristol excursion programme of April 1906.

the first in the country to operate to a timetable. Undoubtedly the road motors provided the inspiration in Great Britain for the provision of 'halts' as railway stopping places, designed to bring the railway services closer to even the smallest communities. The halts were served by rail motor cars and were usually sited at places of easy access.

Initially a curious language problem arose over them. When, little less than two months after launching the road omnibus service in Cornwall, the Great Western pioneered the first steam rail motor car service on its Stroud Valley line between Chalford and Stonehouse on 12 October 1903 (they were the brainchild of T. I. Allen, the Superintendent of the Line, to whom also should possibly be credited the idea of the road motor omnibus services) the stopping places were publicly advertised as 'haltes'. This French spelling, says Mr C. R. Clinker, was probably decided on because there was then no suitable meaning to the English term 'halt'. By 1905, however, 'halt' in English seems to have taken over, 'probably', adds Mr Clinker, 'as part of the general dislike of "things French" which manifested itself in the early days of the present century'.

The halts swiftly became part of the Great Western scene. Although they were later to appear on other railways, the company between 1903 and 1947 was to open nearly twice as many as all the other railways combined. After their inauguration in the Stroud Valley they appeared in Plymouth in 1904 (where an intensive service of rail cars was built up), Wrexham in 1905 and Oxford in 1908. By the outbreak of World War I, 145 were in general use on individual branches and all sections of the company's main line. Some were temporarily closed in 1915 as a wartime economy, but to meet heavy road competition in the 1920s the 'halt policy' was revived to provide 169 more between 1927 and 1935.

Following closely on the halts and designed to meet a somewhat similar need came the 'platform' (a term the GWR borrowed from Scotland where it had been in use before the end of the nineteenth century), the difference between the two terms providing a nice distinction in railway terminology which time later blurred. The first 'platform' appeared at Rodmarton on 1 September 1904, a few miles from the Stroud Valley halts. They were mainly on branch lines where the rail motor services were not suitable. Providing longer platforms than the halts, they were served by short trains formed of ordinary coaches. Halts were generally unstaffed; platforms were usually served by senior grade porters who booked passengers, parcels and sometimes milk. Altogether the GWR opened about 420 halts and platforms between 1903 and 1947 and took over in addition 36 with the Welsh companies, four of them being on the Cambrian Railways.

A glimpse ahead into the 1920s and later throws into sharper relief the fact that before 1914 steam still reigned supreme. At Swindon, where the population had increased thirty-fold since Gooch had built his first engine sheds, Churchward was altering the appearance and increasing the power of Great Western locomotives to give them a predominance which was to remain unchallenged for twenty years. Behind his 'Cities', 'Saints' and 'Stars', breathing in steam from high-pressure boilers and exhausting it from larger cylinders, ran rakes of new 50ft and 70ft corridor coaches which exemplified for first- and third-class travellers (seconds were abolished in 1910) the solid and unfaltering assurance of the age. Yet only eight per cent of GW carriage stock in the early years of the present century was lit by electricity (which Paddington had first seen in 1880) and most of the rest by gas. Suburban services, which until the end of the nineteenth century had been a Cinderella, were expanded in the years immediately before World War I by the launching of a 'homes for all campaign'. The commuting office worker was tempted to live away from London's rush and noise not only by more convenient trains, but by being given access to a property register which provided essential information free of charge as well as a residential guide to properties in Chalfont country, in Buckinghamshire, then an undeveloped leafy countryside. Yearly over the system passenger traffic increased until by the last half of 1912 nearly 55½ million were carried. The coaches they travelled in ran so smoothly that 'one could shave in perfect safety with a "cut throat" razor in a rear coach toilet', while one delighted traveller is said to have found a sovereign he had dropped on the footboard of a departing coach from Paddington still in the same place when the train arrived at Birmingham.

Nowhere was the resurgence more marked than in the services to the holiday lands of the West Country. Here substantial sections of the old South Devon and Cornwall main line had been doubled by 1905. An inspired slogan, 'The holiday line', had been coined in 1903. By brilliant and sustained advertising, with faster and more frequent trains, the company brushed with prosperity the resorts it served. Newquay had opened what was then the largest hotel in the county to become Cornwall's leading holiday resort, a position it still holds. St Ives (joined to the main line in 1877 by the last piece of broad-gauge railway to be built), as well as Looe and Fowey, had been helped to turn to tourist traffic as their traditional fishing industries declined. Romantic and evocatively named 'after sunrise trips' took trippers from Paddington to Penzance and back in fourteen hours. Torquay and Paignton (the line had been doubled from Newton Abbot by 1911) were nourished by through services from the Midlands, often with restaurant cars which by 1903 catered for all three classes. Torquay's fame (its population then above 30,000) had spread to Europe. Napoleon III, seeking forgetfulness after the Franco-Prussian War, travelled to it by train in 1871 from Paddington. By one of life's little ironies there arrived shortly afterwards by steamer 'the celebrated German industrialist Herr Ernst von Krupp, the gun inventor and manufacturer', whose artillery had helped scatter the French emperor's armies. Herr Krupp brought with him 'a large establishment', including six horses.

The period from 1890 until 1914, more than with any other British railway, was the Great Western's golden age. Between 1903 and 1911 receipts rose by more than 21 per cent. Despite departmental rivalries on the board, no system provided a more complete contrast with its immediate past. Freed from the shackles of the broad gauge, not yet dragged down by the ulcer of industrial decline in South Wales, it reached a pre-eminence in prestige and locomotive supremacy which the twenties were to match but never surpass. Employing 73,000 people, with over 3,000 locomotives working 3,282 miles of track and serving more than 1,000 stations and halts, it was the largest single railway system in the country. Out of Paddington ran three great trunk routes taking passengers farther and faster on non-stop journeys than on any other system. This was the true measure of the company's great awakening. Compared with 1888, the journey time from Paddington to Bristol had been cut by thirty-six minutes, Plymouth, nearly 226 miles away, could be reached an hour earlier. Great Western trains sped to Cardiff—151 miles —in $2\frac{1}{2}$ hours. Birmingham (129 miles) was lapped in two hours dead over a steeper route than the rival LNWR. In the north, Birkenhead, nearly 230 miles distant, was reached in $4\frac{1}{2}$ hours. Under the Severn in 1913 rumbled nearly 18,000 freight trains hauling nearly a million wagons.

More beguiling still were the beckoning vistas opening up by the use of through Great Western coaches running via Victoria to connect at Dover, Folkestone and Queenborough 'for expeditious services to Berlin, Hambourg, Frankfort-am-Main, Cologne, Basle, St Petersburg and Moscow'. The railway through which Brunel planned links with America now found the cities of northern Europe beckoning to it as well. It was a welcoming gesture which proved all too fragile and short-lived, for scarcely had it been extended than a great storm blew, banishing beyond recall the prospect it offered.

CHAPTER 5

Two World Wars—and the End of an Era

1914 AND AFTER

The early summer months of 1914 were long wistfully remembered. The sun seemed to shine all day; there had been scarcely any rain since March. As 'the Holiday Line' the Great Western had seldom been busier. Early in July a great crowd had travelled to Shrewsbury to see King George V open the Royal Agricultural Show. He had made the journey to and from Paddington in the royal train. For Henley Regatta in the same month the company had carried a near-record of some 25,000 passengers. On the Thames and its banks the floppy hats, parasols and gay ankle-length dresses of the ladies weaved a bobbing pattern of colour among the straw hats, blazers and white 'ducks' of the men. Seldom had Henley been so gay or the world in general seemed so peaceful. Earlier in the month the four-funnelled *Aquitania*, equipped with a 'long-distance wireless installation', had begun the first of her weekly calls at Fishguard. More people than ever were travelling to the West Country from the capital, so much so that the Cornish Riviera began to run on Sundays as well as weekdays. A new train introduced tentatively in 1913 as the Devon and Cornwall special had proved such a success that in 1914 it was running in three portions. On the company's northern division, expresses from Paddington offered connections to Llangollen, Dolgelly and Barmouth, and from Birmingham and Birkenhead there were excursions to the Isle of Man. In the Channel Islands a Sunday boat service ran from Guernsey. At the London Coliseum the company arranged a cinema matinee for a film called 'The story

116

of the holiday line'. It made everyone realize, wrote an enthusiastic reviewer 'to what an extent the Great Western holds, as it were, the key to the Empire's most celebrated travel shrines and places of pilgrimage'.

War burst abruptly into the holiday atmosphere on 4 August. As it did so the Great Western Railway, along with 120 other railway systems throughout the country, passed into the hands of the Government for the duration of the war. It was a change that at Paddington ruffled only temporarily the holiday timetables. Within a month cheap day excursion tickets, hurriedly cancelled on the outbreak of war, were back.

In the early weeks the most warlike place on the system was Swindon. Here trucks were converted to carry guns and horses, and coaching stock prepared for ambulance trains. The travelling pharmacies and sick bays were on view to the public for sixpence a time, the money going to the Red Cross. The first troops to leave Swindon had marched off to rousing blasts from the Great Western works hooter, its tone somewhat mellowed since a neighbouring landowner had complained that it distracted his pheasants from hatching their eggs. En route by sea to Genoa, Count Mensdorf, the Imperial and Royal Austro-Hungarian Ambassador to London, wrote to *The Times* expressing his thanks 'to the managers of the Great Western Railway which had conducted our train to Falmouth'.

The rapid return of cheap day excursion tickets helped to emphasize the 'business as usual' slogan of the day, an outlook the *Swindon Advertiser* did its best to foster by still carrying advertisements for the drama classes of the Dresden Conservatoire of Music. As shipping was steered away from south-coast ports for fear of German attacks, the Bristol Channel ports served by the company became increasingly important. Even before the war had started, however, the Great Western's main role in it had been decided. As the chief railway exit from the South Wales coalfields it became the lifeline of the Grand Fleet. Throughout the war years the Navy was to burn nearly six million tons of coal. Of this 90 per cent came from the Rhondda and Aberdare districts, beginning its journey to the ships' boiler furnaces behind Great Western engines. Nothing was allowed to interfere with these 'Jellicoe Specials', as they were

named. Day and night for nearly four years they rumbled northwards through remote Welsh junctions and valleys or eastwards
under the Severn to fuel the ships of the fleet in Scapa Flow or
other harbours. The Great Western hauled the north-bound
trains from Pontypool Road over three different routes to
Warrington. Here the LNWR picked them up and transferred
them to one of the Scottish railways for haulage to Grangemouth on the Forth. By the end of the war 2,500,000 tons of
coal in 13,600 trucks had been sent to Grangemouth and an
equal tonnage to Birkenhead, Devonport, Southampton, London, Hull, Chatham and other ports. It was the greatest sustained coal lift in the country's history.

Great Western steamers helped in the war at sea, some
distinguishing themselves in unorthodox ways. The *St David*
turbine steamer on the Fishguard–Rosslare run temporarily de-
prived the Royal Navy of a much-needed destroyer by acci-
dentally ramming it. The *Roebuck* of the Channel Islands service
had the worst of a collision in 1915 with a French battleship in
the Scapa Flow. The *Ibex* from the same run sank a German
submarine (a feat earning the crew £500) while in the Darda-
nelles the *Gazelle* sank an old ex-Great Western steamer with
which the enemy were trying to run the blockade.

The war reached out to the company in many other ways. At
Banbury, the spectacle of 1,000 thirsty troops rushing out of
their train on a hot September afternoon in 1914 to drink all the
water in the station fire buckets led to the immediate establishment there of what was claimed to be the first ever station war
canteen staffed entirely by voluntary labour. Churchward's
'star' class engine *Knight of the Black Eagle*, commemorating a
Prussian Order of Chivalry, was hurriedly renamed *Knight of
Liege*, a warrior of whom history has no record but who was
thought better to symbolize the Allies' cause. The station staff
at Weston-super-Mare, moved by the plight of 'gallant little
Belgium', pledged themselves to support a refugee, while the
stationmaster at Llawerne jumped on his bicycle to pursue and
capture two escaped German prisoners. The secretary of the
Bristol goods' cartage war fund obtained additional money for
comforts by writing and selling patriotic poems in his spare time.
Encouraged by the management's policy of providing lineside

allotments, guard A. Jones, of Neath, raised 5 cwt of onions from an ounce of specially supplied seed. All the time indiscriminate recruiting bit deeply into the company's manpower. Over 16,000 men had gone by 1916 of whom 1,587 had been killed, had died of wounds or were missing.

The staff remaining had to cope with passenger traffic which, far from decreasing, became heavier each year. Towards this, the company's publicity department, working in its own ivory tower, made a contribution of its own. In 1915, by which time U-boats were operating at will in the English Channel, it published a thoughtful booklet called *Yachting in the West* describing the pleasures to be derived by sailing from Torquay to Penzance. The summer timetable of the same year gave full details of thirty-seven holiday trains making 100-mile runs.

More than any other major railway the Great Western illustrated the astonishing gulf between the fighting man and those at home. In the summer of 1916, when the flower of the nation's manhood was dying on the Somme, seasonal holiday traffic reached such proportions that the 'Cornish Riviera' was leaving Paddington daily in three sections carrying an average of 1,400 passengers. Throughout the whole system during July and August, when the struggle on the Somme was fiercest, excursion traffic so taxed the staff that clerks were called in as emergency porters. Not until 1917 did cuts in the passenger services begin to bite. Then, from July of that year, several expresses were made slower, restaurant, sleeping and slip cars discontinued, passenger train journeys reduced by 9,000 miles and fares increased by 50 per cent.

Austerity then became increasingly the rule as war needs made more and more demands. By the end of the war 88,603 Great Western trains had been run for military and naval purposes; 95 engines and 686 wagons were sent abroad along with 29 miles of complete railway. Over 25,000, or very nearly one third of the total staff employed in 1914, had joined the Colours and 2,525 had died. Only the LNWR and Midland Railway sent more staff to the front. All the same, it is doubtful whether the real significance of the company's war effort was ever understood by the public. Visually the south-coast lines stole the emotional limelight, with Victoria station pictured as the 'gateway of goodbyes'. Coal does not bring tears to the eyes or send the pulses racing. Yet the grimy South Wales coal trains, banging and creaking their way through the night, were as potent instruments of victory as the seemingly endless procession of troop trains leaving Victoria.

The war bit deeply into the Great Western's earnings, coming at a time when the short cuts and other enterprises of the great revival were bringing increasing returns. It had also brought about the closure of a number of little-used branch lines and stations, some of which were never to reopen. Physically, however, apart from four years' arrears of maintenance, there had been little damage. There was no bombing, although Teignmouth in South Devon was momentarily blacked out one night in mistake for Tynemouth. With peace came new hopes and opportunities. Alone among the main-line companies, the Great Western was in the best condition to cope with the demands of a public eager to forget food queues, the long casualty lists and the 1918 influenza epidemic—the war's last vicious kick.

Cheap day-return tickets available by ordinary trains had been inaugurated by the company as early as July 1919. The crowds thronging Paddington for the following August bank holiday were among the largest ever dealt with. The Cornish Riviera Limited, restored in the same year and still making the longest non-stop run in the country, had to be run in triplicate; the holiday routes to Wales were crowded. Train mileage, which by the armistice was only 44 per cent of the pre-war total, had been restored by 30 per cent. Some dining-car facilities were back and slip coaches were seen again at Westbury, Taunton and Exeter. Barely three years after the war (3 October 1921) came a bold experiment. This was a through carriage from Penzance to Aberdeen—a convenience long since denied to the contemporary traveller. It was detached at Westbury from the 11.0am Penzance to Paddington, and worked separately thence to Swindon where a restaurant car working as far as York was attached. It was due at Aberdeen at 7.40am, a journey time of about 21 hours over a distance of 783 miles.

Yet the war had left deep scars. The only extra revenue to meet rising costs came from a 75 per cent increase in train fares and a rise in rates and charges for goods and mineral traffic. South Wales steam coal, for which the company's engines were especially tailored, was averaging 25s 10d a ton against 14s 4d in 1913, and every minute of the day the company burnt 3½ tons. Even lamp oil, the chairman (Viscount Churchill) feelingly complained, was 50 per cent dearer. Wages, too, were up. The war had given the railwayman an eight-hour day and a much improved standard of living. To meet post-war prices he had also been given a bonus of 33s which had added another £4,800,000 to the company's bill. Suddenly, it seemed, all these benefits and privileges were at risk. Rumours spread that the Government planned a 40s a week minimum wage for railwaymen compared with the current 51s and a pre-war minimum of 18s.

The railwaymen's reaction was a sudden strike on 26 September 1919, which took all the companies by surprise and brought 65 per cent of Great Western men out. It was the first complete strike on the system since 1913. It also revealed to the company an ugly spirit of militancy among a staff hitherto noted for its responsible loyalty. Near Wootton Bassett a determined attempt was made to wreck a train by obstructions on the line. Strikers at Swindon tarred and feathered the house of a man staying at work (although they cleaned off the tar on discovering that it was the wrong house), and at Taunton and Durston, on the old Bristol and Exeter Railway system, truckloads of sheep and pigs were left stranded. The stoppage would have been more complete (although in South Wales two million tons of coal were lost) but for the sudden onrush of volunteer labour which surprised the Government as much as it annoyed the men. Out of 8,600 volunteers who descended on Paddington 4,113 were taken on, among them the volunteer porter who apologized to his foreman for being late by explaining that he had been detained on duties as a lord in waiting to the King. Less fortunate was a volunteer officer who, offering himself for signal duties on coming out of hospital, was attacked and left unconscious.

The volunteers got a skeleton service moving, but by 2 October the strike was over. The Government intervened with a settlement which maintained railway pay rates at existing levels. No one was more jubilant than J. H. Thomas, one of the men's leaders. He was an old Great Western man who had once cleaned engines at Swindon. The company was less happy. Its wage bill was now £19½ million—three times that of 1913.

The strike was a nine days' wonder which left the men elated but had no relevance to a far more vexing political problem. This was whether the railways should be nationalized or returned to their owners. From 1914 they had been run by the Government with net receipts divided amongst them in proportion to their 1913 earnings. Although it had taken little account of increased costs in running and materials, this control had not been without certain benefits. Wasteful competition and overlapping had been cut out, pooling of wagons brought in and a small, but much needed, degree of standardization imposed. 'God forbid', exclaimed the outspoken Herbert Walker of the LSWR in 1917, 'that we should ever go back to pre-war working.'

This was very different from the view taken at Paddington where the very thought of nationalization was abhorrent. Walker's outburst was seen there as dangerous talk. With a total revenue of £6½ million the GWR was declaring a dividend of 7¼ per cent. Of all the major companies it was the most self-contained and self-sufficient within its geographical boundaries, and it was more efficiently run than most of them. Moreover, the reviving holiday traffic offered an opportunity of recouping much of the expenditure incurred in the great route shortening works before the war. All this stood to be lost by nationalization. In the boardroom, and among the great majority of the rank and file, the Great Western was solidly against it.

The company was rescued from its anxieties by a Government compromise. Nationalization was abandoned. Instead, in 1921 the railways were handed back to their owners but at the same time ordered to regroup themselves into four regions. If not as drastic as nationalization, regrouping nevertheless changed overnight the country's railway map. Old and proud names like Great Northern, Great Eastern and Great Central and in Scotland the Highland and Caledonian Railways vanished along with their traditions and liveries. In the south Paddington's old enemy the LSWR became the Southern and was allowed, somewhat illogically, to keep its Devon and Cornwall lines. Only the Great Western kept its name and identity intact and retained its

Freight was a vital traffic on any railway until the Beeching era of the early 1960s showed that traditional methods of handling were totally uneconomic. *Plate 23 (above)* The local freight shunted wagons at intermediate stations and sometimes included the railways' own engineers' ballast traffic for distribution as well, as in this short GW goods train headed by a Dean 0-6-0. *Plate 24 (below)* On the Great Western, coal from South Wales was one of the staple traffics; a 2-8-0 arrives at Severn Tunnel Junction yard with a trunk haul of coal for examination, en route to London. *(Locomotive & General Railway Photographs and British Railways)*

The GWR also pioneered other forms of transport, as feeders in some cases to its rail services. In 1903 the first GWR road service was inaugurated between Helston and the Lizard. *Plate 25 (above)* is a Milnes Daimler 16hp wagonette on the Redruth and Falmouth service. By the end of 1906 the GWR had a fleet of eighty road vehicles. *Plate 26 (below)* During the 1930s the main line railways inaugurated air services in conjunction with Imperial Airways. A Great Western air service operated between Cardiff, Torquay and Plymouth. The GWR coat of arms can be seen on the rudder of this machine. *(Richard Angove Collection and British Railways/OPC)*

sonorously titled office of Superintendent of the Line. Under the Grouping Act, which became operative on 1 January 1923, the company augmented its capital by £36 million, extended its geographical mileage by 560 miles, and gained 18,000 new employees and an assortment of over 700 locomotives by absorbing as constituent companies five Welsh coal railways as well as the Cambrian Railways system and some twenty-six smaller associated companies. With the coal railways came their docks, making the company the largest private dock owner in the world with thirty-seven miles of quays. Alarm and fear at Paddington evaporated in a euphoria of optimism and relief. The mood was summed up by a *Western Mail* newspaper cartoon. It showed representatives of other companies being scattered in a gale which left a Great Western employee unscathed and remarking 'Hooray, never even blew me cap off'.

Gleefully hailed as a 'bargain package', regrouping had put almost the whole of industrial South Wales, its ports and the carrying of its mineral resources, into the company's lap, leaving it dazzled with prospects of enormous profits. It all seemed like a large, ripe, rosy apple only waiting to be plucked and eaten. In reality it was an apple that contained a large maggot which was already beginning to gnaw at it.

Even the coal railways, once so prosperous, were not what they seemed. The oldest, largest and most important of them was the Taff Vale, which, with twenty-three branches linking the collieries of eastern Glamorganshire with Penarth and Cardiff Docks, had at one time 271 engines working only 124 miles. It also handled passenger traffic—some eight million in 1921— nearly all of them miners and families living in one of the most densely populated districts of the kingdom. Competing with it for the Rhondda coal, the 88-mile Barry Railway, incorporated in 1884, served the docks of its name and in 1912 had given its shareholders 7 per cent on their ordinary shares. The 51-mile Rhymney Railway, born in 1854, had a notable locomotive works at Caerphilly and from a swarm of connecting links with other railways had run coal trains often nose-to-tail over its own track into Cardiff docks. Two smaller concerns, the Alexandra (Newport and South Wales) Docks and Railway and the Cardiff Railway, although with authority to run over and con-

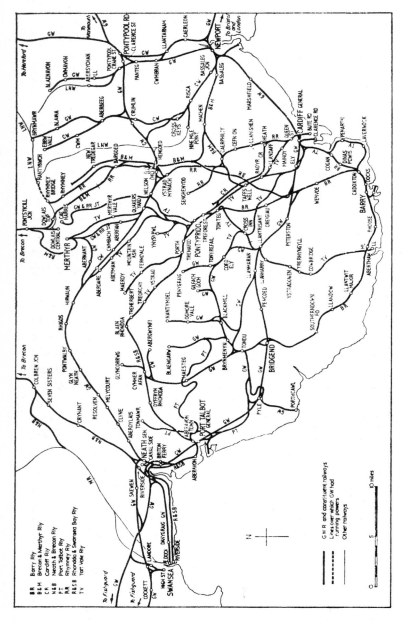

Fig 7 Enlargement of the South Wales area showing the railways in existence before amalgamation with the Great Western in 1922/3.

nect with other railways in the area, were principally dock systems, the latter serving Cardiff's Bute Docks.

Threading the valleys, hills and docks of Monmouthshire and Glamorganshire, these small independent lines made up between them one of the densest rail networks in the country: The Taff Vale approached Cardiff over six tracks and the Rhymney Railway on one section had eleven junctions with six different systems. Only a dedicated rail enthusiast could tell where one railway ended and another began. The odd one out, the Cambrian Railways, had little to do with coal but exploited instead the scenery of east, mid- and north-west Wales. There was less money in scenery than coal, and the Cambrian Railways only marginally prospered. Out of 300 route miles of line only 27 were double, giving the system the longest continuous single track in England and Wales. Possession of the Cambrian, however, gave Paddington the key to the interior of South Wales and enabled the Great Western to make the circuit of four-fifths of the Principality over its own tracks.

The Cambrian system apart, the common factor binding all these railways had been coal and its profits. But the great days of the South Wales coal industry were now in decline; oil was gradually and steadily supplanting it. Never again would the Taff Vale pay its shareholders $17\frac{1}{2}$ per cent. The Great Western had gained the monopoly of the Welsh coal-carrying trade ten years too late. Export markets had been shattered by the war. Europe was beginning to take its coal not from the Rhondda but from the Ruhr and the Saar, squeezed out of the Germans for reparations. South Wales coal production, which in 1913 had peaked at 56 million tons, was down by 10 million tons in 1921 and with brief exceptions was to go on declining. The Taff Vale, which once hauled 20 million tons a year, carried only $8\frac{1}{2}$ million in 1921. Welsh pits were becoming out-dated and worked out; production was increasingly shifting to the East Midlands where coal was easier and less dangerous to mine. The change was slow but inexorable. In consequence an economy in South Wales founded on coal and its ancillary industries, and which was served by 445 GWR stations and halts, was beginning to slide into a decline which in ten years was to make the area a byword for industrial depression. Placed against this background, the 'bargain package' so enthusiastically acclaimed in 1921 was a very suspect article.

This change was only imperfectly grasped at Paddington and was masked by other factors. In 1923 there were still more workers at the coal faces than in any other industry. Moreover, peace had appeared to usher in more stable times, encouraged by a buoyant upsurge of optimism which saw the return on Great Western shares rise to 8 per cent in 1923. In part this was due to increased capital following the South Wales amalgamations, an increase of more than $12\frac{1}{2}$ million in passengers carried (but fares had been reduced to $1\frac{1}{2}$d a mile) and an increase of eight million tons of merchandise. Moreover, the task of grappling with the problems posed by peace and regrouping fell on the shoulders of a new generation of Great Western men. G. J. Churchward retired in 1921. 'It's time the old man got out', he was heard to mutter when confronted with less respectful and more militant trade union attitudes. He had been at the centre of affairs in Swindon for twenty-nine years (see Chapter 6), a virtual dictator in control of one of the largest work forces in Europe and profoundly influencing locomotive design. Still vigorous in mind and body, he lived for another twelve years, leaving no diaries or recollections and keeping his last thoughts about the railway he had served so ably largely unspoken. He died tragically on a foggy December morning in 1933, knocked down by one of the engines of his successor, Charles Benjamin Collett.

Collett began his reign in harness with a new general manager. The war had taken a toll of management as well as the lowlier ranks of the staff. Since James Grierson had become the first to use the style of general manager (1863), Great Western holders of that office had almost without exception been men from the ranks. It was the highest post in the company to which a railwayman could aspire. But in raising up its servants the company's demands sometimes broke them, too. Frank Potter, the beloved war-time general manager and the company's spokesman on the Railway Management Committee, died in 1919 while convalescing in the GWR's Tregenna Castle hotel, St Ives. Like his predecessors, Wilkinson and Inglis, he had been worn out by the strains of office. These same strains, added to the burden of the war years as Superintendent of the Line, had also killed off James Aldington within two years of succeeding Potter. Like Potter, Aldington had begun his career as a railway clerk, and the company looked again within its ranks for a successor.

They found waiting in the wings a remarkable man. Felix John Clewett Pole had started at fourteen in the company's telegraph office at Swindon, working his way forward until in June 1921, at forty-four, he succeeded Aldington to become the company's youngest general manager since the legendary Grierson. Pole was now to give his name to a decade in the company's history. Energetic, imaginative, a born manager of men, he first diminished the influence of the locomotive department over the board—a task made easier by Churchward's disappearance, and he himself at once began to speak in the company's affairs and direction with an authority hardly less than that of the chairman (Viscount Churchill). Pole's management style was personal, positive and dynamic. But it was his fate to reach office at a time when post-war depression and change, the loss of world markets through altered trends in trade, were to leave deep and permanent scars on the face of South Wales. Oil was beginning to supplant coal as a major source of energy; many overseas markets had vanished. Pole sensed this. He was also apprehensive of the overall effect on a region where the economy had been largely based on coal. It was his tragedy, however, to have to carry out the policies and decisions of a board which shared the dangerous illusion that large and lucrative profits could still be made from coal. The legacy of this mistake was to prove a harsh one.

Pole began with furious energy, setting himself the twin tasks of restoring the company's financial stability (compensation from the Government for wartime use was slow in coming through) and welding the concerns acquired in regrouping into an enlarged Great Western. He remodelled the company's timetables, virtually unchanged since 1910, and threw himself behind a £10 million plan to improve stations and signal boxes. In South Wales he pushed on with schemes for improved coal-

Great Western Railway.

NEW & IMPROVED

Passenger Train Facilities

Commencing

MONDAY, APRIL 30th, 1923.

WEEK-DAYS.

TIVERTON JUNCTION, EXETER AND NEWTON ABBOT.

A Rail Motor (one class only) will leave Exeter (St. David's) at 7.30 a.m. for Tiverton Junction, calling at Stoke Canon at 7.38, Silverton 7.46, Hele and Bradninch 7.50, Cullompton 8.0, arriving at Tiverton Junction at 8.7 a.m.

A Rail Motor (one class only) will leave Tiverton Junction at 8.35 a.m. for Exeter (St. David's). calling at Cullompton at 8.42, Hele and Bradninch 8.52, Silverton 8.56, Stoke Canon 9.6, arriving at Exeter at 9.13 a.m. This Motor will connect with the 7.45 a.m. Train from Hemyock to Tiverton Junction.

The 8.20 p.m. Taunton (9.35 p.m. from Exeter) to Newton Abbot will call at Dawlish Warren at 10.0 p.m.

TAUNTON AND MINEHEAD.

The 7.20 a.m. (Mondays and Saturdays) Taunton to Minehead will run each week-day.
The 9.30 a.m. (Mondays and Saturdays) Minehead to Taunton will run each week-day.

NEWTON ABBOT, TORQUAY AND KINGSWEAR.

The 9.0 p.m. Kingswear to Newton Abbot will start at 9.20 p.m. (Dartmouth depart 9.5 p.m.), leave Churston at 9.33, Paignton 9.43, Torquay 9.51, Torre 9.57, Kingskerswell 10.4, Newton Abbot arrive 10.8 p.m. **and be extended to Dawlish,** Newton Abbot depart 10.13, Teignmouth 10.24. Dawlish arrive 10.30 p.m.

NEWTON ABBOT AND MORETONHAMPSTEAD.

The 8.10 p.m. (Saturdays) Moretonhampstead to Newton Abbot will run each week-day.
The 9.15 p.m. (Saturdays) Newton Abbot to Moretonhampstead will run each week-day.

SUNDAYS.

EXETER AND NEWTON ABBOT.

The 9.15 a.m. Exeter (St. David's) to Newton Abbot and Paignton will call at Exeter (St. Thomas) at 9.20 a.m. and Dawlish Warren at 9.35 a.m.

The 9.45 a.m. Exeter (St. David's) to Plymouth will call at Exeter (St. Thomas) at 9.50 a.m. and Dawlish Warren at 10.5 a.m.

The 12.35 p.m. Dawlish to Newton Abbot will start from Dawlish Warren at 12.30 p.m.

The 11.25 a.m. Newton Abbot to Dawlish will be extended to Dawlish Warren, arriving at 11.45 a.m.

PADDINGTON STATION,

April, 1923.

FELIX J. C. POLE,

General Manager.

6,000. WYMAN & SONS LTD., Printers, Fetter Lane, London, E.C., Reading and Fakenham.— 607a.

Fig 8   Attention to detail. Some of the train service improvements of April 1923. Did that 9.0pm from Kingswear really terminate at Dawlish or did it go empty to Exeter?

tipping appliances, particularly at the out-dated Bute Docks. Railway facilities which had grown up piecemeal (at Cardiff, for example, the Taff Vale and Barry lines competed with the Great Western for limited space) were co-ordinated and orders were placed at Swindon for a new design 0–6–2 tank engine for working Welsh traffic. At Caerphilly the works of the Rhymney Railway were reorganized for repairing and maintaining engines working the coal routes. Virtually single-handed, he courageously launched a campaign to substitute 20-ton all-metal wagons for the wasteful and obsolete 10- and 12-ton coal wagons. An amused but incredulous American delegation had called them 'dinky little trucks'. Despite this taunt the colliery masters, partly from apathy, but also sometimes because the high cost of altering the clearances of the colliery screens would fall on them, were slow to replace them. A train load of 20-ton wagons, Pole argued, could carry a pay load of 500 tons occupying only 612ft of track, against 1,009ft by the standard wagons carrying less coal. He stumped South Wales lecturing chambers of commerce on their advantage and offering 50 per cent reductions on dock dues for shipments from fully loaded 20-ton wagons. As an encouragement the company itself ordered 1,000 of the new trucks, and the first trainload, fifty in all, arrived at the Severn Tunnel junction in 1924.

Pole worked hard for South Wales, but he was trying to blow life into dying embers. The old pre-war coal export markets were collapsing. By September 1924 the export of coal from Bristol Channel ports had declined by three million tons. In 1925 a loss of nearly six million tons in freight traffic originating on the company's system was almost entirely due to coal, the output of which over the whole area had declined by $11\frac{1}{2}$ million tons since 1913. As coal and mineral traffic amounted to nearly 70 per cent of the total tonnage carried by the company, the drain on resources was serious. In 1923 the company itself in taking 1,200,000 tons of Welsh coal became one of the largest single consumers of the commodity it was trying to sell at a profit to others.

The fall in coal exports was exacerbated by the growing use of oil as a fuel. The Navy in 1913 had largely patrolled the seas using Welsh coal; by 1918 it was burning instead nearly 2 million tons of oil and in 1921 needed only 300,000 tons of coal, far less than the company itself used. A few years later the Navy had abandoned coal altogether.

This was a serious blow, for it was reckoned that a coal-burning battleship needed the entire services of one pit as well as several complete coal trains to keep it in commission. Now it needed only to come alongside and suck in fuel through a pipe—but fuel which originated in the Persian Gulf and not the Rhondda. Although Pole was alive to it, the significance of this change from coal to oil was slow in impressing itself on the Great Western board. The Trojan horse in the guise of the Anglo-Persian Oil Company had been given a red-carpet welcome into the GWR's midst in 1922 when a refinery was set up at Swansea capable of dealing with 100,000 tons a year. This trickle rapidly became a flood. By 1926 oil had become the second largest traffic in South Wales, with 950,000 tons imported and a total export of refined products amounting to nearly two million tons a year. A crowning irony was the company's decision in 1924 to specify oil instead of coal for four new vessels for the Channel Islands traffic. Then in 1926 came the General Strike, dealing a near death-blow to whatever prospects of revival there might have been for the South Wales coal industry.

The 1926 strike was a contest with organized labour for which Pole was better prepared. From it he emerged as the strong man of Britain's railway hierarchy, driving the hardest bargain of all with his own employees. When the strike started on 3 May the shut-down on the Great Western, as on other railways, was complete. Again, as in 1919, when the railwaymen came out the volunteers moved in. They became porters and manned signal boxes. Dozens applied to drive engines. The newly-sworn-in railway police volunteers at Paddington proved so enthusiastic that they several times arrested Pole himself. But thereafter the parallel with 1919 ended. In that year it had been the railwaymen on their own making the running and the Government which had given in. But in 1926 the railwaymen, at the call of the TUC, struck not for themselves, but in sympathy with the miners. This was a fatal flaw in their armour which Pole, who had absorbed the lessons of 1919, was quick to see.

For him the strike was to be a game of chess in which he resolved 'to be always one move ahead'. He concentrated on undermining the solidarity of the company's rank and file. Why should railwaymen suffer because of a dispute between miners and pit owners? Each man received a telegram with a simple message: was he prepared to dishonour his contract and ruin the company as well at the call of the TUC? To make sure none missed the appeal, Great Western stations were plastered with boldly printed posters demanding 'Whom do you serve?' and setting out side by side the moral claims of the company and the 'unlawful demands of the TUC'. Although the men still stayed out, Pole's propaganda war was unsettling. Pole also contemptuously defied the strikers by guaranteeing London's milk, of which the Great Western was the largest supplier. If necessary, he warned, signals would be ignored and points spiked into position to bring the milk trains in. The Cabinet, refusing to believe him, insisted on scouring the country for milk lorries. They would have been wiser to have trusted Pole. London got its milk, volunteers at Paddington on the first day handling 8,000 churns. By the strike's end milk was reaching Paddington in such quantities that an appeal had to be broadcast to Londoners to drink more of it.

But the Great Western general manager's leadership was most complete in his opposition to the TUCs 'no victimization' call, a demand which he refused from the outset to entertain. Waverers in other railway managements were steeled by him to act in concert. When the strike ended after nine days, railwaymen went back without a 'no victimization' guarantee. But at Paddington, Pole went one step farther. Strikers had to sign a document pledging that they were re-engaged 'on the understanding that you are not relieved of the consequences of having broken your contract of service with the company'. Apart from a momentary sullen stiffening, especially at Bristol, Great Western men accepted. It was Pole's strongest hour. Never again was a railway manager to act with such absolute power and authority in an industrial dispute.

Nevertheless the strike had cost the company over £4 million; in the coalfields it left a sore which continued to fester. For while the railwaymen, the dockers and the bus drivers went back on dictated terms, the miners sullenly stayed out. In the first half of 1926 coal carried by the company decreased by nearly 6 million tons, or 23·25 per cent compared with the previous year, while dock receipts slumped by £297,000. 'I write the word "dock" every time a grey hair appears' Pole had earlier told an audience at Barry, which in normal times exported a third of the coal shipped through the Bristol Channel ports. It was becoming clear that in looking for profits from South Wales coal the company had hitched its fortunes to a burnt-out star. A dividend of 7 per cent declared in 1927 following an improvement of trade (compared with the strike year) proved the herald of a false dawn. Pole's grey hairs were soon to appear on other heads.

The 1926 strike aggravated a decline in mineral and freight tonnage which was to hit the company hardest in the world slump of the early '30s. But throughout the 1920s and 1930s the Great Western Railway in the eyes of the general public was not a system wrestling with economic depression but the railway of the Cheltenham Flyer, the 'Castle' and 'King' class locomotives and the Cornish Riviera Limited. More than all else it was the 'Holiday Line', a title which, despite growing road competition, it enlarged and made uniquely its own. It was a slogan inseparable from an image of chocolate and cream coaches drawn by gleaming engines with burnished copper chimney bands. It conjured up the magic of leisured, palm-fringed promenades and the wide golden sands of the Cornish shore and the Welsh coastal resorts.

This picture owed much to solid engineering and locomotive achievement, but almost as much, also, to Pole's adroit appreciation of publicity. The Great Western's general manager was a born public relations officer. In March 1927 passengers had been vexed and delayed by a mishap with a slip coach in Sonning cutting. On the following night they found on their seats an apology and an explanatory leaflet complete with diagrams. Pole had himself prepared it. Such touches endeared the company to its public; they felt they were being taken into its confidence. Behind this constant awareness of the value of publicity was a deliberate campaign to burnish the company's image until it outshone all others in appeal and brightness.

No new passenger engine classes had been developed at

Swindon since Churchward's two- and four-cylinder 'Saint' and 'Star' classes had appeared before 1914. In boiler and cylinder design they still held their own. It was behind the two-cylinder 4–6–0 *St Bartholomew* that the 'Cheltenham Flyer' made its début. Before the publicity department, under Pole's prompting, were given their head this was an unremarkable nine-coach afternoon up-express from Cheltenham via Swindon to Paddington, incorporating a tea car. But on the afternoon of 9 July 1923 it steamed into history by being accelerated to make the 77¼ mile journey from Swindon to Paddington in 75 minutes. At an average speed of 61·8 miles an hour it became the fastest start-to-stop express in the country, just beating the record of 61·7 over 44 miles start-to-stop held since 1902 by the LNER.

While this was an achievement well within a 'Saint's' capacity, the 'Cheltenham Flyer' was to go on to greater triumphs hauled by an engine that was not of Churchward's design. Restoration of pre-war speeds in 1921, more regular non-stop trains and heavier passenger traffic on holiday routes (the 'Cornish Riviera', for example, was regularly hauling 400 tons, against 380 in pre-1914 days) suggested a bigger passenger engine. Collett responded in 1923 with his four-cylinder 4–6–0 'Castle' class, arguably the best all-round passenger engines ever produced in Britain. Handling them when new, said their crews, was like driving a Rolls-Royce. Burnished in the full splendour of pre-war livery, they marked the emergence of the company's locomotives from the austerity of the war years to help maintain a pre-eminence in passenger train running unapproached until the middle 1930s.

The success of Collett and his design teams at Swindon was now matched, with Pole's enthusiastic encouragement, by the publicity department at Paddington. The first of the new engines, *Caerphilly Castle* (a nice compliment to the absorbed Rhymney Railway), was put on show at the Wembley Exhibition in 1924–5. It attracted delighted cries. Those unable to see it at Wembley could read about it for a shilling in a book by W. G. Chapman. This threw in for good measure a history of Great Western locomotives of which *Caerphilly Castle* was the newest example of a distinguished line. Within a month 30,000 extra copies had to be printed to supplement the first 10,000.

Pole, now firmly in the saddle at Paddington, enlarged the dimension of this publicity by arranging a series of trials or locomotive exchanges with a vaguely comparable LNER engine (see Chapter 6). The 'Castle' won hands down, establishing for Swindon a clear lead in design, performance and economy of locomotive operation.

Headed by a 'Castle', the 'Cheltenham Flyer' now riveted public attention to itself with a series of record-breaking runs, generating an excitement which still tingles after the passage of more than forty years. They began on 8 July 1929 when, after a temporary withdrawal, the 'Flyer' burst upon the railway world with an eye-popping performance. Whirled along by Collett's *Launceston Castle*, the nine-coach train of 280 tons reached Paddington from Swindon in 70 minutes, an average of 68·2 miles an hour. Within a mile from the start 70 had been reached and 80 was on the dial within 11 miles between Challow and Wantage Road. As it drew into Paddington with the merest flurry of steam about it, a wildly excited crowd thronged the platform capturing the gleaming engine in the lenses of dozens of cameras. 'A close study of the timetables on French and American railways', soberly noted the August 1929 *Great Western Magazine*, 'does not suggest any doubt that the new schedule is the fastest in the world'. Slightly nettled by subsequent taunts about a 'stunt run' over a road that from Swindon was mainly downhill, Paddington carefully made it plain that the 1929 summer timetables 'contained in all six start-to-stop bookings at 60mph so that *Launceston Castle* was not a mere freak timing for the purposes of advertisement but indicates the company's recognition of the value to the public of high speed and their determination to provide it'.

But in playing for supreme stakes the Flyer could not rest upon its laurels. To keep its lead it was accelerated in September 1931 to 69·2mph and a year later to 71·4mph, making it the first 70mph train to appear in any British timetable. To the public it was now indisputably the 'Cheltenham Flyer', and the engine carried a headboard with the proud legend, 'The World's fastest train'. The gauntlet so provocatively thrown down was soon picked up. First the Germans with the diesel-hauled 'Flying Hamburger' (the Germans had not overlooked oil) obliged the 'Flyer' to moderate its claim to that of the fastest steam train in the world. Then subsequent events on the other side of the Atlantic forced even that honour to be relinquished.

By now Pole had gone (his last day with the company was 6 July 1929) but the 'Cheltenham Flyer' and the publicity surrounding it had served the Great Western well. However naive this saga of speed seems today, it brought a bright splash of colour and excitement into a world then hag-ridden by slump and unemployment. The name of a Georgian spa had become synonymous in the minds of the travelling public with a new era of railway speed. Nor were the 'Flyer's' achievements a mere flash in the publicity pan. Day in and day out it continued to run with punctual regularity, at speeds of often 80 and sometimes 90mph.

If the 'Castles' were Collett's brainchildren (with some assistance from Churchward), Pole could take some credit for being the godfather of the 'Kings'. The 'Castles' had been launched with the dubious claim that they were the most powerful engines in the country. The boast did not go un-noticed. The everwatchful Southern countered in 1926 with their four-cylinder 4-6-0 *Lord Nelson*, initially a less successful engine but superior in tractive effort. Caught in the toils of his own publicity, Pole cast around for a way out. He found it in the realization that the 'Castles', good as they were, did not supply the complete answer to the problems presented by the company's heavy, long-distance, non-stop passenger trains. In designing them Collett had been tied to a 19½ ton axle load, the supposed weight limit of the bridges on the permanent way. 'Give me an axle load of 22½ tons', he said in effect to Pole, 'and I will give you a very fine locomotive.' Pole called in J. H. Lloyd, the Great Western's chief civil engineer. Lloyd brought surprising tidings. For years, he blandly explained, the company's engineers had been building bridges capable of taking 22 tons. Although Lloyd did not then say so, and it was not his fault, the 'highly departmentalized position of affairs that existed at Paddington for so many years' (to use Pole's words) had been the cause of this vital information not being passed on. The astonished Pole now went back to Collett. The latter, reminded of his promise, was asked to provide a new passenger engine for the 1927 summer traffic. Collett

proved as good as his word; within six months he was back with
a trump card—the 'King' class locomotive. It was big and
powerful enough to give the Great Western a clear lead over all
rivals. King George V lent his name to the first of the class and
the Baltimore and Ohio Railroad set about spreading its fame
around the New World.

This American publicity was Pole's masterstroke. The Baltimore and Ohio, 'the grandfather of United States railroads',
was celebrating its centenary in 1928. Pole was sounded about
getting from England some examples of old and new locomotives
for an exhibition to illustrate travel development. His response
was some shrewd horsetrading. Provided the Great Western
was the only railway to be invited, the Baltimore company could
have *King George V* as well as the replica *North Star*, which had
been reconstructed at Swindon for the British Empire exhibition
at Wembley in 1924–5. Thus while it was still being built 'the
greatest achievement of the Great Western mechanical department' was earmarked for America to be exhibited at the Fair of
the Iron Horse, the culminating pageant of the centenary celebrations. Its arrival after a hair-raising sea journey had been
preceded by some of the most lyrical publicity ever accorded a
British mechanical achievement. 'Breathes there a man with a
soul so dead', rhapsodized the *New York Herald Tribune*, 'that
doesn't thrill a little at such news. Especially when he learns that
this engine now under construction will be capable of 80 miles
an hour, the most powerful locomotive ever built for an English
railway.'

If this was hard on the 'Castles', which were proving themselves capable of 90, it was magnificent publicity for the 'Kings'.
Engine 6000 *King George V* took the Americans by storm. Back
in England, its success led to the organization of regular excursions to the Swindon works to see the remaining 'Kings' being
built.

Within little more than two years after the first appearance of
the 'Kings', Paddington knew Pole no more. He had been
wooed into becoming chairman of the newly formed Associated
Electrical Industries, although for a short time he continued to
act in a consultative capacity for the GWR. Pole's tenure at
Paddington had been exciting and picturesque. He had opened

many windows, was always accessible, and had striven hard against nepotism. He left an enduring mark on the company's between-the-wars history. Joined with Sir Herbert Walker of the Southern, Sir Ralph Wedgwood of the LNER and Sir Josiah Stamp of the LMS, Pole, who had himself been knighted in 1924 for railway advisory services in the Sudan, made up one of the most impressive quartets ever to reign in British railway management. When he went, more people knew more about the Great Western and its trains than at any time before or after. His last seven years were clouded by total blindness which he overcame at seventy by mastering braille. A 'Castle' class engine bearing his name was unveiled at Paddington by his son in 1956.

RIDING THE STORM

Within eighteen months of Pole's departure the world economic storm had burst. His successor, James Milne (knighted in 1931), was less outgoing as a public figure but more penetrating as a statistician. Milne's grip was strong and positive, but if he lacked something of Pole's sparkle and exhilarating daring, he had a valid excuse. Until 1929 despite strikes, rising expenses and increasing competition from road hauliers, the company had held its own. In that year the total revenue was £36,184,053, sufficient to nourish a $7\frac{1}{2}$ per cent dividend on ordinary shares. This was the highest of any of the four main-line companies. Despite a reduction in total earnings of more than £1,800,000, a dividend of 5 per cent was paid for 1930. It was a figure not seen again in the following decade. In the next year the full rigour of the economic blizzard struck the country, and nowhere was its breath harsher than in South Wales 'where the business of the Great Western is very much dependent on the coal, iron and steel trades'. The 'bargain package' of the 1921 Act was now more like a millstone round the company's neck throughout the '30s. Coal production and exports, the cornerstone of the package, tumbled; ancillary industries were almost at a standstill. Out of forty-five blast furnaces on the company's system only five were working in 1931. In the following year the company had lost over £3 million in revenue, a reflection of the 'unprecedented depression in trade and industry', and had to draw over £1 million from reserves to pay 3 per cent. Between 1929 and 1932 almost half of the decrease of £5 million in gross receipts was accounted for by coal and ancillary traffic. The total loss from freight and passenger traffic (the latter due to unemployment) in South Wales was larger than on any other part of the company's system. Faced with a decrease in revenue over three years of nearly £7½ million, Milne publicly called attention to a scale of losses 'unparalleled in the history of the company'.

A sector where these losses were particularly acute was the dock system that the company had taken over through the Grouping Act. Although £21 million had been invested in them, the receipts from Swansea, Cardiff, Barry, Newport, Port Talbot and Penarth were scarcely sufficient to cover working expenses. An ordinary commercial company, the chairman declared, would have closed them, a fate which temporarily befell Penarth in 1936 after losses 'totally inadequate to its receipts'. Yet the plight of the docks only brought into sharper focus a situation of slump and decay which had made over 36 per cent of the working population of South Wales unemployed. Around Merthyr Tydfil, which the old Vale of Neath Railway and the original Taff Vale line had been built to serve, there began to grow up the largest derelict area of any community in the United Kingdom. Miners whose fathers had hewn steam coal to fire Churchward's boilers were singing 'Land of my fathers' in London streets or seeking work as waiters. Since 1929 the Great Western, which alone normally employed 27,000 in the area and paid a wage bill of nearly £4½ million, had been forced to stand off nearly 5,000 of its workers. The effects of the slump in loss of revenue and profit resembled a blood-letting which was to sap the company's enterprise for the remainder of the 30s and was to prove the unacknowledged spectre at the feast during its centenary celebrations.

One man destined not to see these was Viscount Churchill, the company's chairman, who died on 3 January 1934, aged sixty-nine. For nearly twenty-six years he had guided the company's fortunes—the longest holder of the office of chairman in Great Western history. Page of Honour to Queen Victoria, Lord in Waiting to Edward VII, Master of the Buckhounds and of the Robes at the Coronation of George V, a Conservative whip in

The Great Western Railway has had its share of special occasions. *Plate 27 (above)* A scene at Paddington during the general strike of 1926 with volunteers handling milk churns. *Plate 28 (below)* With its royal connections at Windsor, the GWR and Paddington have always been associated with royal journeys including the sad occasions of royal funerals. The procession accompanying the gun carriage at the funeral of King Edward VII leaves Windsor station on 20 May 1910. *(Radio Times Hulton Picture Library)*

The Great Western Railway rightly acquired the title of the 'holiday line', for with its many Devon and Cornish resorts it carried the most concentrated long-distance holiday traffic in the country. *Plate 29 (above)* Star train to the West was the Cornish Riviera Express, which with slip coaches and through portions served many resorts in the South-West. Here King class 4-6-0 No 6015 *King Richard III* near Westbury heads the up Cornish Riviera composed of the new wide-body stock built for the centenary of the company in 1935. *Plate 30 (below)* Holiday crowds at Paddington Station in August 1924. *(Locomotive & General Railway Photographs; Radio Times Hulton Picture Library)*

the Lords, Edward Victor Spencer Churchill, the third baronet, had entered the railway and business world through the portals of the Court. A small, compact, incisive man, he had known Wilkinson and Inglis in the heady, early days of the century. He had held the ring with wary tact in the great feud when Churchward refused to subordinate his authority to Inglis. Autocratic, irritated when interrupted (as Pole once found out), he was also 'the boss' to the great majority of the company's employees in a particularly affectionate and paternal sense. How far he had any ideas of his own which helped shape the policy of the 'dear old Great Western', as he liked to call it, is less clear. Pole suggests that he played some part in discouraging the continuance of a promising all-Pullman service to Torquay and Paignton. Without the intellectual range of Stamp or the brash energy of Walker, he typified the reliable and solidly conservative image of the Great Western. But the world in which he was most at home was beginning to change before he died. The abrasive thrust of trade union and labour troubles in the 1920s had left him perplexed and ill at ease.

The new chairman, Viscount Horne, had humbler origins but a profounder business expertise. A son of the manse, Horne had been successively Minister of Labour, President of the Board of Trade and Chancellor of the Exchequer (1921–2), a more commanding background for a railway chairmanship than court appointments. Among Horne's first tasks was the agreeable one of piloting the company through its hundredth birthday festivities. Churchill had died as the lowering clouds of economic depression had begun to lighten and could take some credit for having steered the company through the blackest period. In 1934 income had risen by over £856,000, although the £90,000 brought in by 2½ million more passengers (largely from third-class tickets at 1d a mile) had meant running a million more train miles. Meanwhile George V, surviving a critical illness, was preparing to share his jubilee year with his people. Amid these sunnier omens the railway over which the King's grandmother had made her first train journey and which served a countryside from which his son, as Duke of Cornwall, drew substantial revenues, advanced into 1935 to become the first British railway to celebrate 100 years of corporate existence.

I

This was an occasion for feasting and speech-making. Along with congratulatory articles in the railway press and a thoughtful leader in a *Times* Supplement, there was a London banquet at which the Prince of Wales was the guest of honour 'not only as a traveller but as a landowner and indeed customer of the line'. A more relaxed and interesting feast was the earlier 'family party' at Bristol where one of the guests was an *enfant terrible* who aroused mixed feelings. This was the Rt Hon J. H. Thomas, now a Socialist Lord Privy Seal. In 1901 Thomas, then an engine driver, had caused consternation by beating his own superintendent in an election for a Swindon council ward. He had urged on the company's employees in the 1919 strike and had led the railwaymen in 1926. Since then he had come a long way, and at Bristol that evening rubbed shoulders with his old employers as a member of the Establishment. It was an occasion Thomas enjoyed. 'Where else in the world', he asked his temporarily apprehensive audience, 'would a great commercial and capitalist institution invite to its birthday as a representative of his Majesty's government one who had formerly been employed as an engine cleaner, fireman and driver.' The ex-cleaner earned a long round of applause.

Away from the glitter of the banquets, however, the celebratory trumpets were more muted. The company's sole contribution to its locomotive heritage was to shorten the journey time between Paddington and Bristol by fifteen minutes and order some luxury centenary stock for the 'Cornish Riviera' express. It was very good stock indeed, but the strong-willed assertion to be first rather than second which, less than ten years earlier, had led Pole to order the 'Kings' was missing. When the LMS over a longer route cut the journey time between London and Birmingham by a full five minutes compared with Great Western timing, it brought no competitive answer from Paddington. Instead it was LNER and Gresley who showed how the centenary might have been linked with the Jubilee rejoicings. Scarcely had the new Bristolian express begun running than Gresley launched his streamlined 'Pacific'-hauled train 'Silver Jubilee' which whirled away non-stop the 232·3 miles between King's Cross and Darlington in 198 minutes at 70·4mph. From then on the glamour of new engine designs and the thrill of high speed

Restaurant Cars

TARIFF
(Ordinary Trains)

Breakfast (Table d'Hôte)		3/6
Luncheon ditto		2/6 and 3/-
Ditto ditto (Cars on Services operating between the G.W. and L.M.S., L.N.E., and Southern Lines)		3/6
Dinner (Table d'Hôte)		5/-

TEAS.—Pot of Tea or Coffee, with Cut Bread and Butter,
per person, 9d.

Full Tea Tariff exhibited in the Restaurant Cars.

N.B.—The charge for Table d'Hôte Luncheon served on the "Cornish Riviera Limited" and "Torbay Limited" Expresses is 4/- per head.

Passengers are requested to note that Dogs are not allowed in the Restaurant Cars.

GENERAL ARRANGEMENTS

RESERVING SEATS.—To secure a seat for breakfast, luncheon or dinner in the restaurant car, it is necessary to obtain a ticket from the Conductor in charge of the car. The seats are numbered to correspond with the numbers printed on the tickets. The attendants will inform passengers when the meals are ready, and conduct them to their seats in the restaurant car. Seats can only be occupied during the time a meal is being served.

RELAYS.—If all the passengers requiring a meal cannot be accommodated at one sitting, further meals will be served if time permit, and tickets for "First," "Second" or "Third" meal issued accordingly. The Company cannot undertake to provide for every passenger in the train.

CORRIDOR COMMUNICATION.—Passengers requiring a meal *en route* should see before starting that access to the Restaurant Car is possible from the compartment in which they propose to travel, as communication throughout the train is not always provided. Passengers travelling in slip coaches cannot obtain access to the Restaurant Cars.

PAYMENTS.—It is particularly requested that all payments be made to the Restaurant Car Conductor, and a receipted bill obtained from him and retained.

Fig 9   Restaurant car tariff of the early 1930s.

records deserted Swindon for the north. At Crewe, drawing on his earlier Great Western experience, Stanier began to bring out the 'Princess' Pacifics for the long-distance expresses of the LMS, while Gresley in 1937 with the 'Coronation' overtook the 'Cheltenham Flyer' with a higher speed over a much greater distance. In the following year with *Mallard*, one of his A4 streamlined 'Pacifics', he took the world's record for speed with a steam locomotive. By contrast the railway of Brunel, Gooch and Churchward in its centenary year opted out of competition to rest complacently on its prestige, content to watch from the sidelines as the world of locomotive achievement sped by. The frightful losses in South Wales had taken their toll; the 'bargain package' had become an empty husk. Dividends were only being sustained by raiding reserves of which there were now scarcely any left. One crumb of consolation was that in the three years 1935–7 the LNER could not pay any dividends at all.

By the time the centenary celebrations had ended, the world was only four years away from another war. Nevertheless, the 1930s, despite their strains, were not without achievement for the company. The difference from the past was that no gauntlets were thrown down for others to strive after, although there was at least one unusual gesture. In 1931 the company's chocolate and cream livery took to the air between Plymouth and Cardiff (extended the following year to Birmingham), bringing South Devon holiday resorts within fifty and seventy minutes of Cardiff. This service was operated in conjunction with Imperial Airways Ltd, which supplied the pilot, the ground staff and the six-seater, three-engined Westland Wessex plane.

Although the first to take advantage of powers obtained in 1929 by the four main-line companies to run air services, the flirtation with the skies was little more than an eye-catching sideline for a company firmly anchored to the permanent way. It still remained, above all, the 'holiday line', boldly and imaginatively catering for the holidaymaker who preferred the comfort and certain arrival of steam travel to the uncertainty of landing and departing from small, primitive and often mist-bound South Devon airfields. Despite the depression, holiday season ticket issues rose from 2,873 in 1930 to 46,995 in 1934. A 15s ticket allowed free travel at will for seven days. Four- and six-day 'land cruises' (originally instituted in 1927) combined road and rail journeys to beauty spots and historical buildings in the Wye Valley, Wales, Devon and Cornwall. One of the Welsh tours even included a trip up the slopes of Plynlymon in an experimental six-wheeled Morris bus. Among the regular holiday trains of the country, the Cornish Riviera Limited was still supreme, an extra train being introduced in 1936 to take its surplus passengers. In 1938 the loads became so great that even the 'Kings' had to be assisted over the South Devon line. Compared with the more democratic LMS, however, the 'Cornish Riviera's' third-class passengers, their baggage spilling over into the corridor, still travelled in cramped discomfort on long journeys, reminiscent of the plight in earlier days of those 'in the lower stations of life'.

At last, too, the company recognized the significance of oil with the introduction in 1933 of diesel cars between Paddington and Didcot. They proved so popular that in the following year a diesel railcar express service, chiefly for businessmen, was inaugurated between Birmingham and Cardiff. They were the first diesel railcars in Britain. Nine years later the company had thirty-eight such vehicles and was using diesel cars for excursion traffic as well as on several branch and local services.

Elsewhere, a £4½ million works programme aided by a government grant (1929) for unemployment relief helped to improve stations and iron out bottlenecks. Paddington was extended (and the interior of its hotel spoiled), Cardiff and Taunton were given completely new stations (although Banbury, and Oxford which badly needed 'rearranging', remained untouched) and the capacity of Temple Meads was doubled. Automatic train control, first introduced in 1906 and in the opinion of driver J. W. Street, of 'Cheltenham Flyer' fame, 'the best thing that was ever done for locomotive men', was extended to the greater part of the system. Electrically operated from a ramp between the rails, the device in its earliest form gave an audible warning to the driver in his cab when he passed a distant signal. It had now been improved to apply the brakes automatically as well. In the West Country the building of avoiding loops to by-pass Frome and Westbury had improved the overall average speed of West of England expresses by ten miles an hour.

Great Western Royal Hotel
Paddington Station, London, W.2
Telephone: 8961 Paddington.   *Telegrams*: " Padotel, Rail, London."

TARIFF

Apartments—

BEDROOMS (PER DAY)

	Single.	Communicating Bathroom.	Double.	Communicating Bathroom.
Ground Floor	10/- & 11/-	—	16/6	—
1st „	10/- to 13/-	13/-	18/- to 25/-	18/-
2nd „	10/- to 13/-	13/-	15/- to 19/6	18/-
3rd „	10/- & 11/-	13/-	15/- & 16/6	18/-
4th „	10/-	13/-	15/-	18/-
5th „	8/-	—	—	—

SITTING ROOMS from 12/6 PER DAY.

Suites 3 Rooms—1st Floor	44/-	49/6	—
„ 2 „ 2nd „	26/6	28/-	—

Reception or Meeting Rooms from 21/-

BATHS—Hot or Cold in Bathroom ⸰ ⸰ ⸰ ⸰ 1/-
Hip Bath in Bedroom ⸰ ⸰ ⸰ ⸰ 1/6
FIRES—Morning or Evening ⸰ ⸰ 2/-   Whole day ⸰ ⸰ 4/-

VISITORS' SERVANTS

Bedroom ⸰ Per night 7/6   Board ⸰ Per day 10/-

DOGS

Animals are not allowed in the Hotel, but accommodation can be provided at the stables at a charge of 2/- per day.   No risk is accepted by the Company.

EARLY MORNING TEA

Tea, Bread and Butter, or Biscuits ⸰ ⸰ ⸰ Per person 1/-

BREAKFAST. DINING ROOM
(Served 8 a.m. to 10 a.m.)

Table d'Hôte ⸰ 3/6   Plain Breakfast ⸰ 2/-
Plain Breakfast, with 2 Boiled Eggs ⸰ ⸰ ⸰ ⸰ 3/-
Breakfast served in Bedroom 6d. extra

LUNCHEON. DINING ROOM
(Served 12.30 p.m. to 2.45 p.m.)

Table d'Hôte ⸰ ⸰ ⸰ ⸰ ⸰ ⸰ ⸰ 3/6
A la Carte Luncheons also provided

Fig 10   Tariff for the Great Western Royal Hotel at Paddington, 1933.

The early '30s also saw a compromise with competing road services. An irregular relationship with road passenger transport had dogged the company from the pioneering days of its Helston–Lizard buses. In 1904, according to Pole, powers to prevent pirate concerns working in any of the company's areas could have been had for the asking. The Post Office, in return, however, demanded that the buses should also carry mail. The company refused to do so, thus missing a chance to protect itself from road competition that was never to recur. By 1928 Great Western-controlled buses were operating 168 services, utilizing 300 buses, carrying over 8 million passengers without any specific powers to do so or to oppose competition. Under a new arrangement this anomally was ended in 1928 and the company's bus fleet was gradually dispersed amongst road operating concerns in most of which the Great Western had a substantial financial interest.

The last years before the war also saw the high noon of the company's ocean liner traffic, which, since the fading out of Fishguard, was concentrated almost entirely upon Plymouth. Although never more than a poor relation of the Southern's Southampton, Plymouth during the later 1930s dealt with an average of 500 liners a year, landing 30,000 to 40,000 passengers and 200 bags of mail. In 1937—a peak year—the Cunard's *Queen Mary*, proudly displaying the Atlantic Blue Riband, called nine times and her rival, France's *Normandie*, four. Landing at Plymouth could bring a passenger to London twenty-four hours earlier than from Southampton, but trans-Atlantic liner captains with tight schedules chafed at the two-hour delay that the Plymouth call entailed. In bad weather it was quicker and easier to by-pass the port.

When passengers did land they were whirled to London non-stop in lightly laden boat trains at privileged speeds. But by the summer of 1939 the ordinary traveller too, on the company's main trunk routes, had a choice of nineteen trains running at 60mph. At the height of its running efficiency in the later 30s the GWR could get a passenger from London to Looe, 250 miles away at the end of a remote branch line in Cornwall, at an average speed of 40 miles an hour despite two stops and a change of trains. It was another story if he tried to cross the company's system from south to north. The journey between Plymouth and Birmingham (226 miles) in the '30s was made at an overall average speed of 40·8mph. Even between Plymouth and Bristol (127 miles) the speed of the fastest train averaged only 47·8—not much better than broad-gauge days. An impatient traveller from Cardiff to Plymouth (165 miles) dawdled at 33·15mph, and even he was a shade better off than one from Liverpool to Torquay, between which the average speed was 32·9mph. Some commentators have suggested that better services were not called for, but poor cross-country times to and from South Wales, the Midlands and the North in fact were a repeated source of complaint with many West Country chambers of commerce. Much of this slowness, especially on the North and West services, arose from the company's policy of effecting mileage economies by cutting out daytime parcels train services and using mostly passenger trains instead. Unfortunately, it gave an edge to the taunt of Southern Railway enthusiasts that the Great Western obstinately remained as it was conceived—a railway between London and Bristol. Today British Rail do things better. In 1938 the average time at platform of trains calling at Bristol Temple Meads was eighteen minutes; now, with a complete reversal of policy, it is only four minutes.

Nevertheless even had there been the will to shorten station stops and improve things in 1938 too little time then remained to do so. As the war edged nearer other problems obtruded. Although total receipts of £32½ million in 1937 were the best since 1930, the effects of the world slump still affected South Wales to a greater degree than anywhere else in the United Kingdom. Exports from the company's docks in 1938 were more than 3 million tons down, 'a decline, I believe, unparalleled in our history', declared the worried chairman. Coal production was still lagging and its rising price (it had climbed 32 per cent between 1934 and 1937) had earlier led (February 1938) to the extraordinary announcement that the company which five years earlier had pioneered diesel traffic was considering electrifying all its lines west of Taunton at a cost of £4 million. The plan, worked out in detail, remained an exercise on paper, which was perhaps all it was ever intended to be. One other problem—the loss annually of 240,000 cups through serving teas on trains—

was intriguing rather than serious. Cups stamped GWR were reported to have been seen in the Khyber Pass and in the Sudan strapped to soldiers' kits. They were soon going to be seen in the same kits nearer home, for air raid precautions had started in 1938. In the following year holidaymakers on some of the 800 additional trains put on for them saw another ominous hint of perils to come. These were station advertisements hinting to industry that it was safer in the West!

TO WAR AGAIN

When war came in September 1939 it was without 1914's excitement and fervour. Rather there was an air of sombre, forlorn resignation, as Horne observed at the company's annual meeting in the following February. 'Those of us', he said, 'who went through four years of the last conflict have an unhappy feeling of waking up after an interval of broken sleep to find the war which began in 1914 still in progress.'

It was a feeling heightened, as then, by handing over the running of the railways to the State, and Milne, like his earlier predecessor, Frank Potter, became a member of the Railway Executive Committee charged with running them. But there, for the GWR, the similarity with the earlier war ended. Instead of fuelling the Fleet, the company found itself providing trains for the greatest mass movement of women and children in the country's history. From Ealing Broadway alone 163 trains carried 112,994 evacuees in four days to a safer West Country, while thousands more left unofficially in other trains. As they travelled behind Churchward's old 'Stars' and Collett's newer 'Castles', 'Kings' and 'Granges', hundreds of children saw for the first time green fields with cows and sheep through their carriage windows, and at their journey's end found frustrating trials in rural remoteness and the absence of a fish and chip shop round the corner.

In the summer of 1940 troops rescued from Dunkirk supplanted the refugees. The Southern brought them back from the Channel ports to Redhill from where 37 per cent of the trains passed to the Great Western and 13 per cent to the northern companies. At sea four Great Western steamers, the *St Andrew*,

WORKING OF EVACUATION TRAINS FROM ACTON AND EALING B'WAY.

When circumstances necessitate the use made of the empty trains may not be strictly in accordance with the following programme. Locomotive Department to be prepared to adjust working of Engines accordingly.

FIRST DAY.

TRAIN NUMBER.		EMPTY STOCK.		LOADED TRAIN.		DESTINATION.	Empty Stock returned for same day's working.	
		Acton Yard.	Old Oak Common.	Acton.	Ealing Broadway.			Acton Yard.
		dep. a.m.	dep. a.m.	dep. a.m.	dep. a.m.		dep. a.m.	arr. a.m.
101	L	7†15	—	—	8 30	Maidenhead	9†30	10†35
102	L	7†30	—		8 39	Oxford .. .	10†50	p.m. 12†30
103		—	7†30	From Paddington		St. Austell	—	—
104		8†0	—	—	8 48	Chippenham	p.m. 12†5	p.m. 2†30
105	L	8†10	—	—	8 57	Henley-on-Thames ..	a.m. 10†5	a.m. 11†10
106		8†30	—	—	9 7	Frome	p.m. 12†40	p.m. 3†20
107		8†35	—	—	9 16	Highbridge ..	—	—
108		8†45	—	—	9 25	Dorchester ..	—	—
109		8†55	—	—	9 34	Bath	12†40	3†55
110		9†5	—	—	9 43	Devizes	12†45	2†55
111		9†25	—	—	9 52	Weston-super-Mare ..	—	—
112	L	9†30	—	—	10 2	Oxford	12†5	1†45
113		9†40	—	—	10 11	Taunton	—	—
114		—	9†35	—	10 20	Bridgwater ..	—	—
115		9†45	—	—	10 29	Swindon	1†35	3†30
116	West London	10†0		10 30	—	{Totnes .. .. / Kingsbridge ..	—	—
117	L	10†0	—	—	10 38	Slough	a.m. 11†35	12†10
118		10†20	—	—	10 47	Trowbridge ..	p.m. 2†0	4†25
119		10†30	—	—	10 56	Weston-super-Mare ..	—	—
120		10†40	—	—	11 6	{Watchet .. .. / Minehead ..	—	—
121		10†45	—	—	11 15	Axbridge ..	—	—
122	L	10†55	—	—	11 24	Maidenhead ..	12†25	1†5
123		11†5	—	—	11 33	Bath	—	—
124		—	11†5	—	11 42	Malmesbury ..	—	—
125	L	11†15	—	—	11 51	Oxford	2†0	3†40
126		11†25	—	—	p.m. 12 1	Swindon	—	—
127		11†35	—	—	12 10	Wellington (Som.) ..	—	—
128	L	11†55	—	—	12 19	Wantage Road ..	2†30	4†10
129		p.m. 12†5	—	—	12 28	Banbury	—	—
130	West London	p.m. 12†0		12 30	—	{Teignmouth .. / Newton Abbot ..	—	—
131		12†10	—	—	12 37	Weston-super-Mare ..	—	—
132		12†15	—	—	12 46	Taunton	—	—
133		—	12†15	—	12 55	Chipping Norton ..	—	—
134		12†20	—	—	1 5	Langport East ..	—	—
135		12†30	—	—	1 14	Uffington ..	—	—
136		12†40	—	—	1 23	Weymouth ..	—	—
137	L	12†50	—	—	1 32	Oxford	—	—
138	L	1†0	—	—	1 41	Newbury Town ..	—	—
139		—	1†0	—	1 50	Bath	—	—
140	L	1†5	—	—	1 59	Culham	—	—
141		1†20	—	—	2 9	Warminster ..	—	—
142		—	1†50	—	2 18	Weston-super-Mare ..	—	—
143	L	1†50	—	—	2 27	Witney	—	—
144	West London	2†0		2 30	—	Dorchester ..	—	—

L—Non-corridor stock.

Working of Evacuation Trains from Acton and Ealing Broadway—continued.

First Day—continued.

Train Number.		Empty Train.		Loaded Train.		Destination.	Empty Stock returned for same Day's Working.	
		Acton Yard.	Old Oak Common.	Acton.	Ealing Broadway.			Acton Yard.
		dep. p.m.	dep. p.m.	dep. p.m.	dep. p.m.		dep.	arr.
145		2†0	—	—	2 36	Bicester	—	—
146		—	2†15	—	2 45	Cirencester	—	—
147		2†10	—	—	2 54	Bruton	—	—
148		—	2†25	—	3 4	Bath	—	—
149		2†30	—	—	3 13	Andoversford	—	—
150		—	2†45	—	3 22	Wells	—	—
151		3†5	—	—	3 31	Swindon	—	—
152		—	3†0	—	3 40	Savernake	—	—
153	L	3†25	—	—	3 49	Bridgwater	—	—
154	L	3†30	—	—	3 58	Oxford	—	—
155		3†35	—	—	4 8	Weston-super-Mare ..	—	—
156		3†50	—	—	4 17	Shepton Mallet ..	—	—
157		—	3†45	—	4 24	Bath	—	—
158	L	4†5	—	—	4 33	Henley	—	—
159	West	London	4†0	4 30	—	Weymouth	—	—
160		4†10	—	—	4 42	Swindon	—	—
161		—	4†10	—	4 51	Devizes	—	—
162	L	4†25	—	—	5 0	Maidenhead	—	—
163	L	4†30	—	—	5 9	Theale	—	—
164		4†50	—	—	5 18	Swindon	—	—

L—Non-corridor stock.

NON-CORRIDOR SETS—FIRST DAY.

No. 1.

6†55 a.m. Southall .. Acton 7†10 a.m.
8.30 a.m. Ealing .. Maidenhead 9.0 a.m.
9†30 a.m. Maidenhead .. Acton 10†35 a.m.
11.51 a.m. Oxford .. Oxford 1.30 p.m.
2†0 p.m. Oxford .. Acton 2†40 p.m.
5. 0 p.m. Ealing .. Maidenhead 5.30 p.m.
6†0 p.m. Maidenhead .. Southall 6†25 p.m.

No. 2.

7†0 a.m. Southall .. Acton 7†20 a.m.
8.39 a.m. Ealing .. Oxford 10.10 a.m.
10†50 a.m. Oxford .. Acton 12†30 p.m.
1.59 p.m. Ealing .. Culham 3.15 p.m.
3†50 p.m. Culham .. Southall 5† 5 p.m.

No. 3.

7†15 a.m. Slough .. Acton 7†45 a.m.
8.57 a.m. Ealing .. Henley 9.45 a.m.
10† 5 a.m. Henley .. Acton 11†10 a.m.
1.32 p.m. Ealing .. Oxford 3. 5 p.m.
3†35 p.m. Oxford .. Slough 4†45 p.m.

No. 4.

7†40 a.m. Slough .. Acton 8†35 a.m.
10. 2 a.m. Ealing .. Oxford 11.35 a.m.
12† 5 p.m. Oxford .. Acton 1†45 p.m.
4.33 p.m. Ealing .. Henley 5.20 p.m.
5†50 p.m. Henley .. Slough 6†30 p.m.

No. 5.

7. 0 a.m. Paddington Hayes 7.34 a.m.
8†20 a.m. Hayes .. Acton 8†50 a.m.
10.38 a.m. Ealing .. Slough 11. 5 a.m.
11†35 a.m. Slough .. Acton 12†10 p.m.
1.41 p.m. Ealing .. Newbury Town 3.0 p.m.
3†30 p.m. Newbury Town West London 5† 0 p.m.

No. 6.

9†25 a.m. Hayes .. Acton 9†50 a.m.
11.24 a.m. Ealing .. Maidenhead 11.55 a.m.
12†25 p.m. Maidenhead Acton 1† 5 p.m.
2.27 p.m. Ealing .. Witney 4.40 p.m.
5†10 p.m. Witney .. Hayes 7†40 p.m.

No. 7.

9†55 a.m. Slough .. Acton 10†50 a.m.
12.19 p.m. Ealing .. Wantage Road 1.45 p.m.
2†30 p.m. Wantage Rd. Acton 4†10 p.m.
5. 9 p.m. Ealing .. Theale 6.10 p.m.
6†40 p.m. Theale .. Slough 7†20 p.m.

No. 8.

2†45 p.m. Southall .. Acton 3† 0 p.m.
3.58 p.m. Ealing .. Oxford 5.35 p.m.
6†20 p.m. Oxford .. Southall 7†50 p.m.

Fig 11 Extract from the emergency evacuation programme organized for the early part of the second world war.

St Helier, St David and *St Julien*, ran a shuttle service to and from stricken Dunkirk. The *St Julien*, bombed, machine-gunned and shelled but miraculously escaping unhit, brought 10,000 allied troops to safety, while the *St Helier* on 2 June sailed into Dover with 2,000 weary men—the very last remnants of the British Expeditionary Force.

While the soldiers re-equipped, the Germans overran France, making Great Western routes and ports more vulnerable and crowded. The Severn tunnel became a bottleneck where every coal train displaced three faster-moving passenger trains. Conditions became so bad that wartime needs overrode peacetime safety fears. The long block section between the tunnel's east and west signal boxes had long called for intermediate colour light signals to break up the distance, but the Ministry of Transport, fearing that steam might obscure them, had refused to put them in despite the company's wish to do so. Now they bowed to the war's demands. By November 1941 the signals were installed and they came into use on that date with specially intensified lights. Elsewhere, as the air attack grew, stationmasters and signalmen received instructions on how to report enemy aircraft. To help them they were given 16 out of the 100 wireless sets the Government rushed to the railways. For fear of being overheard, messages, it was insisted, must be relayed in Morse, which few railwaymen—other than signalmen on lines in some parts of the country where telegraph instruments were still used—knew or understood. Fortunately they never had to be used. In Berkshire Beenham Grange became the Great Western's headquarters with other departments scattered over the adjoining countryside. In all a total of £8 million, most of it Government money, was spent on war emergency improvement schemes including the quadrupling of the line between Gloucester and Cheltenham. This was roughly two-thirds of the £11·5 million spent on railway improvements during the war.

In the lengthening winter nights of 1940–1 the enemy bomber fleets came. Bristol, Birmingham, Birkenhead and Plymouth, where an engine and tender were blown off the line, all felt the fury of Hitler's blitz but kept their stations open. Fires as well as bombs ravaged the company's South Wales docks, Swansea being most heavily hit. Although 52 GWR men were killed and

241 seriously injured in air raids, one of the worst incidents of the early war years did not arise directly from enemy action. In a derailment on 27 November 1940 at Norton Fitzwarren, twenty-seven were killed on the night Paddington West of England express, which had been running on the relief line and whose driver misread signals clear for the adjoining main line. Norton Fitzwarren was a haunted spot. In the same month fifty years earlier a broad-gauge up mail train struck a goods train standing in its path on the up line, forgotten by the signalman, killing ten people.

As the enemy pressed his assault from the skies, Swindon turned out in bewildering array the tools to hit back. As in 1914, one of its first tasks was the conversion of passenger coaches to ambulances. Swindon also completely furnished and equipped the train in which Eisenhower and his staff travelled nearly 97,000 miles on British railways. By the war's end Swindon had fashioned boiler tubes into Home Guard cudgels, and manufactured thousands of components for nine types of aircraft, 400 mountings for 6-pdr naval guns, searchlight projectors, midget submarine superstructures and gun shields. Its workshops redesigned the turntable structure for the 13·5in guns on the Kent coast, the country's only means of hitting back on land in the first few weeks after Dunkirk. Finally, as the allied bomber fleets grew, the sheds that had turned out castings for 'Castles' and 'Kings' made the casings for the first 2,000lb and 4,000lb bombs to be dropped by the RAF.

While Swindon worked round the clock, the memory of an old railway rivalry was revived far away on the borders of Devon and Cornwall. The one-time LSWR's Waterloo main line running alongside the GWR track at St Budeaux, Plymouth, was linked to its former competitor to provide a vital alternative route to London during the worst of the Plymouth raids. When these were at their height in 1941–2 the Southern, through new links with the Great Western at Lydford, Launceston, and Yeovil, was running more Great Western trains over its tracks than its own Towards the war's end, D Day in 1944 brought its own special problems. One of them was the routing of 3,036 special trains for troops, stores and equipment. From June till August, 167 of the trains ran in a reverse direction carrying prisoners of war. Before the tide finally turned in France there came the last great ordeal, the terror of the flying bombs. In this the company was luckier than its Southern neighbour. Although forty-five flying bombs fell on or adjoining Great Western territory, only two of its staff lost their lives. The Southern mourned 63 killed and 767 injured. Throughout the war 14,483 Great Western men joined the forces of whom 444 never returned.

THE LAST DAYS

With the war's end, scarcely three years of independent life remained to Britain's railways. Nationalization, talked of since Gladstone's day, and which had almost come in 1921, was now in the immediate programme of an all-powerful Labour government. At Paddington, too, a new chairman reigned, the third in five years. Viscount Horne had died unexpectedly in 1940. His successor, the banker Sir Charles Hambro, resigned in 1945 to be succeeded by Lord Portal. Portal had no illusions about South Wales, having participated in 1934 in a government-sponsored survey of the distressed areas. Now he faced another problem. Unlike his predecessors, he found himself ruling over a railway empire in the west destined soon to be taken over. But even as the shadows of nationalization steadily lengthened there came from Paddington a last defiant gesture of independence which showed that the old instinct for eye-catching publicity was as strong as ever. In the publication *Next Station: A railway plans for the future* there appeared, among other promises, the resounding statement that 'the Great Western intends to maintain its position of leadership in the application of new forms of energy to railway traction'. The new form of energy was gas turbine propulsion with which F. W. Hawksworth, Collett's successor in 1941, had been experimenting. But Hawksworth's experiments were never completed. By the time *Next Station* was published (its author, the talented Christian Barman, was recruited from the London Transport Board as assistant to Paddington's chief publicity officer) nationalization had been decreed and the British Transport Commission in due course opted for diesel traction. Hawksworth's chief offering to Great Western history was not the gas turbine but the two-cylinder

4–6–0 'County' engines for mixed traffic. Sober, like the times, in their dark livery, they were destined to be among the last purely Swindon-designed engines.

Yet outwardly, until nationalization arrived, Lord Churchill's 'dear old Great Western' still seemed pre-eminent and permanent throughout its territory. The 'Castles' and 'Kings', helped out by Hawksworth's 'Counties', still proclaimed the power of steam. Within a year of the war's end GWR locomotives were performing a hundred or more daily runs at a faster average speed than those on other systems. Building of the 'Castles' had been resumed in 1946, some being fitted with double blast chimneys which took away their symmetry but added to their performance. What changes and differences there were arose from altered conditions and travelling habits. The end of the dominance of coal (exports from South Wales ports had dwindled to 5 million tons in 1945) could be clearly seen in the empty sidings at the approaches to the coal docks and the industrial dereliction around Merthyr Tydfil. Coal supplies became difficult. They had been so at the end of World War I when the company had had only three weeks' instead of nine weeks' supply on hand. In the winter of 1945, however, coal was so scarce that not only were engines in South Wales being fired with American coal but a large number of locomotives were being modified for oil burning. This, too, had been done experimentally in the earlier war. At Plymouth changed transatlantic travel habits had reduced the company's passenger docks, improved in the years immediately before the war, to a mere shadow of their former importance. Atlantic liners and their passengers were now a wistful memory of a vanished age. Instead of American travellers, Plymouth's largest dock landings in 1946 were 646 Australian brides of British servicemen. Gone, too, were the days of the great mail train runs. For all practical purposes they ended on 14 December 1946. On that day 27,000 bags of mail were landed from an American ship, the largest single cargo of mail ever to be handled at the port.

In 1947, the last full year of its existence as an independent railway, the Great Western earned a comfortable dividend of 5 per cent. In March 1948 its shareholders met together at the Paddington Hotel for the last time.

The Times of 15 March 1948 carried the following report of
the meeting, under the heading 'Great Western Railway Company—Termination of a Proud Record'.

A GENERAL MEETING of the Great Western Railway Company
was held yesterday at the Great Western Hotel, Paddington,
London, W.

The RT. HON. VISCOUNT PORTAL, P.C., D.S.O., M.V.O. (the
chairman), who presided, said:—For 112 years these meetings
have been held continuously—in good times and bad and even
in the face of enemy action. They have, on occasions, been the
scene of conflict of opinion between individual stockholders and
the board, especially in times of industrial crises, but I think I
am justified in saying that at by far the greater number of the
meetings the atmosphere has been most cordial and the efforts
of the directors to establish and expand the Great Western Railway Undertaking in the interests of those it serves have invariably met with encouragement and enthusiasm when the support
of the proprietors has been sought. Today's meeting is unique in
that there are no resolutions requiring the stockholders' approval
but the directors felt that it would be the wish of many of the
proprietors that they should have the opportunity of meeting together once more before the company with its proud record
ceases to exist. The Transport Bill received Royal Assent on
August 6th last and I feel sure you all know the efforts which
were made to obtain more favourable terms for the stockholders. The fundamental principles of the Bill remained unchanged, however, and on the 1st January last the undertaking
of the Great Western Railway passed into the ownership of the
British Transport Commission.

MAIN REVENUE SOURCES

As the accounts no longer need the approval of the proprietors they have been circulated in an abbreviated form and
they explain how the directors have decided to distribute the
total amount which is available in accordance with the provisions of Section 20 of the Transport Act, 1947, in respect of
the years 1946 and 1947. This amount is made up of the main
sources of net revenue of the company during Government
control, which were:—

(1) The fixed annual sum payable by the Government under
the control agreement with minor adjustments for interest on
capital.

(2) The net revenue from undertakings excluded from the
control arrangements, consisting largely of dividends on the
company's investments in omnibus and cartage companies.

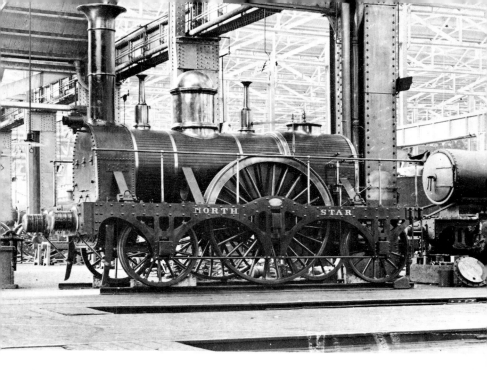

Representing the first and last steam locomotives on the Great Western are
Plate 31 (above) the replica 2-2-2 *North Star* built in the 1930s to replace the
original GWR *North Star* which had been preserved but broken up during
Churchward's regime in 1906. *Plate 32 (below)* The last regular steam
working on the Western Region with Castle class locomotive No 7029 *Clun
Castle* heading the 4.15pm Paddington–Banbury on 11 June 1965. (*Locomotive & General Railway Photographs; E Wilmshurst*)

Great Western preserved: *Plate 33 (above)* The first of the King class 4-6-0s, No 6000 *King George V* has been preserved by Bulmers of Hereford and has been maintained in top class working order and is permitted to run over BR main lines on special workings. It is seen here with some of the Pullman cars also owned by Bulmers on the first of the return to steam trips on 7 October 1971. *Plate 34 (below)* Numerous other GWR locomotives have been preserved, either at depots or museums or as here on a complete preserved GWR branch. 2-6-2T No 4588 heads the 12.30pm Kingswear–Paignton on the Torbay & Dartmouth Railway, one of the two lines owned by the Dart Valley Light Railway Ltd, the other line being the former Ashburton branch preserved between Buckfastleigh and Totnes. *(G F Gillham)*

(3) Profit on realization of investments.

(4) Additional revenue arising from the exact ascertainment of the company's revenue previously estimated for years prior to 1941 when the control agreement was amended to provide for the fixed annual sum.

The net revenue from the first two of these sources for the two-year period has been certified by the auditor appointed under the Act. The first item is not variable except to the extent of the minor adjustment for interest. In the case of the second item there is a substantial increase in 1947 compared with 1946, due to additional and increased dividends in respect of the associated road undertakings.

The Transport Bill as originally drafted precluded the company from distributing amongst the stockholders the proceeds of profit on realization of investments and amounts attributable to pre-1941 financial adjustments, £542,540 was brought into our 1946 accounts in this respect but was not then distributed and a further sum of £31,460 arose in 1947. We were, however, ultimately able to convince the Minister of Transport of the justice of the stockholders' right to these moneys and subsection 8 of Section 20 was embodied in the Act providing for the additional payment to the Great Western Company of £574,000.

No Compensation to Directors

I should here like to mention that several stockholders have been good enough to suggest that a resolution should be submitted to this meeting asking for approval to the payment of a reasonable sum to the members of the board in consequence of their loss of office and I need hardly say that this was a gesture which we greatly appreciated. The board feel that any payment of this nature could quite properly have been made out of the other assets which pass to the commission, but as the Act does not permit this, the directors preferred not to accept any compensation, since the alternative would have been to reduce the final payment to the stockholders, many of whom are, we know, persons of limited means whose incomes will already be cut as a consequence of the conversion of their holdings into the British Transport Commission 3 per Cent. stock.

Balance Available

After providing for the final dividend on the Preference stocks, and the interim dividend of 2 per cent. already paid on the Consolidated Ordinary stock, the balance available for distribution amongst the holders of the Consolidated Ordinary stock is £2,267,616 and it permits of the payment of a final

K

dividend of £5.282158 per cent. making £7.282158 per cent. for the year.

The chairman closed the meeting by thanking the proprietors for

... the kindness and consideration which they have always extended to the directors and to me and my predecessors who have occupied this chair. To many of us the well-being of the railways has been part of our heritage, almost from boyhood days, and whatever changes the future may bring about we shall always remember with pride and affection the part which we were privileged to play in dealing with the administration of the company's affairs and the many friends we made amongst all classes of the community whilst acting in that capacity...

... It is a very sad day for us all, but we took the view that things must be carried on in the most efficient way possible, and so we wish everyone well in whatever takes place in the future. (Applause.)

After the shortest annual meeting on record they said goodbye to each other within earshot of the great station where Brunel's fingerprints still defy time and change. With them they took home in round figures a final dividend on Great Western shares of 7¼ per cent.

As a meeting it was a formality which confirmed a death that had taken place constitutionally three months earlier on 1 January 1948. On that date some 100,000 Great Western employees, seven dock undertakings, 3,856 steam locomotives, 38 diesel rail cars, one diesel electric shunter, and all stations, hotels, fixtures, stock and track became the concern not of Paddington but of the British Transport Commission. Gradually over the 3,800 route miles of line from Paddington to Penzance, from Bristol through to Wales and from the Mersey to the Severn, there appeared on Great Western engines a strange and bizarre device. In place of the familiar roundel and the weaving arabesques spelling out the motto 'Domine Dirige Nos Virtute Et Industria' there stared out what appeared to many to be the image of a starved lion. It was the house badge of British Railways, the Great Western Railway's new owner.

So passed into the hands of the State after 123 years of independent corporate existence the great and majestic railway which Isambard Kingdom Brunel had called the 'finest work in England'. For thousands of others it had always remained so.

CHAPTER 6

Men and Machines

THE TRIUMPH OF GOOCH

Brunel neither designed nor built the first GWR engines. Instead he laid down for them certain stipulations about piston speed, steam pressure and engine weights, leaving the manufacturers to conform as best they could. The stipulations, particularly about piston speeds, appear to have influenced the manufacturers far more than he originally intended. The result, to paraphrase E. L. Ahrons, was the greatest assembly of freaks ever seen on any British railway. Brunel has been much blamed for this. But it is important to remember that at this stage he was primarily a civil engineer. Not only was he largely in the hands of the manufacturers, but it is questionable, when it came to ordering locomotives for the new railway, whether he should have been expected to do more than specify axle and other weights. The GWR directors appear to have been alone, among companies setting out to equip their railways in those early years, in not sending one of their number to seek the advice of the manufacturers or the services of an engineer through one of them. Whether therefore the directors should not also share some of the blame for the inadequacies of the early engines is a matter which can still provoke fierce argument. But whatever the rights and wrongs of the matter the outcome led to one of the great ironies of railway history. For the engines of Daniel Gooch, which rescued the GWR from ignominy and established its supremacy in the early 1840s for speed and smooth running, sprang from a design perfected in the workshops of Robert Stephenson, Brunel's greatest rival and the engineer for the London and Birmingham Railway, the Great Western's most formidable competitor.

For the opening of his railway Brunel had ordered nineteen engines from six different makers, stipulating piston speeds (280ft a minute at 30mph) and engine weights (up to 10½ tons in working order) which were far below those of most narrow-gauge engines of the day. Keeping the speed of the piston in the cylinder down to Brunel's limit forced the manufacturers to build engines with small boilers and large driving wheels. Although carrying a pressure of 50lb/sq in, the same as other engines of the day, they developed 30–50 per cent less power.

The engine *Vulcan*, delivered in 1837 and the first to be tried in steam on the railway after being lifted from a barge on to the track by block and tackle suspended on a handy elm tree, had a slim boiler barrel 8ft 2in long and 3ft 6in wide. This was slung between 8ft driving wheels and 4ft carrying wheels. The 14in cylinders developed a 16in stroke. She was the forerunner of six engines all somewhat similar in design, dimensions and appearance built by Charles Tayleur of the Vulcan Foundry, Newton-le-Willows. Ahrons dismissed them collectively as the 'best of a queer lot'. How queer some of the others were becomes plain in illustrations and descriptions that have survived of them. Among six engines delivered by Mather Dixon and Co of Liverpool between November 1837 and September 1839 was *Ajax* with 14in by 20in cylinders but with 10ft driving wheels built up from riveted pieces of boiler plate instead of spokes. They looked like war shields of Homeric proportions, and against a strong cross-wind the engine could scarcely make headway. Even Brunel was staggered by their size. *Ajax* worked for only two years. *Snake* and *Viper*, two engines supplied by the Haigh Foundry of Wigan, looked almost as nasty as their names. With boilers 9ft long and only 3ft 6in wide, their motion was 'communicated to the driving wheels by means of toothed gearing'. Two other engines making an early appearance on the railway were not so much freaks as monsters. Called *Thunderer* and *Hurricane*, and built under a special patent, each had the boiler and motion on separate carriages with a third making up the tender on to which the train was tacked. Ahrons says the whole thing 'resembled a sort of procession'. To meet Brunel's requirements, *Thunderer*'s four 6ft coupled wheels were geared up to give the equivalent of more than 16ft diameter. The boiler was also unusual in being divided into two parts with separate firedoors. On starting up one fire tended to burn briskly while the other usually went out. Both engines, described by the startled Gooch on first seeing them as 'immense affairs', were total failures in service.

With locomotives like this Brunel had calculated for a 'minimum velocity of 30mph', a speed which many scarcely exceeded at their maximum. They broke down, ran off the rails and developed a multitude of mechanical defects. The first weeks of working with them brought about the near-collapse of the company's train service. Charles Saunders told the Parliamentary Committee on Railways in 1841 that in 1838 the Great Western 'found the engines so inefficient that the timetable working was hopeless; one or two engines might keep time; the other eight or ten were always out of time. So we suspended the timetables until the locomotive power became more efficient.'

The one conspicuous exception to this accumulation of mechanical failures was Robert Stephenson's *North Star*, delivered in November 1837. For more than a year it was the company's only reliable engine. Built for the 5ft 6in gauge of the New Orleans Railway, it was a typical Stephenson six-wheeled locomotive of the time uncomplicated by any of Brunel's theories. Weighing over $18\frac{1}{2}$ tons 'without water, fire or men', it carried a boiler pressure of 50lb with 16in cylinders working a similar stroke. Left on the hands of Stephenson's firm when a financial crisis hit the American company, it was snapped up for £2,150 by Brunel 'as a splendid engine . . . a beautiful ornament in the most elegant drawing room'. With axles extended and driving wheels enlarged from 6ft 6in to 7ft for the broad gauge, it drew the first passenger train on the GWR. Eleven somewhat similar 'Stars' were ordered between 1839 and 1841.

North Star was not only the most famous of all early Great Western locomotives, but was to prove an engine of destiny. In the troubled December of 1838 the directors, going over Brunel's head, ordered Gooch to prepare his own designs for better engines. Faced with this stern test of his capabilities, he turned to *North Star* as a ready-made model. Thus Robert Stephenson's engine became the parent of all future broad-gauge passenger engines and its distinctive Stephenson feature of outside slotted sandwich frames (iron plates between which wood was sandwiched) was to persist in one type of Great Western engine until 1937.

An able but cautious engineer, Gooch, rather than tinker with a well-proved design, did what Collett was in some measure to do more than eighty years later with Churchward's 'Stars'. He kept the basic design of *North Star* along with the double frames to support the engine should the crank axles break (a not infrequent happening in those early days), but enlarged some of the engines' leading dimensions. Gooch took great pains over his work, giving every detail, he tells us later, 'much thought and consideration'. A close eye was kept on manufacturers to ensure standardization and quality of workmanship, and the makers were held liable until each engine had performed 1,000 miles with proper loads.

The result in March 1840 was the engine *Fire Fly*, forerunner of a class of sixty-two built over the following two years with 7ft driving wheels and 15in by 18in cylinders. The first of Gooch's standard engines for the Paddington–Swindon run, they differed in appearance from *North Star* in having a high dome-shaped or 'haycock' type of firebox (the image of the horse age was hard to shake off) with steam space in the casing top. The chimney was narrow, tall and flared at the top. For passenger traffic over the hilly route between Swindon and Bristol, twenty-one smaller engines (the 'Sun' class) were built, but with 6ft driving wheels, and for goods work eighteen 2–4–0 engines and four 0–6–0s (aptly named the 'Hercules' class), these being notable as the first six-coupled engines to be employed on the Great Western.

The 'Fire Flies' were the most powerful engines of their time and Gooch was proud of them. He wrote later: 'I may with confidence after these engines have been working for 2⅝ years say that no better engines for their weight have ever been constructed either by myself or others.' He was right. With them Gooch transformed the locomotive fortunes of the broad gauge and at one stride stepped into the front rank of locomotive designers of the day.

Most of the 'Fire Flies' lasted for more than thirty years and were capable of average start-to-stop speeds of 50mph. Queen Victoria made her first railway journey behind one of them (an engine with the ungainly name of *Phlegethon*), while another,

Ixion, as earlier related, beat all narrow-gauge competitors in the gauge trials. To celebrate the completion of the Bristol–Exeter main line Gooch drove another of the class, *Orion*, with a 50 ton train attached, from Paddington to Exeter and back in just under ten hours, stopping only for a celebration lunch at Exeter. Having stood most of the way, he complained the following day of severe backache!

Driving these early locomotives was not without hazard. The 'Hercules'-class engine *Goliah* (a mis-spelling for Goliath) was wrecked at Plympton, Devon, in 1849 when the boiler blew up. The report was so loud 'that it sounded as if a piece of ordnance had been discharged'. The driver, who died, was attempting to tackle the 1-in-40 Hemerdon Bank. Gooch hurried down to attend the inquest. He heard a 'railway inspector' explain that so much steam 'had to be packed into the boiler to help the train up the steep slope it must be expected some of the tubes carrying the steam would explode from time to time . . . but it was most unusual for the whole boiler to explode'.

By the early 1840s Gooch had given the Great Western a remarkably homogeneous family of passenger and goods engines. Experience with their working led him in 1846 to produce an engine remarkably more advanced in design and power. In that year the Swindon locomotive building depot had been established, its opening coinciding with the renewal of the gauge war. Anxious to keep the broad-gauge lead in speed, Gooch, with the directors behind him, pushed ahead in a hurry. Working only from a few centre line drawings he had the first passenger engine to be turned out in the new shops completed in thirteen weeks. With 8ft driving wheels, 18in cylinders working a 2ft stroke and a boiler developing 100lb pressure—twice that of *North Star*—the new engine was named *Great Western*. In June 1846 it ran 194 miles between Paddington and Exeter in 208 minutes and took only three minutes longer on the return journey, a performance far beyond that of any other engines of the time.

The best of Gooch, however, was still to come. Extensive trials with the *Great Western* (later altered, after breaking an axle, to become the company's first eight-wheeled engine) bore fruit between 1847 and 1855 in the eight-wheeled 'Iron Duke' class, one of the classic early Victorian locomotive designs. With

8ft driving wheels they were the ultimate refinement of the enlarged *North Star* and the largest engines running anywhere in the world when they appeared. The first of Gooch's engines to have a recognizably modern look, they handled the best of the broad-gauge expresses until the end of that era, frequently attaining speeds of over 70mph. The domeless boilers with a 100lb psi pressure (later increased) had a raised fire box casing, and the 18in by 24in cylinders, taking steam from a long perforated pipe in the top of the boiler, extended into the smoke box. In all twenty-nine were constructed of which twenty-four were renewed or completely rebuilt in the 1870s. Their crews were given cabs, but unfortunately no attempt was made to modernize the engines to show the full capabilities of the broad gauge. In some the diameter of the boiler was even reduced. Yet, although representing a design nearly forty years old, they remained, even in their last days, strikingly impressive, powerful-looking machines. The top of the boiler was almost as high as the coach roofs and the copper-topped chimney towered 15ft above the track. The celebrated *Lord of the Isles*, which long figured in miniature on the strap buttons of Great Western enginemen's caps, survived at Swindon until 1906 when it was broken up.

When Gooch left the GWR in 1864 to lay the first Atlantic cable he had been locomotive superintendent for twenty-seven years, designing 340 engines none of which had been outright failures. He had built not only the largest but, in his day, the fastest passenger engines in the world. His celebrated 'eight footers' drew the famous 'Flying Dutchman'. On the South Devon Railway his 4-4-0 saddle tank engines conquered Brunel's fierce inclines, and for the tunnels of the London Metropolitan Railway he built in 1862-3 the first condensing tank engines in the country. But Gooch did more than design engines; he took pains to study the conditions under which they ran. To test performance and wind resistance over measured lengths of track he perfected the world's first dynamometer car. It not only recorded the mileage travelled but calculated the force of the wind by a gauge placed 5ft above the top of the carriage and connected by pencils to a chart. Over the Bristol and Exeter Railway track in the 1840s he could be seen sitting on the buffer beam of an engine travelling at 60mph checking his indicator bars. It was uncomfortable and dangerous, but the detailed knowledge he obtained gave him a practical insight into locomotive performance fifty years ahead of most engineers of his time.

Gooch's subsequent chairmanship of the GWR was a later saga in a long life which complemented, but never surpassed in achievement, his pioneer work for the broad gauge in engine design and performance. Yet the man who rightly thought of himself as the father of express trains liked best to take long country walks and press between thin paper the wild flowers he picked on them. Gooch was not a great experimenter. Once having found a good design he stuck to it. But within those limits, and they were not petty, he was a remarkably far-seeing engineer and ahead of most others in giving his engines ample boiler power. When he died *The Times* said of him:

> He was more remarkable than is generally known. He made surprisingly few mistakes at his work. Genius is a good thing; understanding is better as in the case of Stephenson. Both were combined in the same individual whose death the whole profession will regret.

Today he remains not only undervalued but without a standard biography.

JAMES PEARSON'S MONSTERS

While Gooch was still at Swindon there appeared between Bristol and Exeter some of the most extraordinary engines ever to run over the broad gauge or any other railway. These were James Pearson's 9ft singles built for the Exeter expresses of the Bristol and Exeter Railway. The latter for the first few years of its life had been leased by the GWR, running Gooch's own engines. In May 1849, as told in a previous chapter, the B&E began running its own traffic, and a year later James Pearson, who had been atmospheric superintendent of the South Devon Railway, became its engineer.

Pearson was a Quaker who shied away from bright colours, but with his eight monster 4–2–4 well and back tank engines he made up in size and appearance what he avoided in display. They weighed forty-two tons in working order, seven tons more than the 'Iron Dukes'. The massive 9ft driving wheels were flangeless and without counterweights but were cushioned by two brass cased runner springs. The 16½in cylinders worked with a 2ft stroke and drew steam from a comparatively small boiler 10ft 9in long and 4ft 0½in in diameter. Burning less than 22lb of coke per mile, they were guided by Gooch's 4ft ball and socket type bogie, braking being trustfully confided to blocks between the wheels of the trailing bogie. Looking as if they had been hurriedly run up in a country blacksmith's shop, Pearson's giants clanked when moving 'as if the whole machine was ready to fall to pieces'.

In appearance and size these engines were totally unlike any others in the country and for long were the only tank engines hauling main-line expresses. Ahrons regarded them as among the boldest departures 'made up to that time from the accepted canons of locomotive design'. Others took a less charitable view. G. N. Tyrrell, the GWR's Superintendent of the Line, regarded them as 'nasty, dangerous things'. The footplate was reached by a steep doubled-railed ladder, and crews needed a head for heights when clambering nine feet or more over the curved, narrow splashers to reach the top of the boiler. Yet these clumsy-looking juggernauts proved far more nippy on the track than many more orthodox-looking engines, putting up some of the fastest speeds in the country over the level track between Nailsea and Durston. Their highest recorded speed was 81·8mph down the Wellington Bank. The B&E timetable for 1865 shows the 'Flying Dutchman', which they hauled, booked for the 75½ miles between Bristol and Exeter with a stop at Taunton doing the journey in 92 and 102 minutes respectively.

Despite, or perhaps because of, their size, Pearson's giants were not particularly long-lived, being replaced or renewed by 1873. Pearson then turned them into coal-burning engines with 18in cylinders and knocked two inches off the driving wheels. In this form, weighing forty-nine tons, four were absorbed by Swindon. Then after an accident at Long Ashton in 1876 which killed the driver and fireman, the remaining three were redesigned as 4-2-2 tender engines. With 8ft driving wheels, bringing them into line with Gooch's 'Iron Dukes', they shared the London–Newton Abbot run with Gooch's 8ft engines.

Pearson designed a number of other more orthodox tank and

tender engines, but he was not responsible for *Fairfield*, a combined engine and carriage on six wheels which the B&E used on its Tiverton, Clevedon and Weston branches. Possibly the prototype in this country of all steam rail cars, it was built by W. B. Adams at their Fairfield works. The Great Western, before passing it on to the B&E, tried it over the West London Railway where Gooch noted that 'it was a very small engine and carriage all in one frame but was of little use'. The B&E in turn got rid of it in 1856.

ARMSTRONG AND DEAN

Rebuilding Pearson's 'nine footers' as tender engines was one of the tasks of Joseph Armstrong, Gooch's successor. There is little today in the Great Western museum to remind us of Armstrong, who came to Swindon when the broad gauge was at its greatest extent in mileage and locomotives. By the time he died, thirteen years later, it was confined almost entirely to the West Country. This meant for Armstrong a difficult balancing act between meeting dwindling broad-gauge needs and increasing standard-gauge demands. It fell to him to build (as distinct from renewals) the last purely broad-gauge locomotives, which were six 0–6–0 tank engines for the Metropolitan Railway. Nor was his task made easier by the company's decision, after being turned out of Oxford, to build its own carriages and wagons at Swindon rather than take them from private builders. Armstrong thus found himself responsible for rolling stock as well as engines and became the first carriage and locomotive superintendent of the GWR.

Armstrong came from a celebrated railway family and learned his trade in the Wolverhampton shops of the standard-gauge Shrewsbury Railways. He is credited with building simple, orthodox designs, but it was from his time that standard-gauge engines on the company's system began to approximate in power for the first time to the broad gauge. Appearances altered, too. The steam dome began to replace Gooch's raised firebox casing, notably for the first time on the six-wheeled goods engines which began to appear in 1866 and of which by 1877 more than 300 had been built. Armstrong's best-known standard-gauge passenger engines were the large 7ft single drivers he built for the Paddington–Wolverhampton run. The cylinder dimensions were similar to Gooch's 'Iron Dukes', to which they were superior in weight and tractive effort but not in boiler power.

Armstrong died suddenly in 1877, a victim, like Brunel, of overwork. A tall, patriarchal man, with a bearded Old Testament face, he left a mark at Swindon more as an administrator than as a locomotive designer. The town which Gooch and Brunel had established between them Armstrong not only enlarged but humanized, transforming it, in the words of H. E. Holcroft, 'from the semi-wilderness in which he found it to the model settlement in which he left it'. To do this he lived and worked among his men. Gooch had kept an eye on them mainly from London, although he gave £1,000 out of his own pocket towards a hospital for them. Armstrong made the accident-prone Swindon shops safer, improved workers' housing, provided swimming and washing baths and better hospital facilities. The tradition of prominent Great Western officers actively involving themselves in municipal affairs grew up, says Holcroft, with Armstrong. His sudden death brought an expression of grief remarkable and widespread even for those days, 6,000 attending his funeral. His memory afterwards was kept green in an unusual way. Money from a spontaneous public subscription was devoted not to providing a memorial in stone, but to buying a lifeboat. Named after him, it was stationed at Cadgwith, on the Lizard Peninsula in Cornwall, the county which was one of the last strongholds of the broad gauge.

William Dean, who followed Armstrong at Swindon, bridged three generations of Great Western motive power—the broadgauge Gooch engines with their domeless boilers (some of which he rebuilt), his own brass-domed 4-2-2s (the first eight-wheeled passenger engines to run on the company's standard gauge) and Churchward's bleak prototypes with their high-pitched boilers and Belpaire fireboxes (so named after their Belgian designer). Despite this, the gulf finally separating Dean from Churchward was enormous. In 1899 Dean, who retired in 1902, was still building single-wheelers. By 1906 Churchward had established his two- and four-cylinder 4-6-0 designs as standard engines already being produced in quantity. The latter made much of Dean look almost prehistoric. But if Dean represented a vanished locomotive age, no one had graced that age with a more sensitive eye for proportion and adornment, nor has any locomotive designer better contrasted iron, copper and brass. The engines which came after him were bigger, more powerful and complex, but they were seldom as handsome as the best of Dean.

Dean experimented widely, producing more than a reasonable share of flops and some remarkably ugly engines such as the clumsy and partly experimental 'Krugers', used for South Wales coal haulage. They were so named because of their fancied resemblance in profile to the grim features of the then President of the Boer Republic. In the early 1880s Dean built the first two compound engines (one each for broad and standard gauge) ever to be tried on the Great Western. Both were 2-4-0s with four cylinders arranged in tandem. Both were also failures, one of them blowing into fragments three of her cylinder casings at the entrance to Box tunnel. Sharing the Great Western partiality for tank engines, he made a number of experiments to increase their water-carrying capacity. An eight-wheeled engine designed in 1880 for the standard gauge had tanks carried forward to the smoke box. It was followed by a ten-wheeled express tank with 7ft 8in driving wheels and side tanks holding more than 2,500 gallons projecting beyond the smoke box. A startling freak, liable to derailment, it was kept out of sight until converted to a more conventional six-wheeled tender engine. After this Dean seems to have lost heart, reverting to tender engines for passenger work.

He then showed his powers in the handsome and justly famed 7ft 8in singles for express passenger running. First appearing in 1891 as 2-2-2s, they were finally embodied in the so-called '3000' class of eighty engines and altered to 4-2-2s after one of them, *Wigmore Castle*, broke an axle in Box tunnel. Taking on from Gooch's 8ft singles, they were Dean's most striking tribute to the reign of the single wheeler. Many have thought them the most handsome engines ever built and they were worthily matched by the clerestory stock Dean built for them. Legends grew up about them. Working with a 24in stroke and 140lb pressure, they were likened to 'knights in shining armour' as they headed the West of England trains. The skirts of their double frames hid the motion, giving them the appearance at

speed of gliding along the track. Nor was speed a relative term
with them. No 3065 *Connaught Castle* on 9 May 1904 pulled a
120-ton Plymouth–Paddington mail train over 188½ miles from
Pylle Junction (Bristol) to Paddington in 99 minutes 46 seconds,
a maximum speed of 91mph from start to finish. It was a performance unsurpassed until the Bristolian express was introduced in 1935. The '3000' class disappeared from 1908 onwards
before the growing weight and complexity of traffic demanding
something heavier than the 4–2–2 type. By 1900 a temporary
answer to this problem was being increasingly found with
coupled 4–4–0 engines which afforded greater adhesion.

The engines of Dean which lasted longest, however, were his
six-wheeled standard goods of the '2301' class. Introduced in
1883, no less than 260 were built, some remaining in service for
eighty years. With them Dean replaced the almost universal side
tank for goods engines with a tender and gave the crews some
protection with a cab. Churchward left them unaltered and the
type was perpetuated after regrouping in a new class of 0–6–0s
which Collett built to release Dean's stalwarts for lighter duties.
In World War I, sixty-two of them went overseas for military
railways and 109 of the class 're-enlisted' in 1939, almost all of
them being lost in the fall of France.

The passenger engines of Dean's last period were not wholly
typical of him. The bigger boilers and uglier profiles showed the
thinking of Churchward who, while still nominally under Dean,
used the latter's authority for experiments which were soon to
transform GWR motive power. Thus many of the 4–4–0 'Badminton' class of twenty engines appearing between 1897 and
1899 increasingly showed less of Dean but more of the gaunt
austerity characterizing early Churchward. Their Belpaire fireboxes struck one observer as hideous. In 1900 came a new
4–4–0 series, the parallel boilered 'Atbaras', the class name being derived from one of Kitchener's Sudan battles. Although
nominally of Dean's design, the image was that of Churchward.
Steel instead of copper topped the chimney while the flashing
brass dome, which the new type firebox with its increased steam
space rendered superfluous, disappeared for good. Finally, in
1902, the year of Dean's retirement, came the first Great
Western two-cylinder 4–6–0. The stately, old-fashioned grace of

Dean, whose mind was now clouding, had been left behind for
ever in an engine which, although still experimental, was the
first complete statement of Churchward's principles. Its two
outside cylinders employed a 30in stroke, a record for any
British engine, and its boiler was a standard type designed for
future ten-wheeled locomotives. Known as GWR No 100, its
designer named it *William Dean*. It was the herald of the Churchward revolution.

THE CHURCHWARD SAGA

Churchward's name is part of the Great Western legend, as
securely linked to it as Stephenson's to the *Rocket* or Boulton's
to Watt. He came to Swindon when it had one of the most
varied collections of locomotives of any company; he left it
with a closely knit family of standardized classes unsurpassed in
the country for their tasks. Allied with patient experiments, he
skimmed the cream of American and continental design to produce engines which were not only ahead of their time, but remained without serious challenge for nearly two decades.
Churchward's four-cylinder 4–6–0 'Star' class passenger engines, appearing within four years of Dean's departure, represented in their final form one of the peaks of British locomotive
design, embodying ideas that were still being studied with profit
when the steam age ended on British railways some thirty years
after Churchward's death in 1933.

George Jackson Churchward came from a family without any
previous engineering background. Born on 31 January 1857 at
Stoke Gabriel in South Devon, he was of yeoman stock and retained throughout life a countryman's physique and tastes. After
a schooling in which he was 'brilliant' at mathematics, he became at sixteen a pupil of the locomotive superintendent of the
South Devon Railway at a time when it was still broad-gauge.
Transferred at nineteen to the GWR drawing office at Swindon,
he was successively manager of the carriage works and then
Works Manager and Chief Assistant to Dean whom he succeeded as Locomotive, Carriage and Wagon Superintendent at
forty-five. The title of Chief Mechanical Engineer was not
bestowed until 1916.

Professor W. A. Tuplin has written that in the 1890s the Great Western locomotive stock 'was a collection of oddities—picturesque, perhaps, but still oddities'. By the time Churchward had finished, Great Western engines were neither picturesque nor oddities, but supremely functional, standardized machines. With Dean's post assured to him, he set out at the end of the century to draw up a scheme restricting engine classes to less than a dozen, with standardized boilers, wheels, cylinders, motion and tenders. The key feature was to be a two-cylinder engine powerful and flexible enough to meet all Great Western needs for the foreseeable future. But midway through realizing this programme Churchward swung away from the American influence which had dominated much of his earlier thinking and came under the spell of the French. This radically altered his ideas about the number of cylinders, with memorable and far-reaching results.

Churchward's reforms began in the boiler. While still under Dean he evolved four standard types, each a larger or smaller version of the other to suit his engine classes. Dean's round-topped firebox disappeared, to be replaced by the flat-topped Belpaire type with a narrow sloping grate to burn the fiery Welsh steam coal and large water spaces to give more steam at the hottest part of the boiler. In turn the boilers were wholly or partly tapered to help steam formation around the firebox tube-plate, and the tapering was extended to the firebox to give a better look-out. This tapering or coning, a reflection of American practice which influenced Churchward at this time, was one of his most visual and instantly recognizable 'trademarks'. American thought, too, influenced the design of the smoke box or 'front end' of his engines. It was made larger and projected farther forward than in most contemporary engines. Henceforth Great Western locomotives could never be mistaken for those of other companies.

Less obvious to the eye, but probably of even greater importance, were the results of Churchward's experiments with the valves which let steam in and out of the cylinders. He gave them conspicuously longer travel but with a high piston speed at a time when a low speed was favoured. This, together with generous admission and exhaust ports and his high-pressure, free-

A spotless named express with a green locomotive and chocolate-and-cream stock at speed with express headcode on single track. The *Cambrian Coast Express* is hauled by 'Manor' class No 7811 *Dunley Manor* near Bow Street. (*Colour-Rail, T. B. Owen*)

The autocar is no longer in chocolate and cream but otherwise this is still a very Great Western view of Brunel's *pièce de résistance*, the Royal Albert Bridge at Saltash before it became overpowered by the adjoining Tamar road bridge. Well into BR days the suburban service across the river was among the Western Region's busiest. The locomotive is 64xx No 6420. *(Colour-Rail, T. B. Owen)*

steaming boilers, made possible ample power at high speeds. Churchward's designs were unfussy, simple but logical, and only adopted after proved by considerable experiment and trial. He insisted, too, on high-quality workmanship and generous bearing surfaces. His engines were expensive to build, a point unwisely commented on by a Great Western director who wondered why contemporary North Western engines were cheaper. 'Because', Churchward is said to have retorted 'one of mine could pull two of their bloody things backwards.' Whether or not the retort was ever made in those words, it was not untypical of Churchward, whose engines rarely failed in service.

The first recognizably Churchward engines to appear as a complete class were the two-cylinder 'Cities' introduced as 4–4–0s in 1903, which helped the Great Western to throw off the LSWR challenge for the Ocean Mail traffic from Plymouth. Developed from the 'Atbara' class engine *Mauritius*, the 'Cities' were given by Churchward a partly tapered boiler and 20 per cent more steam pressure, making them the largest and most powerful of his inside-cylinder passenger locomotives. They were renowned for fast running. The *City of Truro* became the first in the world to draw a train at 100 miles an hour, a feat not publicized by Paddington at the time for fear, it is said, of public reaction against anything going so fast. Despite certain doubts which have never been completely resolved, this timing, when working an Ocean Mail special on 9 May 1904, was accepted as a world record until overtaken in 1935.

Only twenty of the 'Cities' were built, but the 4–4–0 formula was carried on for immediate traffic needs in the more controversial 'Counties' with outside cylinders and a 30in piston stroke, compared with the 'Cities' inside cylinders working a 26in stroke. They were powerful but swung their crews around alarmingly, earning the nickname of 'Churchward's rough riders'. Although introduced as a standard class they were comparatively short-lived and perhaps the least successful of all Churchward's designs.

While the 'Cities' and 'Counties' were being launched, more prototype engines were being built at Swindon as Churchward felt his way towards the six-coupled engine as the ideal for fast passenger work. Each of the new prototypes had one of his standard boilers, the design of which had now been largely established, and all had two cylinders and a working pressure of 200lb.

Until 1903 much in these engines still showed Churchward looking at American practice. Now a dramatic change occurred. His attention, shifting across the Channel, was caught by the claims for fast and smooth running being made for the four-cylinder de Glehn compound 'Atlantic' (4–4–2) engines of the French Nord Railway. In the de Glehn system steam was taken through an external pipe to the outside, high-pressure cylinders working the second coupled axle and then passed to the inside low-pressure cylinders driving the leading coupled axle. Through his cylinder arrangement and crank setting de Glehn achieved an almost perfectly balanced compound engine.

Compound engines had never been very popular in England where the principle—that of using steam twice over, first through high, and then through low, pressure cylinders before exhausting it into the atmosphere—had in fact originated in about 1850. The advantages claimed for it of using less water and coal had never found much favour in a country short of neither, nor had British locomotive engineers been much impressed by Francis Webb's compounds built at Crewe for the LNWR. In France, however, compound engines had reigned supreme since the 1880s. By the early 1900s de Glehn's four-cylinder compound 'Atlantics' had brought this type of engine to what at that time was probably its greatest pitch of perfection. Churchward kept a sharp eye on foreign locomotive development. What he heard about the French engines made him curious. To test de Glehn's four-cylinder arrangement with his own two-cylinder engines he persuaded his board to buy some of the French engines for comparative tests.

On 19 October 1903, three large packing cases were unloaded at Poplar Docks. In them were parts of a de Glehn 4–4–2 compound locomotive which, when assembled and slightly modified at Swindon, was given the name *La France*. Apart from the cylinder arrangement it differed also from Churchward's newest prototype in working at 227lb boiler pressure against his own 200lb. Two more French engines with slightly larger leading dimensions were bought in 1905 and named *Presi-*

dent and *Alliance*. Meanwhile, to compete with *La France*, Churchward had built a two-cylinder 4–6–0 with boiler pressure raised to 225lb, but after a year's running altered it to a 4–4–2 to compete more closely with *La France*. The French connection was then tied closer by naming her *Albion*. Subsequently, to help decide between the merits of the two wheel formulas, nineteen more engines similar to *Albion* were built, thirteen as 4–4–2s and the remaining six as 4–6–0s. With twice the power of the 'Cities', they were later embodied in the 'Saint' class of two-cylinder 4–6–0s for secondary main line work.

Churchward's tests between his own and the French engines are remarkable, and outstanding in British railway history. Never before had a British locomotive engineer so thoroughly studied continental engine performance, nor had any company so closely integrated 'foreign' locomotives into its daily services. Over Brunel's old main line via Bristol *La France* on 1 July 1904 ushered in a new era in holiday traffic between Paddington and the West Country by heading a new train, the Cornish Riviera Limited. On the journey down to Exeter she attained 84·9mph 'by sheer force of steam'. Served by English crews, the 'Frenchmen' regularly handled the West of England fast trains as well as the Worcester and Wolverhampton expresses. Each ran well over 700,000 miles and *Alliance* was not finally scrapped until 1928.

By the end of the tests Churchward had satisfied himself on two points. Four cylinders meant smoother and better balanced running at high speeds than two, but for British express work compounding offered no advantages over 'simple' steam. His own boilers achieved much the same thermal efficiency as the French and there was little to choose in coal consumption. These conclusions decided the next step. In 1906 there emerged from the Swindon sheds GWR engine No 40, later given the name of *North Star*. With this engine, built as a 4–4–2 but later converted to a 4–6–0, Churchward substantially achieved his goal. The boiler was now tapered over its whole length and pressure was established at 225lb. The French cylinder arrangement was adopted, but a 4–6–0 wheel layout was preferred to the 'Atlantic' arrangement as offering twice the adhesion on gradients. Thus *North Star* in the form of a four-cylinder 'simple' engine not only revived a famous name but became the fore-runner of the ten-wheeled, six-coupled 'Star' class designed for non-stop long-distance running.

In all seventy-three 'Stars' were built (twelve after World War I), the design being progressively improved over the next seven years from No 40's first appearance. In their final form, weighing some 75 tons with 6ft 8½in coupled wheels, Waelscharts valve gear and four 15in cylinders working a 26in stroke, they represented the crown of Churchward's achievement in express passenger engine design. Gresley and Stanier learned lessons from them; Collett's 'Castles' and 'Kings' were virtually 'Stars' enlarged. The last of them ran in 1957. Today only *Lode Star* (put in service in 1907), its fire long drawn and its boiler cold, survives to reign in burnished but static splendour in the GWR's Swindon Museum, showing to the eye the proportions of Churchward's masterpiece and the scope of the revolution he brought about in steam locomotive design. Yet for essentially British engines the 'Stars' had a remarkably polyglot set of relations. American, Belgian and French practice were all embodied in the final design. Churchward even adopted the de Glehn coil spring bogie in preference to his own and the de Glehn design of 'big end'. Finally, when superheating, which eliminated condensation in the boiler, was later adopted for them, it was Churchward's variant of the German Schmidt system.

The 'Stars', by far the most powerful engines then running in the country, were followed by one of Churchward's most puzzling engines and his only real flop. The *Great Bear* (GWR No 111) had no precedent or successor on the GWR. The first 'Pacific' (4–6–2) ever built in this country when it appeared in 1908, it was the heaviest steam locomotive ever to run on the GWR. Huge, short-lived, undistinguished in performance, the reason for its building when the 'Stars' had ample power for all immediate and foreseeable needs has caused more conjecture than anything Churchward ever did. He himself preserved a sphinx-like silence about it, although perhaps because of the awe in which he was regarded nobody ever seems to have had the courage to ask him.

With its wide firebox and boiler nearly half as big again as the 'Stars', the *Great Bear* was some 55 per cent more powerful and

30 per cent heavier than the 'Stars'. It was not only the longest and heaviest engine in the country, but heavier by nine tons than Collett's future 'Kings'. If this restricted its use to the Paddington–Bristol route, its size was turned to advantage in other ways. Looming over the track like a brooding giant, 'Britain's first "Pacific" ' was seized on by Paddington as a prestige symbol, which was perhaps the reason for its building. It occupied pride of place in the company's literature, photographs of it appearing in every popular book on engines between 1908 and 1922. To its crews, however, it was a giant needing careful handling. It was prone to derailment on sharp curves. While reversing to a west-bound train at Paddington, misjudgement of clearances led to part of a platform being sheared away. At Swindon a hapless fireman was so confused by the extended cab roof that he jammed the fire pricker between it and the grate. The united efforts of three men were needed to free it. Restricted in running because of its axle weight, and despite the awed wonder and even affection of enthusiasts, it remained largely a white elephant until the arrival of Collett's 'Castles' robbed it even of its prestige value. In 1924, needing heavy repairs and no longer earning its keep, it was cut up by Collett to make a 'Castle'. Churchward, who by then had left, is said to have been upset.

Churchward left his mark on the Great Western's freight and general-purpose engines which all benefited from his standardization plan. Two remarkably successful freight engine designs were the '28XX' 2-8-0, a heavy goods engine type, which initially appeared in 1903 and was still being turned out with only slight modifications in 1938 and 1942, and the '43XX' 2-6-0. Versatile and free running, these engines on occasion worked the Cornish Riviera Express, but were equally handy hauling coal trains. In the carriage department his 1904 'Dreadnought' stock (so named after the battleship of the time) was revolutionary in design and length—70ft long and 9ft 6in wide. It proved too revolutionary to be entirely popular. More lasting were the high rounded 'elliptical' top light coaches he produced to replace the clerestory type brought by Dean to late Victorian perfection.

Churchward's overall achievement at Swindon remains in

scope and influence one of the great personal sagas of British steam. Perhaps it was too all-embracing, for in appearing to have solved in essentials all the Great Western's motive power needs he daunted his successors, wedding them to steam when earlier thought might have been given to other forms of power. He was almost alone among British locomotive engineers in his close study and interest in American and continental practice. Without slavishly copying them he improved on others' ideas, but his perfection of long-lap, long-valve travel was entirely his own and perhaps the most significant contribution to the revolution he brought about in the design of the steam locomotive. He was without doubt the greatest locomotive engineer of his time and there were many who acknowledged it. Yet for all his work he was regarded somewhat coolly by the Establishment. In the sovereign's Honours List of 1918 George Jackson Churchward received a bare CBE, the reward of any conscientious civil servant. Less than two decades later Gresley of the LNER and Stanier of the LMS (the latter a Swindon man) received the accolade of knighthood.

COLLETT'S CONJURING TRICK

The task of following Churchward would have daunted most men, but Charles Benjamin Collett who did so in 1922 not only secured his own reputation within a year but gave an extra polish to the Great Western's locomotive image. He did this by a remarkable conjuring trick with the 'Stars'.

Churchward and Collett were two very different men in manner and appearance. Churchward could be autocratic but carried it with a natural dignity and a personality set off by soft trilby hats, country tweed suits and a blunt, often earthy style in conversation. Collett was stiffer, more reigned-in, sometimes waspish. He clung to a hard bowler hat and tightly rolled umbrella. Churchward, also, could be exacting about standards and so too could Collett, but in a more intense way. He is said to have looked on a well-turned crank axle with the wrapt admiration others keep for a prize bloom.

Collett came at time of change. By 1922 the 'Stars', while still equal to most traffic demands, were no longer the most powerful engines in the country. Heavier passenger and goods traffic on West Country lines pointed to a larger engine. The problem was to keep such an engine within the main features of Churchward's standardization scheme. The latter in 1919 had planned a larger boiler for the 'Saints' and 'Stars', but had been told that this would make them too heavy for many bridges.

Collett and his design teams solved the problem by an inspired compromise. The wheelbase of the 'Stars' was retained but the rear frame was lengthened to provide a deeper firebox, and weight was saved on the boiler by introducing a new standard design. This, although three inches wider, remained the same length and retained Churchward's front end. Although cylinder diameter was enlarged to 16in, stroke, wheel sizes and motion were kept the same. The overall result was an engine 10 per cent more powerful and in calculated nominal tractive effort (31,636lb) the most powerful express engine, it was claimed, in the country.

The 'Castles' were Collett's masterpiece, confidently challenging and easily beating the older North Western six-coupled 'Claughtons', 'Princes' and 2–4–0 'Precedents'. Although their acceleration was said to be 'dignified', they had great staying power and could keep up high speeds with heavy loads for great distances. For driver Street of 'Cheltenham Flyer' fame, *Tregenna Castle* was 'the finest engine I ever had' doing almost all her work at 15 per cent cut-off on the valve travel. Less austere than the 'Stars', not as massive looking as the 'Kings', they were the most successful, and certainly among the most sturdy, locomotives ever produced in this country and as ahead of their time as Churchward's 'Saints' and 'Stars' had been. *Caerphilly Castle*, the first of them, burst upon the railway world in artistic lined-out panels and boiler bands and polished brass cab and splasher headings—the first engine to be so turned out at Swindon since World War I. Her gleaming splendour was matched by brilliant publicity in a range of books that has continued to the present day and which the performance of the class as a whole fully justified.

Launceston Castle in competitive trials in 1926 over LMSR metals on the 299 miles from Euston to Carlisle (including the fearsome Shap Fell climb) knocked some nineteen minutes off the scheduled time for the run and burnt less coal doing so. In the preceding year *Caldicot Castle*, the second of her class and new from the shops, competing with the LNER *Victor Wild*, but this time over Great Western track, not only made better time than the 'Pacific', which hauled the Cornish Riviera, but again used less coal. Results such as these led Gresley on the LNER and Fowler the new CME of the LMS to follow Churchward's ideas on valve setting with marked improvement in the coal consumption of the former's 'Pacifics'. Carrying titles of Castles on the Great Western system, 171 were built, the last ten as late as 1950. The very last from the Swindon shops (August 1950) bore, appropriately, the name of *Swindon*.

Three years after launching the 'Castles', Collett faced another demand. Heavy summer loadings showed that they had little reserve to draw on. Moreover, the claim for them, based on nominal tractive effort, of being the most powerful engines in the country had not gone unnoticed. By 1926 R. E. L. Maunsell of the Southern Railway (and an early admirer and follower of much of Churchward's teaching) had gone one better with his four-cylinder 4–6–0 *Lord Nelson*, which if not a particularly good engine at that stage was superior in tractive effort (33,500lb) although working with 5lb less steam pressure.

Wriggling in the toils of its own publicity, Swindon, as earlier related, had to produce a new engine at speed if it was to remain in the forefront of locomotive performance. This was Collett's dilemma. Called upon for the second time within three years for a new design, he had little room for manoeuvre and was also in a hurry. For the earlier 'Castles' he had turned to the 'Stars'; he now enlarged the 'Castles' to produce the 'Kings'. The boiler was lengthened to 16ft and given a pressure of 250lb, a record for any engine of that time in Britain. The cylinder stroke was increased to 28in, but the coupled wheel sizes were reduced to 6ft 6in (the 'Castles' were 6ft 8½in). The overall tractive effort was improved to 40,300lb, far in advance of any other design. With adhesion and engine weights of 67½ tons and 89 tons respectively, both then unprecedented in the British Isles, the 'Kings' easily became the most powerful ten-wheeled engines of that date in the country.

Thus Collett established Swindon's prestige with a six-coupled engine, but one embodying all the proportions of a

'Pacific'. The 'Kings' were the Great Western's most visual contribution between the wars to the power and legend of steam. Their regal appearance was enhanced by brass safety valves, casings and brass beading on the splashers and, of course, the copper chimney band. The first of the class, *King George V*, so dazzled the Americans in design and performance that the Baltimore & Ohio and the Hudson Railroad Companies paid the compliment of modelling engines on her. The former even copied the front end, and 'we endeavoured to copy the stack but do not believe we got that quite right in the shape of the copper top'. This was a tribute to the 'King's' remarkably tidy profile, contrasting with the mass of external ironmongery which characterized many American engines.

The 'Kings' were not a numerous family. Only thirty were built, the last in 1930. Unassisted they could haul 500 tons between Paddington and Taunton, against the 455 tons of the 'Castles' and the 420 tons of the 'Stars'. They chopped the Cornish Riviera's twenty-year-old timing of 247 minutes between Paddington and Plymouth to an even four hours, an average speed of 56·3mph. Yet Swindon used them timidly. Not until after World War II were they seen West of the Severn tunnel. By then their reign was nearly over.

Collett carried on Churchward's standardization scheme in the 4–6–0 mixed-traffic engines he produced. Thus the 'Halls', numerically the largest class on the system and dating from 1928, resulted from the experimental rebuilding of Churchward's 'Saint' class *St Martin*. In 1936 came the 'Granges' for mixed traffic and in 1938 the 'Manors' for running where the 'Halls' and 'Granges' were not permitted. All three worked with a 30in stroke in 18in cylinders and with a boiler pressure of 225lb. The 'Manors' were the first 4–6–0s to work over the Cambrian Railways system where curved and long stretches of single track presented problems.

Like Churchward, Collett and his design teams also left their mark on the GWR's coaches, notably with the 1931 Pullman or Cunard stock. These GWR 'personally styled Pullmans', named after the Royal Family, were expressly tailored for American travellers on the Plymouth boat train and were probably the most individual and handsome stock of the time in the country.

Panelled in walnut, fitted with Wilton carpets and with windows shaded by silk damask curtains, they provided a standard of luxury travelling and comfort for which the company demanded a supplementary charge of 10s on top of the first-class fare. Four years later, to mark the GWR's centenary, Collett built not a new engine but the celebrated 'centenary stock' for the Cornish Riviera Limited. The first GWR coaches to have large compartment windows, they were the widest of all main-line coaches in Britain but largely restricted to the Riviera's route.

World War II was two years old when Collett retired at seventy. He is a slightly puzzling figure, darkened somewhat by Churchward's shadow. His 'Castles' have been dismissed as enlarged 'Stars' and the 'Kings' as larger 'Castles', and his 'Halls', 'Granges' and 'Manors' as Churchward's 'Saints' with smaller wheels. Collett, it is said, should have followed on from the *Great Bear* and built a 'Pacific' as Stanier did, although Stanier's first 'Pacific' was virtually a GWR 'King' enlarged. Yet Collett's achievement was not a mean one. He left the company with a remarkably homogeneous and individualistic family of 4–6–0 locomotives, and his designs were generally sound. Few engines have been freer from teething troubles than the 'Castles' and fewer still produced in so short a time as the 'Kings'. Moreover, not many would now disagree with Collett in shrugging off streamlining.

WHAT MIGHT HAVE BEEN

After Collett's retirement the Great Western had little more than six years of independent life. F. W. Hawksworth, his successor in 1941 as Chief Mechanical Engineer, became a man of unfulfilled destiny. In the short time left to him Hawksworth brought a further development to Churchward's two-cylinder 'Saints' with his ten-wheeled 'County' series, the last passenger engines, although not the last locomotives, to be built for the independent GWR. They revealed two intriguing departures from long-established Swindon features in an unusually high boiler pressure of 280lb, the highest ever used on the GWR, and 6ft 3in coupled wheels, a distinctly non-standard GWR size. Had the railway remained independent, both might have been portents of Swindon's next logical post-war step from the 'Stars',

'Castles' and 'Kings'. This, according to how one interprets the signs, might have been a 'Pacific' 4–6–2 or a 4–8–0 locomotive. Such a dream, if it ever existed, remained unfulfilled; Hawksworth, instead, built the 'Counties' of which a further distinctive feature was a new-pattern, straight-sided tender. The 'Counties'' calculated tractive effort of nearly 32,580lb was almost the same as that of the 'Castles', although their two cylinders made them cheaper to produce. Built with a special eye for West of England gradients, they were not in the end greatly superior to the 'Castles'. To Hawksworth also fell the distinction of designing the final class of GWR pannier tanks, of which No 9400, among the last locomotives to be built for the company, can be seen today in the Swindon museum.

With Hawksworth's retirement in 1949, Swindon's independent locomotive history virtually ends. The Wiltshire railway town, built according to legend on a site Gooch and Brunel selected when the latter tried to see how far he could throw a railway sandwich, had been forged by a succession of engineers —most notably by Churchward—into one of the great power houses of locomotive design and construction. 'Made in Swindon' was more than a nameplate. It was a hallmark. In turn, the railway ruled not only the town, but dominated and regulated the life of its inhabitants. It even followed them into their homes. Pride of place on the walls of the best rooms of many of its railway houses went not to family portraits, but to pictures of Great Western engines. They, along with the names of Gooch, Brunel and Churchward, were part of the warp and woof of 100 years of continuous railway working which had been woven not only into the name of Swindon but into the character of its people. When the Great Western finally surrendered its independence Swindon lost its soul. Although the M4 motorway today has supplanted the railway that raised the town, Swindon still remains a town of railway ghosts wandering in limbo.

CHAPTER 7

What Has Gone and What Remains

Today Great Western nameplates in the company's distinguished Clarendon Bold letter-face are changing hands at £800 and £1,000 each. A three-aspect Great Western signalling lamp in working order is now worth more than £10 (more still if made of copper) while the lucky possessor of a GWR-type pill-box cap (introduced in 1900 and still used by senior uniformed staff after World War II) will guard and treasure it as closely as a philatelist a rare stamp.

Together with porters' buttons, policemen's staffs, glass and cutlery, clocks, direction and warning signs, station furniture (particularly if the initials GWR are entwined in the bench ends or seat supports), old and forgotten luggage labels, tickets, time-tables, bills and posters, they are all today eagerly snapped up to minister to the strange paradox that while fewer and fewer people travel by railways interest in their steam working days has never been greater.

But such things, along with a monogrammed cup and saucer and a button from an engineman's cap, are the trivia of rail-way working and history. The legacy and heritage of a great trunk system are better seen in its stations and bridges, in its effect on the towns it served, the harbours it brought into be-ing and nourished and even the road over which its engines travelled.

The most enduring memorial of the Great Western Railway and of Brunel as its engineer, and one which will last as long as railways themselves, is still the original main line he laid down between Paddington and Bristol more than 130 years ago. He sited its stations, designed its bridges and bored its tunnels. He even landscaped its embankments. It was the trunk from which the Great Western system grew. Straighter and more level over a greater distance than any other in Britain, and still laid on its original foundations, it stands out in profile on a map like a perfect ellipse, 'as flat as the arches which carry it over the Thames at Maidenhead'. And it used to be said, and was until recently believed, that the sun when it was shining still peered momentarily through Box tunnel on its builder's birthday—and on no other day in the year. Alas, science has now disproved this legend, although devotees and believers are still known to huddle at the entrance to Box tunnel to see it happen. The story was that Brunel deliberately lined the tunnel up east and west so that the sun would shine through it at dawn on 9 April. But an astronomical expert has now proved that this is impossible on a fixed calendar date. Nevertheless it is a Brunellian legend that is likely to long go on being related.

The Great Western has lost much of its past. Some of it has been through change, but a great deal more of the most precious through unthinking destruction. The greatest loss of all is the complete absence of any comparative examples of the engines and stock that made up its broad-gauge glory. (*Tiny*, the 0–4–0T South Devon engine at Newton Abbot, and the 1925 replica of *North Star* at Swindon hardly count.) The almost entire destruction at Swindon after 1892 of what then remained may perhaps be condoned, if not forgiven, in the light of the times. But the deliberate breaking up of *Lord of the Isles* in 1906 because it was taking up too much room at Swindon was not only vandalism but robbed history of one of the great locomotive ornaments of the broad gauge.

Later times have been marginally more enlightened. If nothing of Armstrong or of Dean's stately 7ft singles survives, there is at least a reminder of Dean in the '2301' class goods engine preserved in the GWR museum at Swindon and reflecting, if only faintly, a period when Gooch's influence still hovered over the company. Near it the Churchward revolution of the early 1900s can still be studied through the two-cylinder *City of Truro* and its ultimate design transformation in the four-cylinder *Lode Star*, a sister of the engine *North Star* through which its builder made his gesture to the French.

In the Science Museum the best of Collett can be seen in *Caerphilly Castle*, shining in full livery and selected to illustrate the last days of steam, while *Pendennis Castle*, built in 1924 and the victor of the 1925 exchanges with the Gresley 'Pacifics', is preserved, but in Australia of all places! *Clun Castle*, a late-comer in 1950 and the last 'Castle' to run in service, has been acquired by the Standard Gauge Steam Trust and can be seen on display at Tyseley. Altogether some forty Great Western engines are still in steam (if only occasionally) or preserved on a number of sites by British Rail, the Great Western Society (at Didcot, Caerphilly, Taunton and Bodmin) or in museums (at Swindon and Tiverton).

But it is Collett and not Churchward who is mostly seen on the track. No 6000 *King George V* (one other remaining 'King', No 6023 *King Edward II*, now lies forlorn and cannibalized in the breaker's yard at Barry) along with its famous bell still makes occasional and festive appearances in steam, drawing crowds of the order that generally rush to greet film stars. Collett's 'Halls' and 'Manors' are eagerly sought after by enthusiasts running revivified branch lines. *Dumbleton Hall*, rescued in the nick of time from Barry, is the latest acquisition (1976) on the Dart Valley Railway in South Devon. This independent company keeps the Great Western tradition in being by running trains between Totnes and Buckfastleigh over the old Ashburton branch railway. It has also reactivated the Paignton–Kingswear line although, interestingly, it now calls the terminus Dartmouth Ferry as if acknowledging that the ancient port ought originally to have been the main station. The engines which survive on this and other former Great Western lines still arouse not only loving enthusiasm but strong protective instincts. When an earlier and battered 'Hall' was rescued from the Barry graveyard and rebuilt at Swindon, fitters and painters long in retirement clamoured to restore her and reproduce the old Brunswick Green livery. Such is the continuing lure of Great Western steam.

Others find an equal fascination in stations. No one interested in railways can depart from Paddington or Bristol Temple Meads without an overwhelming feeling of the Great Western's past. At Paddington it may be remembrance or anticipation of royal occasions, for no other London terminus has a longer or more intimate association with royalty. Although twice remodelled, Paddington is still, except for the northernmost bay, essentially as Brunel designed it, a reflection of Paxton's Crystal Palace. The great roof with its lofty aisles and transepts, originally designed as traverses for rolling stock from one side of the station to the other, remains outstanding of its kind. If Paddington was Brunel's achievement it was left to another architect, Philip Charles Hardwick, in the 1860s, to superimpose on its front one of the first hotels to be designed as an integral part of the station it served. Instead of perpetuating the Tudor style of the entrance to Temple Meads, Hardwick chose Baroque, with results that have excited Professor Pevsner. The building still serves its original function but with many of its best interior features smoothed away through 'modernization' and 'improvements'.

Between them Brunel, Hardwick and Digby Wyatt, who ornamented Paddington's interior, still impose on it an air which helps to make Paddington the most individual of the great London railway termini. Less cosmopolitan than Victoria, friendlier than Waterloo and not as overwhelming as Euston, it preserves the permanent holiday atmosphere of a station that always seems to be on the threshold of the countryside.

There are good reasons for this. In 1912 the Great Western was publishing for the astonishing price of one penny a 100-page fully illustrated residential guide entitled *Homes for all in London's Western Borderlands*. To tempt people to live out of London, but on the company's system, were pictures portraying scenes of unbelievable rural remoteness and tranquillity within twenty miles of Paddington. Ealing Broadway was then tree-lined and without traffic. There was a water splash at Southall and open meadows at High Wycombe, and along the road to the station at Cowley cows still walked to the milking sheds. Between Reading and Windsor a poultry farm, complete with a six-bedroom farmhouse, cost £500 freehold, and a five-bedroom house within five miles of Reading, standing in six acres with a rabbit warren and paddock attached, cost a mere £3,300. If today this one-time countryside is solidly built over, its overtones still influence Paddington's atmosphere.

Bristol Temple Meads, along with its train shed (although not now used as such), remains the most important surviving example in the country in anything like its original condition of an early railway terminus. Soon after it was built the GWR had to share it with two other railways—the Midland and the Bristol and Exeter—and traces of their 'occupation' still exist. At Temple Meads four styles of railway architecture bridging 100 years can be studied. They are the Perpendicular Gothic of Brunel's original station offices, the Jacobean 'fancy' of the Bristol and Exeter station buildings (now used as general offices), the Digby Wyatt remodelling of 1879, chiefly Gothic in character, and the more modern (and not unpleasing) work of the 1930s when extra platforms, new bays and shelters were provided. This is an extremely varied but vulnerable architectural backcloth continually at risk from the threat of improvement. Although not everybody (Christian Barman, for example, in *An Introduction to Railway Architecture*) wholly admires the 'big Tudor composition at Bristol Temple Meads', it remains one of the most precious relics of railway architecture in the first quarter-century of the steam age. It would be a tragedy if it suffered the fate of Hardwick's great arch at Euston.

Elsewhere in the south and west reconstruction of stations (although Windsor, as yet untouched, still preserves William Tite's Gothic fancies in the royal entrance and the public portion of the station) has long swept away many individual features, among them Brunel's curious 'one-sided' stations at Reading, Slough, Gloucester and Taunton. Gone, too, are almost all of the Brunellian over-all roof stations so long characteristic of the South West. One remains at Frome. Another survives at Ashburton, formerly at the end of the branch line from Totnes, but now a filling station and garage workshop, so completely bricked in as to be scarcely recognizable. The buildings of Exeter St Thomas with their glazed gable ends (a fine example of their kind) disappeared in 1970, although the station is still open for traffic.

The years between the wars saw much rebuilding of stations—notably at Cardiff, Taunton and Newton Abbot—which added to their convenience at the expense of any real architectural merit. The redesigning of Banbury station, although decided on

A classic Western branch line scene. 14xx No 1471 near Brampford Speke on the Exe Valley auto service.
(Colour-Rail, L. F. Folkard)

You can almost hear the escaping steam, the fireman tending the fire in readiness for the climb up Dainton Bank and smell the mixture of steam and mist as 'Hall' class No 5940 *Whitbourne Hall* waits at the down end of Newton Abbot's long platform for the right of way for Plymouth. (*Colour-Print, P. W. Gray*)

by the company before World War II, was a task eventually completed by British Rail.

The litter of abandoned stations and halts and platforms throughout the system is a striking commentary on the vanished commuter traffic of a former age and the changed travelling habits of today. Halts were officially abolished throughout England and Wales in 1969. The last GWR platform, Wootton Wawen, lost its suffix on 6 May 1974. To see at its unhappiest the decline of a railway's influence in an area it once dominated it is necessary to travel to Plymouth, where the number of closed or abandoned stations is greater than in any other town in the country except Greater London. Plymouth is a graveyard of the hopes and enterprise of two systems, the Southern and the Great Western. The Southern has disappeared almost without trace; the Great Western remains, but in a form which only too sadly reveals how once proud hopes for its nationalized future have turned sour. The towering 'asymmetrical composition' of the new £1½ million ten-storey building next to the remodelled station, completed in the early 1960s to house a directing and operating staff which was to hold sway from Taunton to Penzance, was a whte elephant before it was ever finished. 'It's a great mistake', conifessed Lord Beeching before he even opened it. Today it stands painfully under-used by its owners, the working of the railway in Devon and Cornwall controlled not from Plymouth but from Bristol. Scarcely a mile away from it stood Millbay Station, a much older but more characteristic building, marking the one-time terminus and headquarters of the South Devon Railway. Built of hand-cut Plymouth limestone which, after rain, shone like Carrara marble, it has now been completely demolished. The adjoining docks Brunel built to serve it have been turned over to road haulage for French roll-on roll-off ferry traffic. Nor are there many relics *in situ* of South Devon's notorious 'atmospheric caper'. Only the fierce inclines between Newton Abbot and Plymouth remind the traveller of Brunel's enthusiasm for it. The pumping house at Starcross, although it still keeps the campanile-like tower which did duty as a chimney, is in a precarious condition. Of the two remaining ones at Totnes and Torre (Torquay), the latter is on the whole the best preserved.

To its midland and northern stations the Great Western

brought no distinctive architectural touches of its own, but elsewhere Brunel's bridges and viaducts still proclaim his eye for
symmetry, whether in the gracefully turned brick arches of the
Wharncliffe viaduct, the still astonishing long brick spans that
leap over the Thames at Maidenhead, or the viaduct out of
Bath through Twerton. Trains still carry passengers and freight
across the Wye at Chepstow and the Tamar at Saltash by the
bridges Brunel built in 1852 and 1859. The Wye bridge, it is true,
was substantially reconstructed in 1962 but its outline remains
the same. The Royal Albert Bridge was strengthened in 1968 for
the heavier diesel traffic, but not so the chains in its suspension
tubes, which are still as strong as they were when Prince Albert
opened the bridge in 1859.

Brunel's methods in building his iron girder bridges still provide thought-provoking chapters in books on bridge building
(notably P. S. A. Berridge, *The Girder Bridge*, 1969), but his
famous timber viaducts in Devon and Cornwall have long since
been replaced, although the curious can still see the remains of
some. They sprang from their designer's immensely painstaking
experiments at Bristol in 1846 into the strength of yellow pine,
experiments which gave him a confidence and boldness in handling timber for bridge building unsurpassed by any other engineer in the country. Resting on stone or timber piers, according
to the type of country crossed, the wooden beams radiated 'like
four fingers of an outstretched hand' to support the longitudinal
baulks carrying the road. Each unit could be replaced quickly
and cheaply and they carried the entire main-line traffic in
Cornwall until 1908. The stone piers of some remain because
they were too strong and expensive to demolish. Look out of the
coach door window as the train crosses the river valley at Ivy-
bridge, near Plymouth. The four masonry stumps that carried
the graceful timber viaduct—the highest in Devon—on a curve
114ft above the valley can still be seen. Similar stumps still stand
at Moorswater, near Liskeard, on the old Cornwall Railway,
where the stone viaduct built in 1881 is often mistakenly pointed
out as Brunel's original bridge. But the highest of all, St Pinnock
viaduct in the Glynn Valley, 151ft, still does duty on its original
foundations, having been rebuilt by heightening the piers and
laying a steel girder frame across them.

These timber viaducts lasted longest in South Wales. The 14-span Gamlyn and adjacent Dare viaducts on the little-used Dare mineral branch of the Vale of Neath Railway remained in active use until demolished in 1947. The South Wales terrain lends itself to spectacular bridge building and not all the honours are held by Brunel. The great Crumlin viaduct over the Ebbw Vale, west of Pontypool, one of the finest iron bridges in South Wales, was the work of T. W. Kennard. Completed two years before the Royal Albert Bridge, it came to the GWR with the incorporation of the West Midland Railway in 1863.

Wales has many echoes of Great Western dominance. Neyland is at once the most depressing and the most remarkable. Created by Brunel and for fifty years the Great Western's sole packet station for southern Ireland until supplanted by Fishguard, its period of railway importance can still be discovered through its station of local stone and its large hotel, all preserved 'like a fossil' after the passage of seventy years. Fishguard has not worn so well. Its former hotel, perhaps the last purely railway hotel to be built in Britain by a railway company, along with its three-quarters of a mile of formally landscaped gardens, looks out on a harbour which, if still used by the railway, has lost for ever the Atlantic traffic it was so ambitiously engineered for—a melancholy reminder of railway enterprise undertaken at a time when most companies were contracting rather than expanding.

Indeed Wales in general is a case book of Great Western hopes and ambitions—and of the decay of many of them. It is there that the end of the dominance of the coal traffic that figured so long for good and ill in Great Western balance sheets can best be seen. Abandoned and almost lost mineral branch lines, the bleak truncated station at Pontypool (it ceased to be Pontypool Road in May 1972), the grass-grown sidings, long bereft of rails, at Barry and elsewhere, are mute reminders of hopes and enterprise that flourished, but also foundered, on coal. And eastward, as one goes under the Severn tunnel with its memories of Gooch, Richardson and Hawkshaw, there is the reminder that steam no longer even moves the pumps to keep the tunnel free from the ceaselessly flowing waters of the 'Great Spring'. In 1957 the six Cornish beam engines which for eighty years successfully controlled it, pumped for the last time, being replaced by electric submersible pumps. Sadly, not one of the engines is preserved in its entirety.

But it is Swindon (or New Swindon to give it its proper name), never envisaged as a stop in the railway's original prospectus, that still carries the most haunting echoes of Brunel's great railway. Passengers still alight and depart within sight of the works which turned out its historic locomotives, although their importance is now so diminished that lorry drivers sometimes have difficulty in finding them. Their most substantial link with a famous past is a small department which supplies on demand aluminium name and number plates for collectors. And if Swindon's station was never another Temple Meads, something of the proportions of the celebrated first-class dining-room so vividly portrayed in Bourne's print can still be discerned in the meaner atmosphere and appointments of the present self-service buffet, while underneath it there remain portions of the cavernous cellars which did duty as kitchens and storerooms.

Step outside the station and a few hundred yards away are still the rows of cottages for the company's workmen built of the pleasant Bath stone excavated for Box tunnel. They are still known as 'Company Houses'. Many have now been taken over by the district authority and house university students instead of railwaymen and their families, but reminders of their former occupiers are still everywhere to be seen. There is a tavern still called after Daniel Gooch and another with a sign featuring a locomotive with a tall chimney reminiscent of one of his 'Fire Flies'.

There are other things, too, about New Swindon which will last as long as the railway that made it is remembered. For there are still memories among its inhabitants of that pattern of social life forged by its celebrated 'trips', of which the North Country 'wakes' offer the nearest equivalent. They started in 1849 when the directors granted a special train for the purpose. By the 1900s the annual 'trip' was requiring thirty special trains needing a 38-page book of instructions to work and transport 27,000 people to Wales, Weymouth, Weston-super-Mare and London. All Swindon came to a standstill for the 'trip'. But out of it grew social and emotional alliances between families which have been

More broad-gauge memories: *Plate 35 (above)* The West End of Swindon in 1852, Gloucester line to the right. The GWR railway town had taken shape. *Plate 36 (below)* Up express at Bathampton hauled by 4–4–2 *(Both Locomotive & General Railway Photographs)*

Ceremonial and everyday: *Plate 37 (above)* The date is 1 July 1901 and the official caption read: 'The new Great Western Railway Service from Penzance. The Mayoress starting the First Train. The Inauguration of the new Express Service which shortened the journey to London by 40 minutes was witnessed by a large number of spectactors and Penzance was *en fête* for the occasion.' *Plate 38 (below)* Class 28xx No 2844 brings a mixed freight including privately-owned colliery wagons up the incline from the Severn Tunnel at Patchway on 4 August 1938. Almost certainly it would have had a long wait for its turn through the tunnel at Severn Tunnel Junction. The locomotive might well have been pressed into passenger service the next Saturday. *(Both Locomotive & General Railway Photographs)*

maintained for over a lifetime, widening and enriching a community which by the very nature of its work could have become insular.

Hard by the 'Company Houses' still flourishes St Mark's Church for which Great Western directors and shareholders subscribed money in 1845 and which the young Gilbert Scott designed. Here Gooch was among the mourning congregation when Joseph Armstrong was carried by Wesleyan bearers to his brick-lined grave in the churchyard. Dean rode in his coach to its services and Churchward was a worshipper. The tombs in the burial ground and the murals inside the church are a 'stone remembrance book of Great Western men, some proud in their official rank and some humble', but all a lasting and often poignant reminder of a great but now vanished railway.

GREAT WESTERN RAILWAY.

IMPROVED SERVICE

TO AND FROM THE

CHANNEL ISLANDS

Via Weymouth,

BY

The Express Steamers,

"ANTELOPE," "GAZELLE," "IBEX," AND "LYNX,"

AND

THROUGH TRAINS IN CONNECTION,

DAILY (SUNDAYS EXCEPTED).

JULY, AUGUST & SEPTEMBER, 1893.

SHORTEST SEA PASSAGE.

QUICKEST AND BEST ROUTE.

WEYMOUTH TO GUERNSEY	GUERNSEY TO JERSEY
IN ABOUT 4½ HOURS.	IN ABOUT 1½ HOURS.

THE SERVICE BETWEEN

WEYMOUTH AND THE ISLANDS OF GUERNSEY AND JERSEY

IS NOW CONDUCTED BY MEANS OF THE COMPANY'S OWN STEAMERS.

These Steamers have been specially built for this Service upon the most approved principle, possess all the requisite qualifications of first-class ships, are fitted with the Electric Light and all the latest improvements and conveniences.

EXPRESS TRAINS

ARE RUNNING BETWEEN

London & Weymouth

in connection with the Steamers, and direct connections have been established to and from all parts of the Great Western Line.

• **These Trains work to and from the Landing Stage at Weymouth, and enable Passengers to pass direct from the Train to the Steamer, and vice versa.**

Fig 12 Although the GWR ran in connection with Channel Islands steamers, from the opening of the line to Weymouth in 1857, it was many years before GWR boats operated the service. This advertisement comes from the 1893 timetable.

Plympton	dep.	M p.m.	M p.m. 9 3	M p.m.	M p.m. 9 22	M p.m.	M p.m.	M p.m.	M p.m. 9 55	M p.m.	M p.m. 10 24	M p.m.	M p.m. 10 40	M p.m. 10 50	M p.m.	M p.m.	M p.m.	n'gt.	n'gt.	n'gt. 12 41
Marsh Mills	,,				9 22						10 24			10 50			11 22			12 36
Laira Halt	,,						9 30		10 1			10 46		10 55	11 5					
Lipson Vale Halt	,,		9 10	9 27			9 32	9 42	10 4		10 30	10 49		10 58	11 8	11 23	12 23		12 42	12 48
Mutley	,,		9 13	9 29			9 34		10 6	10 32		10 51		11 0	11 10	11 30			12 44	
North Road	arr.		9 22	9 35			9 39	9 50	10 10	10 40		10 55		11 6	11 14	11 35	12 30		12 49	12 54
Millbay	{ dep.	9 20			9 37				10 5	10 18		11 6	11 6		11 10					
Wingfield Villas Halt	,,				9 40				10 18						11 13					
Devonport	,,	9 25			9 42		10 11	10 20				11 6	11 6		11 15					
Dockyard Halt	,,	9 27			9 44			10 22							11 17					
Ford Platform	,,	9 29			9 46		10 13	10 24				11 8	11 8		11 19					
Keyham	,,	9 31			9 48		10 16	10 26							11 21					
St. Budeaux Platform	,,	9 34			9 51		10 20	10 29				11 12	11 12		11 24					
Saltash	,,	9 37			9 55		10 24	10 32				11 20	11 20		11 30					
Defiance Platform	arr.						W					11 23			11 32					

L—Third class only.   M—Rail Motor Car, one class only.   W—Defiance Platform arr. 10.27 p.m. except on Saturdays.

Fig 13 The suburban railway home after a night out in Plymouth

Bibliography

Anyone who writes about the Great Western Railway does so against a background of a proliferation of books covering so much of the Great Western Railway, its equipment and practices. Inevitably E. T. MacDermot's History, originally published in two volumes in 1927 and revised by C. R. Clinker in 1964 with a third volume by O. S. Nock in 1967, is the classic work on the company, covering its history until nationalization in 1948 and is a valuable work of reference.

Apart from Archibald Williams' *Brunel and After*, published by the company itself in 1925, the only published history of the GWR available, for example, to Sir John Clapham for the earlier volumes of his *Economic History of Modern Britain* (3 volumes, 1926–38) was G. A. Sekon's *History of the Great Western Railway* published in 1895. Sub-titled 'The Story of the Broad Gauge', Sekon's book was not so much a history as an explosively opinionated apologia for Brunel's experiment. Few today would dare to write in Sekon's style of imperial arrogance and assuredness, but if the general untidiness of his book, as well as its prejudices, can be overlooked, Sekon still has his uses and is not to be despised.

I have made much use of the *Great Western Railway Magazine*, an often overlooked and underrated source of material. In its pages in the period between the wars the company wrote about itself with a fullness and candour remarkable even by today's standards, and much of this material has formed the background of Chapter 5.

As well as the *Railway Magazine* the following works are among many that have been consulted:

HISTORY

J. B. Latimer *Annals of Bristol*, published in 1887 (marred by prejudice against the GWR and Brunel and contains some factual errors, probably arising from its main sources being contemporary newspapers, but any researcher would be the poorer for not consulting

Latimer); F. Pole *Felix J. C. Pole His Book* (1954) (this is a personal memoir written by Pole for his friends, and perhaps should be judged as such, although one wishes he had left a more substantial record of his experiences before and during office); R. J. Woodfin *The Centenary of the Cornwall Railway* (1960); O. S. Nock *The Great Western Railway in the 19th Century* (1962); *In the 20th Century* (1964); and *Sixty Years of Great Western Express Running* (1973); C. Noall *The Battle of the Gauges* (an interesting review in *The Cornish Magazine*, November 1964, of early railway history in Cornwall and particularly of the GWR); R. B. Wilson *Go Great Western* (1970), and *The Diaries of Daniel Gooch*, published in 1972 (the first is an absorbing history of GWR publicity and the second the first full edition of Gooch's manuscript diaries); C. J. Allen *Salute to the Great Western Railway* (1970); *Great Western Progress* published in 1972 (a reprint of *The Times* GWR Centenary issue); D. St J. Thomas *Regional History of the Railways of Great Britain: The Westcountry* (revised 1973); and *The Great Way West*, published in 1975 (an admirable account, with a wealth of pictures, of the way in which the GWR linked Paddington to Penzance).

LOCOMOTIVE HISTORY

In addition to the locomotive chapters in MacDermot's history (which were not written by him), an indispensable reference is *The Locomotives of the Great Western Railway*, a series by several hands published since the 1950s by the Railway Correspondence and Travel Society. Of equal value has been H. E. Holcroft's lucid *An Outline of Great Western Locomotive Practice* (1957). Other books consulted have been: E. L. Ahrons *The British Steam Locomotive* (1925); H. E. Holcroft *The Armstrongs of the Great Western* (1953); W. G. Chapman *Caerphilly Castle* (reprint 1970); O. S. Nock *The Great Western Stars, Castles and Kings* (2 vols 1967–70), and *GWR Steam* (1972); three books by W. A. Tuplin *Great Western Steam* (1958), *Great Western Saints and Sinners* (1971), *Great Western Power* (1975) are attractively and often provocatively written and among the few books about locomotives giving an insight into work on the footplate, particularly by the fireman.

BIOGRAPHY

L. T. C. Rolt *Isambard Kingdom Brunel* (1957); P. Hay *Brunel: his achievement in the transport revolution* (1973); H. Rogers *G. J. Churchward: A locomotive biography*, published in 1975. (Apart from Stanier's appreciation in *The Transactions of the Newcomen Society*, XXX, 1960, this is the most recent, useful and valuable appraisal of Churchward's work.) Sadly, there is no biography of Gooch nor any independent work on Dean or Collett. My references in Chapter 3 to Captain Huish's career are drawn from T. R. Gourvish 'British Railway Management in the 19th century with special reference to the career of Capt Mark Huish', London PhD thesis (1967).

GENERAL BACKGROUND

J. A. Francis *A History of British Railways* (2 vols 1851); W. Hunt *Then and Now*, published in 1887 (Hunt was a West Country journalist with an interest in the contemporary railway scene and he has some interesting, but tantalizingly brief, references to the Atmospheric Railway); L. V. Grinsell and others *Studies in the History of Swindon* (1950); C. Hamilton Ellis *Four Main Lines* (1950), and *British Railway History* (2 vols 1954–9); J. W. Street *I Drove the Cheltenham Flyer*, published in 1951 (an interesting period piece); C. L. Mowatt *Britain Between the Wars 1918–1940* (1955); M. Robbins *The Railway Age* (1962); J. Simmons *The Railways of Britain* (2nd ed 1968); M. C. Reed and others *Railways in the Victorian Economy* (1969); H. J. Dyos and D. H. Aldcroft *British Transport* (1969); H. Perkin *The Age of the Railway* (1970); S. J. Crispin 'Permanent Way and Viaduct History' (from *Journal of Junior Institution of Engineers*, Oct 1970); R. M. Barton's *Life in Cornwall*, published in 1970 (this has several passages, some of which I have used, from the Truro published *West Briton* newspaper, of the impact of railways on nineteenth-century Cornwall); D. Smith *Discovering Railwayana* (1971); Sir Gerald Nabarro *Severn Valley Steam* (1971), and, with others, *Steam Nostalgia* (1973).

Index

Page numbers in bold type refer to illustrations